DATE DUE

JUL 07 2009	

TWILIGHT OF THE TEXAS DEMOCRATS

Number 107:
Centennial Series of the Association of Former Students,
Texas A&M University

TWILIGHT OF THE TEXAS DEMOCRATS

The 1978 Governor's Race

KENNETH BRIDGES

Texas A&M University Press
College Station

All photographs, unless otherwise indicated, are courtesy Texas State Library and Archives Commission.

Library of Congress Cataloging-in-Publication Data

Bridges, Kenneth.
  Twilight of the Texas Democrats : the 1978 governor's race / Kenneth Bridges. — 1st ed.
      p.   cm. — (Centennial series of the Association of Former Students, Texas A&M University ; no. 107)
  Includes bibliographical references and index.
  ISBN-13: 978-1-60344-009-7 (cloth : alk. paper)
  ISBN-10: 1-60344-009-7 (cloth : alk. paper)
  1. Governors—Texas—Election—History—20th century. 2. Texas—Politics and government—1951– 3. Clements, William P., 1917– 4. Political candidates—Texas—Biography. 5. Politicians—Texas—Biography. 6. Political parties—Texas—History—20th century. 7. Political campaigns—Texas—History—20th century. 8. Party affiliation—Texas—History—20th century. 9. Democratic Party (Tex.)—History—20th century. 10. Republican Party (Tex.)—History—20th century. I. Title.
F391.2.B75 2008
976.4'063—dc22

                                                              2007033912

CONTENTS

PREFACE AND ACKNOWLEDGMENTS

HISTORIANS OFTEN ARGUE whether the individual shapes the times or the times shape the individual. Political history often revolves around that question. The answer is not always clear. Why Texas voters rejected a century of political tradition in 1978 in favor of a Republican as governor stems from a combination of factors that had built over several decades in post–World War II Texas. Changes in the wealth and demographics of the electorate, economic changes, an evolution in the political tastes of voters, and a clash of distinct personalities drove the election.

The contest between John Hill, an accomplished and otherwise popular Democratic attorney general, and Bill Clements, a hard-charging businessman and Republican, created an earthquake in Texas politics, yet one that many observers saw coming for some time. For many Texans, Hill represented a promising new direction for the state; while for others, Clements embodied the mythic, larger-than-life culture of Texas that many voters wanted to see in their governor. This study examines those forces that created a change in Texas political culture and hopes to answer the question of why this occurred at that particular moment in history and between these two particular men and what the consequences became for Texas, for good or ill.

The coming together of this study of the 1978 election has been an adventure in itself, and there are many people to thank. At the top of this list I must place the major professor for my Master's thesis, Ray Stevens. His retirement unfortunately left me searching for another Texas historian to sponsor my academic efforts, but happily, Gregg Cantrell, at that time new to the faculty at the University of North Texas, agreed to take on the task. I had never taken him for a class or even met him before I asked him to serve; he had never supervised a dissertation. But it worked, and I'm grateful for his gracious assistance and advice, especially in locating the key players from the 1978 election.

I dived into the topic, trying to put together as much information as possible. My apartment soon came to resemble the Texas History section of the UNT Library, and the stacks of books did not impress my girlfriend, now my wife. As I prepared the interview process in 2002, I discovered that some individuals whose recollections would be important to my efforts had already passed away. However, John Hill, Bob Krueger, Lance Tarrance, and David Dean were very happy to talk with me and were most gracious with their time. The hardest part was trying to explain to them that I did not have much first-hand knowledge of the 1978 election, since I was only three years old at that time.

I spent most of 2003 writing and rewriting the work. I am grateful that John Gossett and Roy deCarvalho agreed to serve on my committee, replacing the wonderful Charldean Newell, who had retired, and Bullitt Lowry, truly a great historian and a great human being, whose passing saddened us all. I must also thank Mike Campbell and Gus Seligmann, who also honored me by serving on the committee. These dedicated educators and scholars enabled me to successfully complete the first phase of this research and writing, and I sincerely wish to thank them all.

Some of my advisors then suggested that I expand my interviews and revise the work, and this book is a result of those revisions—the new and improved version. I talked with Senator Krueger again in spring 2004, and thanks to the good offices of Lance Tarrance, who helped put me in contact with Governor Bill Clements, I was able, after months of trying to arrange an interview, to speak with the former governor, who provided valuable insights into the times.

One of the most interesting things about the research has been discovering how down-to-earth each of these men are in individual settings. The media and campaigns can portray public figures as somewhat unapproachable, but that certainly did not ring true with those I interviewed. I am grateful to all of them for their time and courtesy.

Of course, the most important thanks go to my beautiful bride, Karen, for putting up with the pack-rat habits of a historian and my pacing through the living room as I agonized over the proper adverb. Our sons, Kaleb and Toby, have been wonderful sources of inspiration; all writers should be so lucky. The gang at SouthArk Community College, friends, colleagues, Texas A&M University Press, and many others, of course, deserve thanks as well.

TWILIGHT OF THE TEXAS DEMOCRATS

CHAPTER 1

TEXAS IN 1978

DESTINY CAN ARISE either out of the labor of men or out of the creations of some greater cosmic force. These philosophical questions of whether individuals make history or remain helpless to the forces of time frame many questions over the choices that societies make. Elections typically provide the opportunity for the people either to ratify the status quo or call for a change in their community's approach to problems of society and governance. An election can also signal the beginning of an immense shift in demographics and ideology or confirm that a new way of thinking or population shift has already solidified in the eyes of the voters. The 1978 governor's election in Texas provided such an opportunity.

Texas in 1978 stood in a whirlwind of change that steadily pushed the economy and society in new directions. These same forces, internal and external to the Lone Star State, led many to question their traditional political loyalties. The result of the gubernatorial contest of that year, an election fraught with bitterly divisive debates, would lead to an entirely new type of politics in the state, establishing a viable Republican Party and a shaken and weakening Democratic Party for the next generation of Texas politicians.

Until that fateful year, the Democratic Party had held the governor's office in the state for more than a century. No change seemed in sight. The Democratic Primary pitted Atty. Gen. John Hill and former Gov. Preston Smith against incumbent Gov. Dolph Briscoe. The results surprised many observers with the ouster of the sitting governor. The general election contest between Democratic nominee John Hill against Republican businessman Bill Clements shook the politics of the state to its foundations by ending the Democratic monopoly on statewide offices.[1]

By the late 1970s, Texas had long since evolved into a more complex state than the classic images of cotton farms, dusty cattle trails, and patches of oil derricks. Agriculture and oil still remained a powerful component of the state's economic engine; but finance, real estate, technology, and manufacturing all served to build an urbanized, technological Texas.[2] The traditions that had built Texas, however, continued to shape the character of the state.

The Reconstruction period and the backlash against it had an incredibly powerful impact on the psyche of the state that reverberated into the 1970s. Analysts of Texas politics often mutter the phrase, "For the first time since Reconstruction" to describe the impact of many of the state's recent political developments. After the end of the Civil War in 1865, the federal government over the next decade instituted a series of broad policies to rebuild the shattered former Confederate states and reshape them politically and socially.[3] The Republican Party controlled this process in each of these states. For the newly freed African American population, Reconstruction represented a tremendous opportunity to exercise the most basic civil liberties for the first time. Siding overwhelmingly with the Republican Party for its postwar policies of emancipation and civil rights, African Americans throughout the South voted and won election to office for the first time.

For the population of white Confederates, Reconstruction remained an exercise in unrelenting humiliation. Furious that the federal government had mandated a new social order of racial equality, the former Confederates feverishly worked to reclaim the state governments. By the close of the 1870s, Democrats had forced the Republicans out of office and worked to marginalize them over the ensuing decades.[4] African Americans would see their modest gains vanish quickly.

Texas' voters evicted its Republican governor of the Reconstruction era, Edmund J. Davis, in 1874.[5] Afterward, the last vestiges of Republican power withered away in the state. The disgust many whites felt over Reconstruction aided the Democratic Party in developing almost a complete monopoly over politics. As a result, over the next several decades after Reconstruction, loyalty to the Democratic Party became deeply embedded in the state's political culture.[6] No viable alternative existed to the Democrats before the war, and during Reconstruction the Democrats became the most vocal opponents of the excesses of the Republican governments. Thus, the first time the state voted Republican in a presidential contest resulted from the vitriolic 1928 contest between Secretary of Commerce Herbert Hoover and New York Governor Al Smith.[7] Evangelical Protestants, a clear majority of Texans in 1928, had furiously protested the candidacy of the Roman Catholic Smith, delivering the state to the Republicans for the only time until 1952.

Hoover would carry seven southern states in 1928. Only six states would stay with the Democrats, from Arkansas to South Carolina, all in the Deep South.[8] Oklahoma voted Republican for the first time ever. But like Texas, these states would resume their traditional Democratic voting behavior over the next several elections.

After the collapse of the slave-based plantation economy and society following the Civil War, the state found itself trying to find new industries to sustain itself. The Civil War had left the wealth of many cotton plantations in ruins, but other powerful interest groups, especially the ranching, railroad, and lumber interests, quickly moved in and dominated the state in the seven-decade period from Reconstruction to World War II.[9] Coupled with the recovery of agriculture in the late 1800s, this helped to build and maintain an economic elite to dominate the political apparatus of the state Democratic Party. The economic interests of the state, however, remained fairly evenly distributed. The economic interests of one area of the state never seemed poised against another area, as in other states.[10]

The Great Depression of the 1930s crippled the nation's economy and left countless Texans destitute and desperate. The chaos of the disaster overpowered the traditional avenues of help for the poor and unemployed. With no jobs available and few Texans able to give to charities to help others, more and more residents of the state turned to the government for help. Franklin D. Roosevelt's New Deal programs provided the hope and bare means of survival that many had longed for with a system of economic reforms and public works projects to provide financial security and to provide the infrastructure to help rebuild the nation's finances. The benefits of the programs cut through regional and racial barriers, inspiring many to believe that the government could not only ensure economic viability to everyone but justice and equality for all.

While the federal government and many in state governments across the United States worked for economic recovery, conservatives balked at the long-term prospects of New Deal-era reforms. In the South, conservatives held most of the political influence. The Great Depression and the New Deal relief programs, however, had encouraged working-class blacks and whites to demand relief, but the system of segregation and suffrage restrictions severely limited the possibility of any successful challenge to conservative dominance.[11] Many of these reforms threatened the economic leverage that many in the upper class held over the lower classes and the social system many tried to keep intact.

Opposition to Roosevelt and his supporters increased with each new proposal in the late 1930s, from the court-packing bill to the enactment of the minimum wage to proposed federal anti-lynching legislation. Liberal Democrats, basking in the popularity of Roosevelt, had managed to capture a number of important state offices in Texas, including the election of Jimmy Allred as governor in 1934. When Allred stepped down from the governorship in 1938, conservatives swept into office and continued to control the governor's office into the 1970s. But with fears of another world war looming in 1940, Franklin Roosevelt broke with the tradition that dated to George Washington and decided to seek a third term as president. The decision shook the political establishment and caused many to break with the president, with some believing that no one should seek a third term, and others, who had waited patiently for Roosevelt's second term to end, to seek the position for themselves. Among those included popular Texan John Nance Garner. Garner had hoped to succeed Roosevelt in 1940, but once Roosevelt won his nomination for a third term, many conservative Texans began to turn away from the national party in disgust.[12]

The most conservative Democrats in Texas had begun to rebel against the national Democratic organization. They remained within the party since no realistic alternative existed in the state and the conservative faction controlled the state organization. As conservative Texans recoiled against the New Deal, Texas liberalism faced a crippling series of defeats.[13] The old conservative elites regained control of state government and remained determined for decades to undo Roosevelt's programs and influence in Texas. Throughout the 1940s and 1950s the conservatives tailored the state's political agenda to enact a system with few taxes on businesses, anti-labor laws, continued hostility to civil rights, and a general aversion to expanding social services—all to the disgust of the liberal faction.[14]

Franklin Roosevelt won the election easily in 1940, and the trials of World War II led him to seek a fourth term in 1944. For many conservative Democrats who had stayed with the president but privately questioned the wisdom of the New Deal for years, the fourth term became too much to bear. Conservative Texas Democrats united to fight his renomination at the Democratic National Convention. Hoping to wrest control of the national party from the liberals and New Deal stalwarts, the Texas Regulars emerged as a part of a region-wide movement to reclaim conservative dominance of the party.[15]

Texas liberals, however, pulled themselves together to fight the challenge by the Texas Regulars. For the first time, liberals and Roosevelt supporters organized within the party to fight the conservatives.[16] The conservatives attempted to send an uninstructed delegation to the national convention to condemn the New Deal and the Supreme Court's recent decision to ban the whites-only primary laws in many southern states, only to meet with failure.[17] Furious at the defeat, the conservatives worked to strike back at Texas liberals. Running a separate ticket from the regular Democrats to protest the national ticket, the Texas Regulars hoped this protest would lead to a Democratic defeat in the state to punish Roosevelt supporters. Again, the plot of the Regulars failed. The faction rejoined the Democrats reluctantly. As for the liberals, the fight for Roosevelt represented their last major victory for many years.

The Great Depression and World War II sparked many changes in Texas and the rest of the South. The Lone Star State in particular enjoyed a great deal of growth and the beginnings of greater diversification in its economy. It began to move beyond simply agriculture and oil and into other enterprises. The war brought defense manufacturing plants to the state, many of which continued to operate afterward. New technology altered agricultural operations, sending many into the cities seeking work. Texas cities began growing rapidly into the late 1940s and 1950s. This growth not only transformed the state into an urban landscape but altered the shape of the political horizon as well.

African Americans entered the cities in large numbers after World War II, continuing a trend that began in the 1920s. The status of African Americans, however, did not improve once they moved to urban areas. In urban areas, discrimination, enforced by segregation laws, forced minorities to gather in ghetto communities.[18] Deeply segregated communities forced racial minorities to live in squalid neighborhoods with few services available. The throngs of new residents overwhelmed many communities. Most cities in the South did not cope with the surge of new residents during the 1920s, resulting in severe housing shortages, made even worse by the dislocation of the Great Depression and World War II.[19] As a result, the promise of new jobs dwindled quickly. For most minorities, the only gainful employment available kept them in the most menial positions, in many cases changing little from their lives in the rural communities.

With major changes in the rural economy because of federal farm subsidies and mechanization, and because of defense factories emerging in urban areas by the 1940s, Texas and other southern states began to experience accelerated growth in the cities. With this changing agricultural economy and economic revival generated by World War II armaments enabled southern cities and states to begin urbanizing along with the rest of the nation.[20]

Despite this growth, most urban areas in Texas remained small, compared to the large metropolitan areas of the North. The ten largest cities in the United States all lay in the North through the 1940s and 1950s, each with populations exceeding 800,000. The largest cities in Texas had only a fraction of the population of these communities. After the Second World War, industries surged to the South, attracted by cheap land, cheap labor, and a general absence of labor unions. The cities surged in population and annexed as much surrounding land as possible to accommodate new businesses and residents. This process of growth would completely reshape the major cities of the state in the span of a generation. Small farm communities surrounding these cities would soon become suburbs. As one urban historian notes, "The American city did not evolve so much as it exploded."[21]

Although Texas remained a clear one-party state, deep divisions in the Democracy festered and hardened into two distinct factions: liberal reformers and conservatives distrustful of government and partial to the status quo. The combination of the Texas frontier ethic and southern social conservatism produced an unusual strain of conservatism in the state, feeding off of the romantic ideal of the individual frontiersman to maintain a more traditional southern society. The idea of the Texas frontier ethic has had a powerful impact on the state's image of itself and has fed the state's basic conservatism.[22] Thus, the conservatism that existed in the South had an even sharper focus in Texas. The reform impulse that had swept the larger, older cities of the Atlantic seaboard thus had little relevance or precedent in rural Texas society. The Texas self-identity of a group of isolated figures building civilization on an untouched plain became central to the politics of the state and thus became very difficult for reformers to modify or combat in any significant way.[23] Many in the state fiercely fought against any attempt to change what had already been built, whether right or wrong. The mythic past that had emerged in the minds of many conservatives became almost sacred, increasing in importance as time passed, while moderates and liberals looked at the realities of the past and present and became uneasy at the disparities and injustices in society and rejected the status quo.

As the state attracted more residents from other states, Republicans began trickling into Texas. But in the late 1940s, Republicans remained little more than a curiosity in the state rather than a power in the politics of the Lone Star State. The rest of the South remained much the same. Interestingly as late as 1948, roughly three percent of all southern state legislators belonged to the Republican Party, and five states boasted a Democratic monopoly in both houses of their state legislatures.[24] Only one major area of Texas, the Hill Country, boasted any significant Republican strength. Traditionally known as "the German counties" because of the large numbers of German immigrants into the area in the twenty years preceding the Civil War, these lightly populated counties maintained a strong adherence to the Republican Party and, out of the absence of Republican candidates in many cases, went to the conservative Democratic faction. These settlers had emerged from a Europe struggling toward democratic institutions, thus they rejected slavery and the Confederacy and turned to the Republicans as the only alternative to the secessionist Democratic faction that controlled the state at the time.[25] Nevertheless, the Republican Party remained far from any position to strike at Democratic supremacy in any area of the state.

Opposition to Democratic policies at the national level grew in the state, yet most conservative Democrats remained content with the behavior of the party at the state and local levels. Factionalism grew, but few seemed willing to break with the party that held all of the political power in the state, hoping perhaps that their faction could gain control of the national party. The only two significant post-Reconstruction revolts—the fight by a faction of Protestant Democrats against the nomination of New York Catholic Al Smith in 1928 and the Dixiecrat rebellion over Harry S. Truman's 1948 civil rights program—represented little more than protests against the national organization. No realistic alternatives yet existed in the South outside of the Democratic Party.[26] After each protest by the conservatives, they returned to the party. This kept the South Democratic, but southern Democratic leadership typically remained far more conservative than the national party.

Political observers, however, noted the evolution of the Texas Democratic Party by 1949:

> In Texas the vague outlines of a politics are emerging in which irrelevancies are pushed into the background and people divide broadly along liberal and conservative lines. A modified class politics seems to be evolving, not primarily because of an upthrust of the masses that compels men of substance to unite in self-defense, but because of the personal insecurity of men suddenly made rich who are fearful lest they lose their wealth.[27]

Although liberals remained far in the minority, the state's conservatives had become increasingly vocal. A politics driven by fears of an uncertain future had begun to emerge as the Cold War erupted and threatened to consume the system of freedom the nation had built.

Changes in the Texas economy and living patterns fed the growth of the liberal–conservative divide even further. Rapid industrialization had caused considerable urban development in the state, creating new problems for the cities. In the three decades after 1950, the west south central states and the Mountain states showed the fastest industrial growth, leaving the Northeast stagnating and creating major manufacturing centers in the areas of Texas, Florida, Georgia, Oklahoma, and other Sunbelt states.[28] This also caused problems for the rural areas. Legislative representation began shifting to the larger cities, steadily reducing the numbers of rural representatives. City issues would begin receiving more attention at the expense of the countryside and small towns. Accordingly, this caused a new rift to develop in Texas politics, pitting the interests of rural residents against urban dwellers across a variety of issues.[29]

Conservatives and liberals would be pitted against each other again in the late 1940s and early 1950s over the issue of the Tidelands. Federal courts had ruled that the states only had offshore oil drilling rights to three miles off of their coasts, while the federal government reserved the rights to the remaining eight miles to the limits of international waters eleven miles from shore. This shocked Texans, proud of the wealth they had built from oil and fiercely protective of their rights. The ruling would cost the state considerable funding for its schools it earned from oil drilling. The state's new governor, Beauford Jester, dramatically demonstrated the plight of Texas over the Tidelands threat as he stated that $200 million in Texas school funds would disappear under federal ownership.[30] Furthermore, many state officials pointed out that Texas had a unique claim to the Tidelands, given its status as a former independent republic over a century before. The Truman administration, however, defended the federal position on Tidelands ownership. Texans grew outraged by the stand, and the battle once again pitted the conservatives against the liberals.

When Governor Jester died in 1949, the extremely conservative Lieutenant Governor Allan Shivers ascended to the governorship and took the lead on the Texas fight for the Tidelands. The clash became almost as symbolic as the legendary battle for the Alamo. To oppose or even suggest compromise became unthinkable. Shivers added a list of demands so complex to even the possibility that Texas might yield the Tidelands that it sealed the impossibility of reconciliation.[31]

The liberals, however, had few means of defense by this time. The loss of liberal gubernatorial candidate Homer Rainey in 1946 had cost them all control of the state party.[32] The same defeat had ushered in Jester as governor and Shivers as lieutenant governor. Shivers and his allies remained determined that liberal power could never resurrect itself in Texas, even if it meant shattering the Democratic Party in the process.

Disgusted by President Truman's policies on the Tidelands, desegregation of the military and the national party's continued liberal direction of social policies under the Fair Deal, Shivers broke with the Democratic Party in protest and announced he would run for reelection as governor in 1952 as both a Democrat and a Republican. A 1951 state law allowed Shivers to cross-file in this manner. To leave the party altogether would have doomed his political career in the state, given the extreme weakness of the Republicans. In this way, Shivers could announce his disgust with the national party and still control the only viable political vehicle in Texas, yet battering the state's traditional loyalty to the Democracy in his fight against Truman.[33]

When the 1952 elections arrived, the Democratic presidential nominee, Governor Adlai Stevenson of Illinois, faced a tremendous challenge in the state. Not only did the conservatives control and run the state with an aim to end the reform policies of the New Deal and the Fair Deal, but they had found a powerful weapon in their quest. Stevenson had followed Truman's lead on the Tidelands controversy and backed the federal court rulings. In the frenzied atmosphere of Texas nationalism, such opposition remained extremely dangerous. But in the Republican presidential candidate, Gen. Dwight D. Eisenhower, many Texans found a Republican they could rally behind.

Not only did the war hero support the Texas position on the Tidelands, but Eisenhower also boasted his status as a Texas native. Impressed by these credentials, even some Texas Democrats threw their support to the Republican. The Denison-born Ike easily defeated the Illinois governor nationally. In Texas, Eisenhower stunned the political establishment by becoming only the second Republican ever to win the state. For most observers, the 1952 election marked the turning point in the evolution to a two-party South.[34] Eisenhower had managed to crack open the Solid South for the first time in more than seventy years. Eisenhower's totals represented something far different than Hoover's 1928 vote: a realistic and palatable alternative for southern Republicans to rally around.

Despite the success of Republicans in winning the state for the presidential ticket, they remained frustrated at their lack of progress down ballot. Texans remained satisfied with conservative Democrats in control of the state and Republicans in control of the White House. The Tidelands threat, the Shivers cross-filings, and the conservative agendas of Shivers and Lt. Gov. Price Daniel blunted any significant Republican challenges.[35] However, the political hybrid known as the presidential Republican had emerged and would begin to play a powerful role in Texas politics.

The depth and influence of the conservatives expanded considerably in the 1950s. The success of the Eisenhower campaign in the state inspired more conservatives to break with the Democrats and vote Republican. Radical economic

change in the state as more Americans and industry moved to Texas also affected voting behavior. During the decade, the social effects of industrialization and rapid economic growth further contributed to the increasing radi-
calization among conservatives, that is, the new prosperity against the bitter
memories of the Great Depression only reinforced their fears of losing what
they had gained and became a significant political force in the southwestern
United States.[36] The traditional agricultural economy still existed that had re-
built the Democratic Party after Reconstruction, but it was now complemented
by a burgeoning oil industry and new manufacturing.

Although segregation would remain the law in Texas and the rest of the
South until the 1954 Brown v. Board of Education decision overturned the
practice in public schools, most Texas politicians said little about the subject in
their campaigns in the early postwar period. Liberals, however, could say little
to combat the practice, and conservatives felt confident enough in their own
power to resist race issues in most cases. In fact, segregation had relatively little
importance as an overt campaign issue in the Texas of the early 1950s and in
the period between the Dixiecrat revolt of 1948 and the Brown decision of 1954,
few prominent southern politicians throughout the South campaigned as overt
white supremacists; and none questioned the status quo on segregation.[37]

After nearly a decade out of power, the liberal faction regrouped and prepared to challenge the conservatives again in 1956. Shivers stood aside in the
Democratic Primary but fought to keep his grip on the state party machinery,
to no avail. The liberals had ousted Shivers at the convention.[38] The liberal
victories, however, remained limited; Shivers was replaced as governor by the
equally-conservative Price Daniel, and President Eisenhower easily defeated
Adlai Stevenson for reelection in 1956, again winning Texas by a comfortable
margin.

Segregation had begun to fade away, but many Texans bitterly resisted. In
September 1956, Shivers ordered the Texas Rangers to Mansfield High School
and Texarkana Junior College to prevent integration and restore order as angry
whites fought to prevent African Americans from attending, although other
schools began peacefully desegregating by the next year.[39] Violent resistance
to desegregation never became as widespread as it did other southern states,
and few governors afterward attempted to stage any dramatic showdown to
prevent federal court orders from ending the Jim Crow system in the state. In
fact, "Texas governors after Shivers limited their intervention into local desegregation affairs to verbal expressions of support."[40]

Texans looking for change of whatever variety found some encouraging
signs in these events. Liberal Democrats excitedly pointed to the ouster of
Shivers and the beginnings of progress in race relations. Republicans eagerly
chalked up another election victory. Liberal Democrats in Texas hoped that
the more reform-minded direction of the national Democratic organization,
particularly with its emphasis on social policy and civil rights, would so alien-

ate the conservatives that they would leave the Democracy for the Republican Party. In theory, this would leave a Democratic Party controlled by moderates and liberals, who would make up their losses through the enfranchisement of minorities who would more likely support the party.

By the late 1950s, this new direction appeared to work with the election of the liberal Ralph Yarborough to the United States Senate in a 1957 special election victory. The law at the time allowed Yarborough to win the special election without a runoff, which had usually undermined liberal chances as the conservatives converged on one candidate to defeat the liberal in the runoff. The shift of the most extreme conservative Democrats into Republican ranks had helped Yarborough defeat the conservative William Blakley, a change that liberals had longed for. Unfortunately for the liberals, the strength of the conservatives was far beyond what they had hoped, and the alienation that drove them from the Democratic Party would endanger Democratic opportunities to win in the general election. As one observer notes, "Changes were occurring, the most important of which was a shift in preference toward the Republican Party. This is what the liberals had long hoped would happen, for it would signal an exodus of conservatives from the Democratic Party, which would give liberal candidates a better chance to win the nomination. . . . but it soon became obvious that a Democratic nomination was no longer tantamount to election in November."[41]

Conservative Democrats had begun to leave the party for the Republicans, but at the expense of the Democracy's monopoly on electoral power. The Republican Party steadily gained support from Texas voters. The special Senate election in 1957 proved that the party could now tip the balance of power in the state as the Republicans now drained the strength of the conservative Democrats. Just enough workers, minorities, and small farmers could vote to tip the balance in favor of liberal Democrats such as Yarbrough, while the conservatives split their votes between the conservative Democrats and Republicans.[42]

By 1960, the Democrats had rebounded from the previous decade's reversal of fortune on the national scene. The party's presidential nominee, Sen. John F. Kennedy of Massachusetts, chose Texas's own Lyndon B. Johnson as his vice-presidential candidate. Johnson, the Senate majority leader since the mid-1950s, was a moderate warmly embraced by all factions of the Democratic Party. Republicans, however, tore into Johnson as he attempted to run for reelection to the Senate at the same time he ran for vice-president. Anti-Democratic sentiment had risen steadily in the state for a number of years, particularly in Dallas. By the mid-1950s, Dallas County had elected and reelected a Republican to Congress, Bruce Alger of Dallas. Alger had won with the support of disaffected Democrats, but the oil and financial center of Dallas had grown to such an extent that the Republicans had begun to emerge as a powerful electoral force apart from the conservative-liberal schism. Dallas had become a center for many right-wing groups that held no sympathy for Democrats of either faction.

At a campaign stop in the city, a mob of angry Republicans swarmed upon Johnson and his wife. The Johnsons endured a half-hour of being jostled and spit on by the group as they made their way to a campaign luncheon.[43] The incident enraged many Texans, leaving attendees of the debacle such as Republican Senate candidate John Tower and Congressman Alger, as well as Republican organizers of the affair, perplexed by the outcry. Johnson endured the incident, galvanized the many Texans disgusted by the abuse of a national candidate, and mustered all of his political skill into a narrow win for the Texas Democrats.

But once Johnson became vice-president in January 1961, the Senate seat he had been re-elected to now lay open and required a special election to fill the vacancy. Tower, Johnson's Republican opponent in the 1960 Senate contest, resumed his campaign against an army of seventy Democrats hoping to fill the seat. The Republican Party put all of its energy into the campaign, while the Democrats remained hopelessly divided.[44] The runoff election in spring 1961 threw Tower against the extremely conservative interim Sen. William A. Blakley. Liberal Democrats, disgusted by Blakley, refused to vote for either candidate or voted for Tower to cast off the conservative faction. The results stunned the nation. "In the 1961 special election, Tower won with 50.6 percent of the vote, becoming the first Republican senator from the south in the twentieth century."[45] The election, dismissed by Democrats as a fluke, would become a harbinger of the growth of the Texas Republican Party. The Texas Republican Party had now proven that it was not simply a protest party or a safety valve for the raging Democratic civil war, but a power that the state must recognize. The chasm in the Democratic Party, if not repaired, would simply thrust more Republicans into office over Democrats unable to work with the separate wings of the party.

The Republicans found the breakthrough they had longed for. The Republican Party had emerged as a viable alternative, but would still rely on Democratic defections for victory. With Tower in office, the Republicans hoped to use his stunning win, coupled with the sharp criticisms of the Kennedy administration, into more election victories. The strategy almost worked. The 1962 election saw more wins for the Republicans as a backlash over the Kennedy administration's civil rights initiatives cost the Democrats two congressional seats and the Republican Jack Cox earned 45.6 percent of the vote in the gubernatorial election against the Democratic nominee, Johnson's protégé, John B. Connally.[46] Democratic support had fallen sharply since 1960, but the party had rallied against the Republicans, salvaging its electoral monopoly on statewide offices. The popularity of Connally and Johnson helped bolster Democratic strength weighed down by conservative defections spurred by disgust at the social policies of the Kennedy-Johnson administrations.

Events in other southern states proved that the rise of the Republican Party was more than a local phenomenon and more enduring than a single candidate in a single election. Republicans captured Oklahoma in the 1960 presidential election. In 1962, Henry Bellmon would become the state's first Republican governor, followed by Republican Dewey Bartlett in 1966.[47] Both men would be elected to the U.S. Senate within two years of leaving office.

The rapid changes in the state remained quite unsettling for many. Despite the nation's impressive economic growth in the 1950s, the fears of communism and growing calls for changes in all areas of American social life from across the nation planted grave doubts about the future of the country that many conservatives wanted. In particular, Texas's brand of conservatism fed upon the enormous changes in the decades since the end of World War II.[48] Conservatives had developed a reluctance and mistrust of almost any new initiative, fearing they would make diplomatic and social problems even worse than before.

Some Republican strategists saw the race issue as a wedge in the Democratic Party, one that could help the party's fortunes in the South.[49] Hoping to recapture the White House in 1964, some Republicans began to alter their civil rights stance to make the party more palatable to these politically homeless conservatives and an attractive alternative to the remainder.

Kennedy's civil rights initiatives had foundered until his assassination in Dallas in November 1963. Lyndon Johnson rallied the shocked nation and pushed through many of Kennedy's proposals, including major civil rights legislation. With the landmark Civil Rights Act of 1964 passed, many southerners reacted with horror as the Jim Crow system began to collapse. Johnson realized this would deepen the schism in the Democratic Party, and he worked feverishly to keep the party together. After Johnson's ascension to the presidency in 1963, he worked skillfully to contain Democratic infighting long enough to present a unified front during his 1964 election campaign.[50] Arizona Sen. Barry Goldwater provided a welcome alternative for Jim Crow enthusiasts as he denounced the Civil Rights Act and looked for a Republican opportunity to break into the South. The election proved disastrous to Republicans nationally and in Texas, but Goldwater successfully carried a number of Deep South states for the first time since Reconstruction.[51] He had espoused a new conservative philosophy that resonated with many in Texas. More significantly, when Goldwater criticized the Civil Rights Act, southern white support began to flow toward the Republican Party for the first time in southern political history.[52] The immediate significance paled in the wake of Johnson's landslide, but the trend toward the Republicans would only continue.

As the legal rights of minorities expanded across the nation and more minorities moved into entirely new areas, the politics of the nation also shifted. The Democrats now had to rely more heavily on the minority vote to win elections in the South, and the Republicans now had to rely on disaffected conservatives streaming into their camp. The demographic changes taking place in the nation were dramatic and undeniable. One change almost unnoticed by the rest of the United States resulted in a massive wave of immigration to the cities. Roughly five million African Americans, primarily from the Deep

South, moved into the central cities between 1950 and 1970, while seven million white people moved into the suburbs.[53] As a result, large inner cities thus became increasingly dominated by minorities and more of the most economically distressed rural residents moved away. In fact, on the eve of World War II, approximately one-third of the South's black population resided in cities, and by 1970, that percentage had doubled to 67 percent, though many remained in the lower economic classes.[54] With more African Americans and other minorities living in the cities, the shift summarily altered the politics of both the city and the countryside.

Minorities found new opportunities in the cities, but also found the same prejudices they had faced in rural areas. Nevertheless, the prospect of a better life in the cities, at least in some respects, continued to attract minorities. Despite the promise of a city life, many minorities could find only menial, low-wage jobs. In fact, most African Americans remained concentrated in the lowest urban occupational categories from the until the 1970s.[55] Only with the introduction of major civil rights legislation in the 1960s did discrimination in education and hiring begin to subside and allow minorities to compete for better jobs.

In 1966, buoyed by their success in defeating all Republican congressmen in Texas and having a total monopoly in the state Senate, Texas Democrats hoped to oust the state's leading Republican, John Tower, hoping his election had only been a fluke. The Democrats, however, reeled from bitter criticisms of Johnson, over the war in Vietnam, civil rights, and rioting in major cities across the nation.

Although Atty. Gen. Waggoner Carr had won statewide elections before, he had always faced weak opposition in the fall. Never before had Carr attempted to oust a sitting Republican from as lofty a position as Tower. Tower's forces remained determined to hold their one Republican Senator at all costs. Carr proved as disastrous as Blakley—he remained too conservative and racially divisive for most liberal Democrats to accept. Tower won a full term. Tower had run a campaign financed by Texas and national conservative sources, while Texas liberals and Hispanics were completely alienated by the conservatism of Carr.[56]

This continued the trend of tactical voting that liberal Democrats had employed for some time.[57] With the success of the Voting Rights Act of 1965, the initial results of the experiment seemed to bode well for Texas liberals. Conservatives began to leave the Democratic Party and more minorities began to vote. In fact, before the Voting Rights Act of 1965, only 29 percent of eligible African Americans in Texas had registered to vote, but this number increased dramatically into the 1970s.[58] The new base of minority voters now had access to the polls, and registration totals gradually increased. But too many conservatives had left the party, or those conservatives who had never voted now looked to the Texas Republicans as their new alternative.

Coupled with new civil rights laws that allowed minorities to vote and a growing Republican Party that had begun to provide a realistic alternative to the Democrats, more voters began rushing to the polls across the South. Conservative Republicans now had a reasonable possibility of winning some elections. Interestingly, although the southern population had increased by only 34 percent between 1948 and 1968, voter turnout nearly tripled, up 183.6 percent by 1968.[59] For all of the threats the Republican Party had leveled against Democratic power, they had failed to capitalize before the 1970s. The Republicans had very few primary voters, largely because the Democratic Primary still decided the election in many areas. Studies reveal that from 1965 to 1982, the Republican Primary vote in Texas represented only an average of 11.9 percent of the total Republican vote in the November contest.[60] The strength of the Democrats on the local level resulted in many Republicans voting in the local Democratic Primary elections in order to have a voice in the local races often uncontested by the party. The "Presidential Republican" thus maintained at least a passing loyalty to the Democrats, frustrating Republican attempts to build a sustainable voting base.

Race had driven southern politics for decades, but as minorities began to vote in greater numbers, it became much more perilous to spout openly racist rhetoric as the 1970s wore on.[61] With the lifting of voting restrictions and energetic efforts to register minorities to vote, African Americans had now become a powerful component of the Democratic voting base. This was a base that a Democratic candidate could not afford to alienate and win an election. However, many conservatives still quietly fumed at the federal mandates against discrimination. In increasing numbers, they began to leave the Democratic Party for the Republican Party in response to the strong civil rights stands by the national party and some local Democrats.

The political climate in Texas, curiously, remained much milder on the race issue than other southern states. In 1968, when the race issue remained at its strongest, Texas remained the only state in the South to stay with the Democratic nominee, Hubert Humphrey.[62] The other states lined up with either Alabama Gov. George Wallace of the American Independent Party or Republican nominee Richard M. Nixon. The leadership of Johnson and Governor Connally managed to keep the disaffection of conservative Texas Democrats in check.

In 1968, Connally decided against seeking a fourth term as governor, opening the floodgates for ambitious Democrats to step into the governor's mansion. When the dust settled from the first primary, liberal stalwart Don Yarborough and Lt. Gov. Preston Smith faced each other in the runoff. It became a typical Texas-style election. Smith campaigned across the state combining conservative themes with popular reform proposals, including improved medical care, education facilities, and better highways. In the second primary, the conservatives surged to Smith, while liberals and minorities moved toward Yarborough.

Smith defeated Yarborough to win the nomination, but in the general election, the minority voters and liberals stayed loyal to the Democracy and voted for Smith. In this "reverse-scale" phenomenon that developed in the South, during the primary voters would cast their ballots based on ideology but would vote for their party nominee in the fall out of party loyalty. In particular, Smith won less than 5 percent of the black vote in the 1968 second primary, but more than 80 percent of the upper-class white vote, yet the situation reversed entirely in November when he won barely one-third of the upper-class white vote and more than 70 percent of the black vote.[63]

The upper-class whites had begun to move into the Republican Party, stripping the Democrats of much of the strength they had in the past and robbing conservative Democrats of a valuable constituency they had depended upon for support. Because of the usual lack of significant Republican opposition in the general election, many conservatives continued to vote in the Democratic Primary almost by habit to have a voice in local affairs, strengthening the conservative wing of the Democracy.

Smith won the general election in 1968 but by a less than comfortable margin. Large cities, with affluent neighborhoods and plentiful business opportunities for corporations, had slowly become the base of Republican support. Texas Democrats, historically used to a rural constituency, faced difficulty in connecting with new voters from outside the state and unfamiliar with its politics or political traditions. These new voters had instead brought their own voting traditions with them, rejected the Democrats no matter how conservative or liberal a candidate might appear, and integrated themselves into the new Republican Party for the state. Native Texas conservatives had slowly left the Democrats and those who remained in the party could no longer appeal to these voters. The rural base of the Democratic Party had steadily weakened in the face of massive urban growth. The Democrats continued to register winning vote totals in the cities in most instances, but these margins had declined steadily for years. Smith's totals demonstrate this trend. In his gubernatorial bids, Preston Smith won the large urban counties with a 52 percent majority in 1968 and a 48 percent plurality in 1970.[64]

Smith embarked on a quiet administration, pressing for quiet reforms to the state's social services system but concentrated on maintaining the pro-business climate of the state. Despite the state's almost legendary frontier past, Smith, a Lubbock native, had become the first true West Texan to become governor.[65] The western portions of the state had generally felt underrepresented for many years. One biographer notes, "Smith had prided himself on his availability to ordinary Texans while he served as governor."[66] This personal touch generated many warm feelings for Smith.

The Texas economy now boasted a wealth that the state had never seen. Despite this, the state lagged behind most of the nation in most social services; and Texas and the rest of the South, however, still ranked behind the national average in terms of poverty.[67] Minorities remained especially afflicted economically, still ranking far behind the rest of the nation in terms of median income well beyond the 1970s. By 1969, 18.8 percent of Texans and 20.3 percent of southerners still lived in poverty, compared with 13.7 percent nationally; but in 1975, these numbers had dropped to 15.2 percent, 15.3 percent, and 11.4 percent, respectively.[68] By 1975, Texas had fallen behind the southern average of children in poverty with more than one out of every five children in poverty, compared with 19.6 percent across the South and 14.5 percent nationally. Many Texans had yet to participate in the new age of industrial prosperity that had since arrived.

Growth had become the watchword for cities in the Lone Star State. Over the course of a few short decades, Texas cities exploded in ways that altered their character forever. In fact, the major cities of Texas had all become at least ten times larger in 1960 than they had in 1900.[69] The growth began to alter the politics of urban Texas. The rural character of the state's main political concerns would soon be vastly overshadowed by the problems of suddenly crowded cities. Analysts had predicted this change for decades, as one 1949 analysis suggests. As V. O. Key writes, "The growth of cities contains the seeds of political change for the South. In almost every type of analysis urban political behavior differs significantly from that of the rural areas."[70]

By the 1960s and 1970s, the South no longer represented a pariah for businesses and individuals wishing to relocate from the North. The Sunbelt South, a region of cheap land, moderate climates, and new opportunities had begun to emerge. By the 1960s, for the first time since before the Civil War, more people had begun moving into the South than moving away; and by 1980, one out of every five southerners had been born in the North.[71] The character of the entire South would change accordingly.

Texas's growth in the 1970s had become not just urban, but suburban, reflecting a nationwide trend. The suburbs became the focus of most of the growth of the South and not the large central cities.[72] Texas remained no exception. As many southern cities continued to face rising crime rates and tensions stemming from desegregation, many preferred the lifestyle offered by smaller, typically more homogeneous communities outside the major cities. Once-isolated farm towns quickly began evolving into major urban population centers. Cheap land and easy access to the major cities enticed this growth. In Texas, most of this growth centered on the Dallas–Fort Worth metropolitan area and the greater Houston area. A 1980 report shows that of the ten fastest-growing counties in Texas, four included counties surrounding the Dallas–Fort Worth area and two more included suburban Houston counties.[73] Collin, north of Dallas, had more than doubled its population, adding 77,570 in the 1970s, Denton had increased 89.2 percent, and Hood had nearly tripled in population. Montgomery and Fort Bend counties each added more than 78,000 people each during the decade.

Houston's growth, however, remained quite uneven. Aggressive annexation policies fueled most of the city's population gains, absorbing wide areas of new land and subdivisions. In fact, by 1978, Houston had 50 percent more territory than it did just fifteen years earlier.[74] By mid-century, the city did not necessarily radiate from a central point, but through the annexation of outlying subdivisions and pre-existing communities, communities within Houston spread outward and connected with others.[75] Local leaders fought to encourage new industries to relocate to the area, winning the site for the coveted NASA space center in the 1960s. But its heart still lay in the oil industry. Oil fueled the growth of the city as most of the country's largest oil companies had located major facilities in the area.[76] While cities in the industrial northeast faltered in the 1960s and 1970s, Houston enjoyed no impediments to its progress. Its rapid expansion as a city, however, had come at a considerable price to many neighborhoods. Houston had expanded so rapidly that it had neglected its older neighborhoods in favor of the more affluent areas annexed on its outskirts. The city had worried so much about the new, mostly white, neighborhoods that services in older minority neighborhoods suffered tremendously.[77] City services in historically minority neighborhoods suffered tremendously. Many of these issues did not begin to be solved until the 1980s. In fact, more than three dozen black neighborhoods still lacked indoor plumbing as late as 1985.[78]

Problems of representation also haunted minority neighborhoods. The numbers of minorities registered to vote in the Houston area had risen dramatically since the 1960s but still had not yet realized any electoral gains from their newfound voting strength. Progress in municipal representation lagged significantly. Houston had elected African Americans to the state legislature by 1966, but an African American did not serve on the city council until 1971.[79]

The growth of Dallas became almost legendary. Aided by annexation policies as aggressive as Houston, Dallas surged from a compact community on the banks of the Trinity River before World War II to a major city swallowing most of the county within twenty years. The city grew in area more than sixfold from 1940 to 1960, with a population reaching 680,000.[80] The population would double again between 1950 and 1980.[81]

The Lone Star State charged into the 1970s with the same postwar momentum. Cities grew and industry expanded. The Texas of the 1970s had almost completely changed from the Texas at the turn of the century. It had become an urban, industrialized state and continued to move further from its agricultural roots. A complete reversal in population had taken place from 1900 when roughly five out of every six Texans remained rural; by 1970 the state was 79.7 percent urban.[82] Much of the wealth of the state had come very recently. Of the richest families in Texas in the early 1980s, only a handful had inherited fortunes as far back as the nineteenth century.[83] This had come as a direct result of the oil and manufacturing that had developed fairly recently in the state.

As the 1970s unfolded, it had become clear that Texas had moved far beyond agriculture and oil as the focus of its economy. In actuality, some eleven of the twenty largest Texas-based public corporations were primarily affiliated with the petrochemical industry.[84] More of this new wealth had filtered down to ordinary Texans. Incomes had risen dramatically in just a few short years in the 1970s. Personal income in the state had more than doubled from 1971 to 1977, to nearly $88.5 billion, while the Texas per capita income rose from thirty-second in the nation in 1970 to eighteenth in the nation by 1980.[85] Texas had quickly moved ahead of the national average in terms of per capita income and personal income. This new wealth affected spending and social patterns and gave many Texans a sense that it should be protected by any means.

The 1972 Democratic Primary would produce no major shifts in ideology, but would oust an incumbent governor. The Sharpstown stock fraud scandal had crippled Smith's reelection efforts, and his challengers quickly capitalized on the corruption issue.[86] Although Smith had a reputation as an otherwise honest and kindly figure, the scandal had tainted this reputation during the 1972 election season. The courts would never convict him of any charges, but the voters soundly rejected him. Lt. Gov. Ben Barnes, also implicated in the scandal, faced the same electoral fate in the primary.

The runoff paired State Rep. Frances "Sissy" Farenthold against rancher and former State Rep. Dolph Briscoe. Farenthold, a liberal, had few resources with which to mount a challenge to Briscoe, easily one of the richest men in the state. The Farenthold campaign, underfinanced and understaffed, focused its meager resources on the thirty counties in the state with the largest population, and her candidacy, as a result of its inability to compete, immediately became more of a crusade than a campaign.[87] Hopelessly outspent, her campaign folded in the face of Briscoe's quiet conservatism and deep pockets.

The gubernatorial contest of 1972, however, remained far from complete. Republican State Sen. Henry (Hank) Grover waged a surprisingly strong campaign, aided by the popularity of two Republicans seeking reelection, Senator Tower and President Nixon. Democratic strength drained further when a third-party candidate, Ramsey Muniz of the La Raza Unida (The United People) Party, waged a fierce campaign against the discrimination faced by Hispanics. Muniz targeted the Democratic Party and wealthy farmers and ranchers such as Briscoe who regularly employed Hispanic migrant farm workers as exploitative. Muniz's organization caught fire in South Texas, a region rich with Hispanic voters. In the triangulated race, Briscoe won with 48 percent of the vote—a three-percentage-point victory. Muniz captured 6 percent of the vote. Briscoe had become the first Democratic governor to win with less than a majority of the vote since 1894. With this election, the growing strength of the Texas Republicans had become undeniable. Grover's 45 percent represented far more than a respectable effort but a new trend. In three of the previous six elections, the Republican candidate had earned at least 45 percent of the vote. In 1962, Republican nominee Jack Cox polled 46 percent of the vote; and the nominee in 1968 and 1970, Paul Eggers, polled 43 percent and 47 percent of the vote, respectively.[88]

Democratic control of the governorship to this point had been preserved by relatively popular Democratic governors, intense loyalty to the Democratic

Party, and weak Republican candidates. A change in any of those conditions could prove disastrous for the Democrats. The Democratic nomination for the governorship no longer meant automatic election—a strong fall campaign became mandatory, a sharp departure from the past. The brand-name loyalty that had kept many conservative Democrats loyal to the party almost all of their lives no longer had as much appeal. The national party had changed direction over the years, leaving many conservatives unsure of where they now fit.

The numbers, however, still largely lay on the Democratic side. The 1970 Democratic Primary had attracted nearly ten times the voters of the Republican contest; while in the 1972 primaries, the Democrats boasted 2.1 million voters and the Republicans could only attract 114,000.[89] Despite the voting totals from the May 1972 primaries, Republican Richard Nixon easily won the state's presidential vote and Senator Tower won reelection with relative ease. Dolph Briscoe barely won the fall election. The question remained: How long could the Democrats keep winning by such narrow margins, particularly if their strength began to falter?

The 1974 contest saw a return of Democratic fortunes in Texas. Farenthold challenged Briscoe for a rematch in 1974. Farenthold's attempted rematch, however, faced the same lack of money, and many former supporters remained apathetic to her attacks on Briscoe's record on education funding and other important issues.[90] Briscoe had done little to alienate many Texans, but had not acted forcefully enough for others. With this, Democratic Primary voters renominated their incumbent. As the Watergate scandal encircled and devoured the Nixon White House, Republicans found themselves on the defensive and retreated nationwide. The Republicans nominated a lackluster gubernatorial candidate, Jim Granberry, and watched helplessly as Briscoe swept to a resounding reelection victory—winning by a two-to-one margin.[91]

With changes in the state constitution now enacted, state offices moved to four-year terms beginning in 1974. On the heels of the Watergate scandal that forced Nixon from the White House, the Democrats expanded on their 1974 electoral successes in the 1976 election. Sen. Lloyd Bentsen, who had defeated Sen. Ralph Yarborough in the 1970 Democratic Primary, now easily beat back a Republican challenge. Democrat Jimmy Carter of Georgia won the state by 130,000 votes to capture the presidency. (See appendix F.)[92] The Democrats gained more than 900,000 presidential votes over their crushing loss in 1972 as voters embraced Carter after turning away from the 1972 nominee, George McGovern, in disgust. The Republicans only lost 345,000 votes between 1972 and 1976, reflecting the continuing strength of the presidential Republican voter in Texas.

Even with Carter's regional strengths and with the recent memories of Watergate weighing down the Republicans, the Democratic rebound in the South proved, at best, anemic compared to the party's performance in the past. The Democrats could not return to the days of unquestioned supremacy. One study reveals how deeply the Republicans had begun to entrench themselves throughout the South: "Carter received only 54 percent of the popular vote in the South . . . [and] Republicans accounted for about 23 percent of the members of Congress and about 10 percent of the state legislators in the South."[93] Carter, a son of the South, could no longer appeal to the unbending loyalty of the South for the Democrats. That intense loyalty had faded. By far a minority, Republicans relished each gain and tried to build on each success.

Segregated schools and neighborhoods had remained a delicate problem for the state in the late 1970s. In fact, in 1970 the Texas Education Agency reported that in the San Antonio school system, some 87 percent of the black students still attended predominantly black schools, while the Houston and Dallas districts reported segregation rates of 92 and 97 percent.[94] Housing remained deeply segregated through the 1970s. Houston remained especially afflicted with more than four out of five of Houston's blacks living in predominantly segregated neighborhoods in 1980, and African American families still earning an average of 61 percent of white families.[95] Efforts to desegregate neighborhoods and schools, particularly through court orders, prompted sharp anger from white residents that would continue throughout the 1970s. Thousands of white families fled to the suburbs during the decade to escape the problems associated with court-ordered busing, a phenomenon derided as "white flight."

Although minorities represented an increasing portion of the state's population, these communities could not boast of any significant voice in state or local politics. By 1971, three African Americans served in the Texas House of Representatives but neither blacks nor Hispanics had any representation on the city councils of Houston or San Antonio.[96] Protests by civil rights supporters and a series of court cases forced these cities to alter their representation schemes to allow the voices of minorities to be heard. In Houston, the U.S. Department of Justice ruled Houston's annexations of outlying white areas in 1977 and 1978 to the detriment of minority voting in violation of the 1965 Voting Rights Act, while San Antonio's move to a single-member district form of government allowed Hispanics to dominate local politics for the first time since the days of the Texas Revolution.[97] New voting rights legislation and aggressive voter registration dramatically increased registration rates for minorities across the state. By the late 1960s, the African American voter registration rate in Harris County had climbed to 67 percent, or 85,000 voters—a gigantic leap forward from the 5,000 African Americans registered to vote in the county in 1944.[98] However, with an increasingly competitive Republican Party emerging, whites disgusted with Democratic rule had also increased their registration and turnout by more than 250,000 voters over the same time period. Minority voting power had clearly increased but paled in the face of the new white electoral strength.

Political power steadily shifted to the cities. This posed problems for the Democrats as the strength of the Republicans lay in the large cities. Preston Smith had barely managed to win the metropolitan areas in his 1968 and 1970 campaigns. New families flooded into the cities every day. The Comptroller's

Office noted the astonishing growth of Texas cities. Arlington, although a sub-urb of Fort Worth, had swelled to become one of the state's largest communities, while Austin and San Antonio posted incredible gains in the 1970s.[99] Throughout the entire decade, the state would gain 916,000 new residents, roughly equivalent to gaining a new city the size of Dallas as it existed at that time.[100] Such growth and demographic shifts could not help but alter the state's traditional political alignments. In addition, the suburban communities had begun to grow outside the larger cities, absorbing an increasing Republican population looking for a simpler life away from the big city.

This growth, however, centered on the suburban areas or new, affluent sub-divisions on the outer edges of the major cities. Within Houston's 1940 boundaries, the population dropped between 1940 and 1980, making its growth from annexation; San Antonio faced a similar situation as it lost nearly 55,000 residents from its 1950 borders between 1960 and 1975.[101] This loss of population created problems for the inner cities as they coped with the rise of slums, but the once-isolated farm towns on the outskirts of the cities reaped incredible benefits as thousands of middle- and upper-class residents swarmed to these new communities. Aggressive annexation of unincorporated areas on their peripheries provided Texas cities with the opportunities to fuel new growth to offset any urban decay, allowing the state to avoid the worst of the urban problems that declining—and landlocked—industrial cities faced in the North.

Potential problems began to appear on the horizon. Crude oil production had declined precipitously in the mid-1970s. Combined with the two Arab oil embargos of the decade, many feared for the future energy independence of the nation. These signs of decline worried many Texans whose livelihoods depended on oil. The economic well-being of the state depended upon maintaining a healthy oil industry, state officials warned, with the American bill for foreign oil rising $17 billion between 1973 and 1974.[102]

The South had made incredible strides by the end of the 1970s but still paled in economic strength and wealth compared to the rest of the nation. Texas fared the best of all southern states. The bulk of the nation's wealth still lay in the industrial areas of the northeast. In 1976, the per capita income of all eleven former Confederate states still ranked below the national average.[103] Rural areas faced a sharp decline as agricultural employment dropped from 4.4 million in 1940 to 800,000 in 1975.[104] Farms continued to decline, threatening the future of many rural communities as many left for the bustling new metropolitan areas of the state. The larger farms and ranches, with more resources at their disposal, continued to thrive despite the difficulties that the smaller farmers faced.

Texas would enter the 1978 elections as a modern, urban industrial state. The agricultural base now paled in comparison with the power of the cities. Federal statistics demonstrated how profound these changes had become for the state in a very short time. Non-agricultural employment in Texas had more than doubled between 1959 and 1978, from 2.5 million to 5.2 million in 1978, an increase of more than 300,000 just since 1977.[105] Manufacturing jobs alone had surged from 488,000 jobs in 1959 to 893,500 in 1977 and jumped still higher in 1978 to 954,100.[106] More Texans now worked in manufacturing than in agriculture, a stunning reversal just since World War II. Texas produced a great deal in terms of agriculture, but now paled in the face of its industrial might. Many Texans remained quite anxious to keep this new industrial wealth safe. This began to totally refocus how Texans behaved politically.

The Republicans continued to creep up on the Democrats. Slowly, they gained seats in the state legislature, in the Lone Star congressional delegation, and in various offices at the local level. In the legislature, the Republicans held 16 seats in the 150-seat House of Representatives after 1974 and increased their numbers to 19 after 1976, but they still held only 3 seats in the state Senate.[107] Far from a majority, Republicans played an increasingly important role as they allied with conservative Democrats on important legislation. They steadily made their presence felt. As of 1978, the Democrats had won only four of the previous seven presidential elections in the state. The Republicans claimed one U.S. Senator and only two of the state's twenty-four congressional seats.

The Democratic congressional vote percentage statewide had fallen from 72.2 percent in 1974 to 64.7 percent in 1976.[108] These vote totals had dropped for years. In 1978, the Democrats would face an anxious electorate fretting over the energy independence of the nation and the direction of the state. The increasing disapproval of Jimmy Carter also threatened to weigh down the Democrats. Sen. John Tower would face reelection in 1978, and the Republicans promised to defend their lone senator with all their might. Gov. Dolph Briscoe also faced reelection against a growing Republican Party and a liberal Democratic faction frustrated with his performance.

Both parties entered new territory with the 1978 election year. Texas had transformed itself, creating an electorate increasingly unfamiliar to the traditional political alignments of Texas. It had become an industrial state, but not a unionized state. The Republicans would wage battle from their power bases in the large metropolitan areas, while the Democrats would rely on their faithful voters in the rural areas and minority voters. This represented almost the complete opposite strategy of many states outside the South. And the many voters feared for an uncertain future in what seemed an increasingly anti-American world.

The Republicans waited quietly for their opportunity. The Democrats hoped that tradition and the century of experienced leadership once again would lead the party to victory and keep the Republicans at bay for another election season. The Republicans hoped that 1978 would finally be the year to break the Democratic hold on the state's politics—if everything would fall into place.

CHAPTER 2

THE DEMOCRATIC REVOLUTION

"I SAY IF THEY DON'T LIKE political jokes, they shouldn't elect them," quipped former Texas Gov. Preston Smith as he wandered the dusty political trails of West Texas.[1] Texas politics had always managed to produce eccentric characters and campaigns replete with sometimes bizarre entertainment, either bitterly tragic or morbidly hilarious. The 1978 Democratic primary would carry on that tradition as the incumbent governor, Dolph Briscoe, would attempt to defend himself from the embarrassing missteps of his administration. Smith would try to recapture the governor's mansion that spring, becoming an interesting sideshow as Gov. Dolph Briscoe would campaign for a third term against Atty. Gen. John Hill, who would try to wrest away the prize he had long sought from both. The results of the primary would reshape the leadership and direction of the Texas Democratic Party.

The three main candidates for the Democratic nomination had actually run against each other for governor before. In 1968, Briscoe, Smith, and Hill had become part of a crowded field of ten candidates hoping to succeed Gov. John Connally after he announced he would not seek a fourth term. Smith placed second in the first primary, with Briscoe placing fourth, and Hill finishing a distant sixth. Smith went on to defeat liberal Don Yarborough for the nomination in the runoff and serve two terms as governor. In 1972, Briscoe ousted Smith, while Hill won election to the post of attorney general. In 1974, the traditional two-year terms of state officeholders switched to four-year terms.[2] Briscoe easily won reelection, while Hill faced no opposition in the general election and both looked to new opportunities in the upcoming 1978 contest.

Throughout 1977, the candidates began moving into position for the primary. Since the primary's inception at the beginning of the century, it had essentially become the real election, given that the winner of the Democratic Primary had always won the governor's mansion in the fall contest against a weak Republican candidate. In fact, almost every southern Democratic primary produced greater turnout than the general election.[3] In many areas of Texas, the Republican Party did not exist on the local level and never bothered to offer candidates for office, making many these areas strict one-party communities. The election began and ended with the Democratic Primary. Although the Republicans had made strong attempts to challenge the Democrats before, they had always met with defeat. To most Texas observers, little seemed different about the state political scene in 1978.

Dolph Briscoe would seek a third term that year. He had attracted a loyal group of admirers, but many Texans inside and outside the Democratic Party remained unimpressed with his leadership over the past six years. Briscoe had not won his first term by a wide margin. In the wake of a nationwide Republican sweep in 1972, Briscoe barely won election over a well-organized opponent, State Rep. Hank Grover. Some results on election night alarmed the party faithful with reports showing Briscoe trailing Grover, results that caused many to question Briscoe's effectiveness. Despite Briscoe's clear victory, critics continued to deride him as a "minority" governor.[4]

Briscoe came to the office with a very traditional idea of a limited government. In a speech to the legislature, he repeated his mantra, "Government should do only two things: Safeguard the lives and property of our people; Ensure that each of us has a chance to work out his destiny according to his talents."[5] This attitude played well with most Texans. In 1974, he was elected to the state's first four-year term for governor, winning by a two-to-one margin (see appendix B). As governor, Briscoe worked to build a system of modern highways for the state and to hold down taxes. He often boasted how his administration consistently opposed new taxes and defeated any efforts to raise them.[6]

Upon entering office in 1973, Briscoe called for a restoration of integrity to government as Texans recoiled against the Sharpstown stock scandal that led to the downfall of Gov. Preston Smith and Lt. Gov. Ben Barnes in the 1972 election. Briscoe declared, "We must restore politics to a high level of respect instead of being thought of as a dirty business."[7] He also touched on an issue that he would repeat often, calling for "no new taxes in 1973."[8] The call to stop tax increases became a constant refrain for Briscoe as he boasted about his administration's efforts to avoid raising taxes throughout his tenure as governor. At one point, he declared, "The country is tired of rising taxes and wasteful government. . . . We have one of America's lowest state tax levies and neither a corporate nor a personal income tax. We should keep it that way."[9]

In addition, Briscoe became renowned for his obsession with the state's transportation system. He aggressively pushed for the construction of new highways across Texas. In his 1975 inaugural address, Briscoe painted the transportation issue in very flowery terms. "Each Texan has a right to mobility, the ways and means to transport himself and his goods from one place to another by highway, rail, water or air."[10] For supporters of new highways, the extreme distances within the state and the growing population made the necessity clear. In his first term, the state completed 4,566 miles of new and reconstructed highways and an additional 1,885 miles remained under construction.[11]

By 1977, Briscoe had come under fire by many Texans for this same understated style that won him so many admirers. Much of this criticism had steadily mounted for years. State Rep. Walt Parker, a Denton Democrat, echoed the sentiments of many in a 1973 interview when he noted lack of enthusiasm for Briscoe's performance.[12] Many remained disappointed with the lack of progress on many pressing issues. Liberal Democrats, teachers, ranchers, and Hispanics had all become increasingly agitated by the Briscoe administration. When a scandal erupted over the management of the Office of Migrant Affairs, an organization run by the governor's office through federal funds, many Texans began to believe that Briscoe's days as governor had become numbered as a rebellion simmered in the Democratic ranks.[13]

Even staunch supporters recognized the increasing difficulties that Briscoe faced. House Speaker Billy Clayton commented in 1977, "[Briscoe is] just as honest as the day is long. Now, he's not flamboyant; he may not be as aggressive as some would like to see. He certainly is not one that seeks the press for the press coverage. For that reason, it may be frankly a little detrimental to his political status."[14] Robert Krueger, a two-term congressman from New Braunfels in 1978 and the eventual Democratic nominee for the U.S. Senate, reflected this opinion. "He was an old-fashioned conservative Democrat—not an activist. I had a lot of respect for Briscoe. He was a man of a lot of integrity. . . . He was not a glamorous man."[15]

Almost everyone who knew Briscoe remarked on his honesty. State Rep. Gib Lewis, a Fort Worth Democrat, recalled Briscoe's tenure in a 1979 interview. "I believe that Dolph Briscoe is a very honest man; he was sincere in what he did. . . . He had hired people outside the government that had no knowledge of how the media worked, how the legislative process worked to some extent . . . I think his appointments damaged him very greatly."[16] Briscoe did not publicize his efforts or his successes and did not often call press conferences to respond to his critics.

In the meantime, more Texans quietly looked for alternatives. A rising number of opponents claimed that Briscoe and his supporters "put highways ahead of education," although teacher salaries rose on average from $8,680 to $13,200 between 1973 and 1977.[17] Briscoe argued in response to the attacks by detailing the spending increases on education. "Our state has doubled the money we spend on education," he repeated on numerous occasions.[18]

The area of appointments, however, became Briscoe's greatest embarrassment. By 1978, Briscoe had named almost every appointed position in state government. Relying heavily on an appointments secretary to secure the names of upstanding Texans to serve in these positions, Briscoe did not notice a horrifying mistake the secretary had made. The governor had appointed a dead man to the State Health Advisory Commission. Briscoe's opponents howled at the episode. The popular magazine *Texas Monthly* awarded him a "Bum Steer Award" to highlight the comic dimensions of the appointment.[19]

Briscoe's lead counsel, David Dean, recounted the incident and the political fallout in a 2002 interview. Apparently, a list of eighteen appointees received a nomination, but four months later, a second list had to be submitted for various reasons. "The secretary had sent the names up and didn't do the due diligence of the phone calls and checking up, and one of the gentlemen had died. His widow really didn't appreciate it," said Dean.[20] "The one episode had magnified what John Hill was saying about an 'absentee governor.'" Krueger recalled that this represented Briscoe's "only slip-up that I can think of."[21]

Briscoe came from a background of privileged Texas ranchers. Briscoe County, located in the panhandle, received its name from a prominent ancestor. Formerly a state representative from his native Uvalde for four terms starting in 1949, Briscoe was worth more than $200 million by the 1980s and reportedly had more land than any individual in the state. He had spent over $1 million of his own money on the three races he made for governor, including his first successful one in 1972.[22] As a rancher, Briscoe appealed to the agricultural interests of smaller communities across the state, where most of his supporters resided.[23] His nature exuded the political inclinations that many west Texans had come to develop. Observers have noted that the wide-open, arid region has helped produce a self-sufficient, lonely, and suspicious citizenry, often slow to change or to accept it.[24]

Briscoe's lackluster style had frustrated many members of the state legislature. State Sen. Oscar Mauzy of Dallas commented in a 1975 interview that Briscoe could prove as tough an opponent as anybody when pushed, but he would only fight on a narrow set of issues. "When Briscoe makes up his mind he is going to do something, he can be as tough a son of a b— that I have ever seen," said Mauzy. "But he doesn't make up his mind to do anything very often. He really doesn't like this business of leaning on the members. It's offensive to his lifestyle, his personality. And I don't understand it."[25]

Briscoe had a mixed election record. Although he had won his races in 1972 and 1974, he had lost in 1968. And his victory in 1972 had been embarrassingly close. Many Hispanics had supported a third-party candidate that year, Ramsey Muniz of the La Raza Unida Party (LRU), who received 6.3 percent of the vote.[26] In the 1972 election, the forty counties in South and West Texas saw LRU capture 18 percent of the vote, a sizable defection from Democratic Party ranks.[27] Hispanics would develop a long mistrust of Briscoe in the years that ahead as he fought back against the organization.

The 1972 Republican nominee, Hank Grover, had done well in the large metropolitan counties, but strong Briscoe support in the rural areas helped offset this.[28] But rural power had declined precipitously in Texas for years. In fact, from 1951 to 1967, the number of rural seats in the Texas House of Representatives fell from 95 to 63 out of 150 seats available.[29] With this, the rural districts that had ruled the legislature for generations had now become the minority in favor of the rising metropolitan areas. The trend continued well into Briscoe's tenure as more Texans streamed into the cities. Rural politicians had fought for years to cling to power, often at the expense of the rising urban and suburban populations, and especially at the expense of minority representation in the cities. Changing demographics and new federal protections for voting rights forced Texas politics to reorient itself toward the cities, but rural voters still held considerable power.

The 1974 election year, however, proved far more fortuitous than two years before for Briscoe. Watergate had proved advantageous to Democratic fortunes as Texas Republicans lost two U.S. House seats, and their gubernatorial nominee, Jim Granberry, a former Lubbock mayor, ran the weakest statewide race since 1966.[30] Briscoe won by a wide margin, dispelling the memories of the near disaster two years before.

Briscoe fought back bitterly against La Raza Unida to try to destroy the organization and prevent the movement from spreading beyond South Texas. He had countered LRU with legislative attempts to tighten the requirements for political party recognition. Moreover, he denounced the party as a communist threat and blocked federal funding for Zavala County programs.[31] The fallout from the fight over federal funds for LRU's Zavala County stronghold would affect the 1978 primary fight.

The governor prepared his run for a third term, confident of his record in fiscal affairs. "The Briscoe campaign felt that Briscoe's record of solid accomplishment would carry the day," David Dean, Briscoe's general counsel noted. "Dolph was well-funded."[32] President Jimmy Carter had become a profound disappointment to conservatives, but Briscoe's stands helped separate him to some degree from much of this criticism. A *Dallas Morning News* editorial noted, "Briscoe helped deliver the Texas vote to candidate Jimmy Carter, believing firmly that the future president was committed to deregulation. As we know, Carter was not so committed. And for Briscoe, an honest man, the realization that he was taken in by Carter stands as a keen disappointment. . . . The News applauds Briscoe's efforts."[33] Briscoe's campaigned thus seemed to open on a positive note.

A November 7, 1977, rally for Briscoe in Dallas attracted nearly 7,000 supporters. One prominent Briscoe ally, Jess Hay, praised the governor, saying that the people "know the difference between phony flamboyance and true and effective leadership."[34] Briscoe beamed at the throng, "I've never been more confident of a winning campaign. . . . I like what we have here in Texas and I want to keep it that way."[35]

Atty. Gen. John Hill, however, had emerged as a rival to Briscoe. An East Texas native, navy veteran, and graduate of the University of Texas, Hill received appointment as Texas secretary of state in 1966. After winning election to the attorney general's office in 1972, Hill gained increasing support through his highly publicized efforts on behalf of ordinary Texans. He pushed for greater consumer protection and launched a number of other programs through the attorney general's office.[36] In August 1977, Hill launched a statewide investigation of nursing homes. The shocking abuses of elderly patients in one Dallas facility forced Hill to file a lawsuit against it. Forest Manor thus became the first nursing home placed in state receivership. "This just shows you what can be done if people care," confidently declared Hill. He promised more action in the next session of the legislature to protect nursing home patients.[37]

Hill had sought the Democratic nomination unsuccessfully in 1968. Although appointed secretary of state by Gov. John Connally, he had never run for a statewide elected office before. "Since it would be my first actual campaign for any kind of an office, I gave it a lot of thought," recalled Hill. "I had never run for anything. That gave me a lot of pause."[38] His friends and supporters reassured him that remained not at all unusual in Texas politics for people to run a time or two before they won. He lowered his sights and won election as attorney general in 1972, winning reelection in 1974. As attorney general, Hill began amassing an impressive record as he began his second run for the governor's mansion. He announced his candidacy for governor in late 1977 and determined to make education reform the focus of his campaign. "I thought that we had neglected education and campaigned hard on that issue. Most of my speeches were oriented toward education and health issues. Briscoe's tenure wasn't an issue in the campaign, but the media picked up on it and helped us out," noted Hill.[39] Hill nevertheless believed that Briscoe had served long enough. "No one had served two four-year terms; ten years would be too long. There were some things I wanted to accomplish in education. Some friends encouraged me to run and I did. I thought I could pursue some issues that the people would be interested in."[40] Despite the attorney general's rising popularity, most initially expected a repeat of the usual primary history and for Briscoe to win renomination. Hill faced a daunting task against an incumbent governor, but felt confident of his chances of success. Commented Hill in a 2002 interview, "I had a successful record in the state; I was well-known."[41]

David Dean had gone to work for Briscoe during the transition in December 1972. He was off and on the state payroll during the 1978 campaign. His work had provided him a unique perspective on the Briscoe administration and the governor's relationship with John Hill. Hill and Briscoe had fought bitterly over a number of issues in the state legislature. As a result, the relationship between the two disintegrated, and Dean became more of an intermediary between the two. Dean blamed Hill's well-known dreams of the governorship as partly responsible for the breakdown, as their ambitions clashed. "Hill really coveted the governor's job," recalled Dean. "Dolph Briscoe and John Hill's relationship soured over the years—they did not get along well. Briscoe really relied on the general counsel more and more."[42] Briscoe no longer wanted to deal with Hill.

The battle with La Raza Unida became just one example of how racial issues still simmered in Texas politics. A 1974 report ranked Dallas housing as the sixth most segregated city in the South.[43] In 1975, the federal government placed the state under the protection of the Voting Rights Act in response to its history of discriminating against minority voters.[44] Segregation as a major campaign issue, however, had long since faded since the 1950s. Allan Shivers, the last strong segregationist governor of Texas, left office in 1957, while the last major unapologetic segregationist to run in the Democratic Primary for governor was former governor and U.S. Sen. W. Lee "Pappy" O'Daniel, who attempted political comebacks in 1956 and 1958.[45] By 1972, eleven of the twelve southern states had moderate governors who conspicuously avoided racial rhetoric and had advocated progressive policies in their campaigns, including Texas.[46] The most strident opposition to civil rights progress centered on the issues of court-ordered busing to facilitate the integration of schools and affirmative action programs. These would prove volatile issues with many voters in the 1978 campaign. Despite progress in a number of areas, voting in southern elections remained severely polarized along racial lines.[47]

The Voting Rights Act required that states covered under the legislation had to seek federal approval of laws that could impact minority voting strength. Between 1975 and 1978, Texas submitted thousands of requests for approval, by far more than the rest of the South combined. In 1976, Texas submitted 4,694 requests for Department of Justice preclearance; the state submitted another 1,735 in 1977 and still another 2,425 in 1978.[48] The Department of Justice objected to only 83 requests between 1976 and 1978.[49] This legislation helped increase minority voting power in the state. Texas slowly made progress in electing more minorities to office. By 1971, roughly 736 Hispanics held elective office in the state.[50] In 1976, Texas also had a total of 161 elected African American officials.[51] These numbers, however, paled in the face of the fact that 23,000 elected offices existed in the state.[52]

Beginning in the mid-1970s and accelerating into the 1980s, activists used the Voting Rights Act in successful challenges of the at-large voting structures of hundreds of city councils and school boards, in addition to contesting the boundaries of state legislative districts and congressional districts.[53] Some cities had expanded so rapidly and absorbed white neighborhoods to such an extent that it drowned out minority votes. Aggressive annexation policies threatened minority chances of representation in San Antonio, for example, which prompted the enactment of a district council system in 1977, which would become dominated by minorities.[54]

The Voting Rights Act also opened the way for white moderates to ascend to power in a region where, prior to 1965, any position deviating too far from the doctrine of white supremacy and segregation likely doomed a candidacy. Minorities became a powerful new constituency in the Democratic Party. While African Americans benefited tremendously from voter registration efforts, the results remained mixed for Hispanic communities into the late 1970s, in spite of a great financial and organizational investment in mass registration.[55] The frustration over progress on civil rights led many Hispanics to support the La Raza Unida movement early in the decade. The increasing urbanization of the black population and the increasing numbers of Hispanics has coincided with the use of the Voting Rights Act to increase the political power and representation of these minority groups.[56] As a result of this urbanization of minorities, conservative Democrats often had more difficulty in the primaries in these areas. Briscoe's rancher image and conservatism, for example, did not play well with urban Democrats. In the 1972 primary, Briscoe won a 38 percent plurality of the vote in the large metropolitan counties but lost these counties with 43 percent of the vote in the general election.[57]

The phenomenon of conservative Democrats seeking the support of upper-class whites in the primary only to court lower-class minorities in the general election became known as the "reverse-scale strategy." It had become a strong component of Texas politics and had allowed conservative Democrats to stay in power for years.[58] For example, in the 1968 Democratic runoff, liberal Don Yarborough received 58 percent of the lower-income white vote, 47 percent of the middle income vote, 17 percent of the upper income vote, and 98 percent of the black vote.[59] Preston Smith received the rest, concentrating heavily with the middle and upper-income voters, while capturing almost none of the black vote. In the general election, the trend reversed itself as blacks and lower income voters flocked to the Democratic nominee. In the 1968 fall contest, Smith received 58 percent of the lower-income vote to 42 percent for Republican nominee Paul Eggers, while he narrowly lost the middle income vote by a margin of 49 percent to 51 percent for Eggers, and won the black vote by a margin of 71 percent to 29 percent.[60] This gave Smith a total victory of 57 percent to 43 percent.

When Jimmy Carter burst onto the national scene, he represented the emerging strength of moderates in the southern Democratic Party. Students of the 1976 election point out that southern support for Carter owed more to regional pride than to Carter's moderate ideology. In fact, Carter pushed this theme late in the race as the campaign used several television advertisements to generate regional pride on behalf of the southern candidate as Carter carefully balanced conservative and liberal themes.[61] As the South emerged from the turbulence of the civil rights movement, the people of the region tried to rehabilitate the region's reputation. Carter, as a southerner, put a new face of respectability on the South. He dispelled many political myths that had developed about the South since the 1950s and 1960s, by proving that a native southerner with a modern temperament could win in the region. John Hill had taken this lesson to heart as he prepared his second run for governor.

By the time the 1978 election season emerged, Carter had become steadily more unpopular. The upsurge of the conservative movement, particularly with the rise of Ronald Reagan and the property tax revolt in California, the nagging energy crisis, and renewed tensions with the Soviet Union all added to Carter's problems. Republican operatives hoped that the unpopularity of Pres. Jimmy Carter would finally give the Republicans the opportunity to break the Democratic monopoly on statewide offices by tying them to the president.

Sen. John Tower, running for a fourth term in 1978, kept a careful eye on the state's political scene—especially the upcoming gubernatorial primary. He had commissioned a number of polls to gauge public opinion on the expected candidates. A March 1977 poll asked respondents in which Texas politician did they have the most confidence and whether they approved of their actions. The poll revealed that 17 percent of respondents had the most confidence in Gov. Briscoe, with just 2 percent for Atty. Gen. Hill; Hill had earned a 27 percent favorable rating and a 7 percent unfavorable rating, while Briscoe had a respectable 54 percent favorable rating and a 25 percent unfavorable rating.[62] Any upcoming primary election showed Briscoe with a clear advantage: 57 percent favored Briscoe while 35 percent favored Hill. Hill had a strong following, but Briscoe remained the prohibitive favorite to win a third term. Tower commissioned a second poll seven months later which revealed little change in public opinion. When asked which Texas politician had done the most good for Texas, 12 percent of respondents gave Dolph Briscoe a plurality with Hill at 3 percent and 2 percent for U.S. Representative Barbara Jordan of Houston.[63] Jordan had become a hero to many during the 1974 televised Watergate hearings with her powerful defense of the constitution, but she had no reported interest in the governor's mansion in 1978. The electorate had yet to focus on an election still seven months away, but Tower's internal polls on potential primary match-ups showed that the public clearly had taken notice of Hill.

As Hill and Briscoe prepared to battle for the nomination, a third major candidate appeared on the scene. Preston Smith, whom Briscoe had ousted in the 1972 Democratic Primary, had found himself written off by the political establishment. Nevertheless, the genial former governor had become enraged with Briscoe's performance and decided to challenge him again for the post. Smith loudly condemned Briscoe's fiscal policies. Despite Briscoe's claims to have prevented higher taxes, Smith claimed that he had spent money without restraint. "Briscoe has overseen the wildest spending spree we've ever had in this state," proclaimed Smith as he dismissed Briscoe's chances for renomination. "I damned sure do think there is a possibility that Briscoe won't make the runoff," he declared.[64]

Smith began his political career in 1944 when he won election to a state representative seat in a nine-county West Texas district.[65] From there, he gradually worked his way up the political ladder. In 1963, Smith became lieutenant governor under John Connally.[66] Despite the power of the lieutenant governor's post in Texas, Smith had little visibility when he aspired to even higher office as Connally prepared to step down.

At the beginning of Smith's first campaign for governor in 1967, very few Texans could identify him.[67] His low standings in the polls did not daunt him, and he worked feverishly to overcome his early polling handicap. Similarly, Smith hoped that history would repeat itself ten years later. In the 1968 runoff, Smith had earned the endorsements of both Briscoe and Hill against Don Yarborough.[68] Neither would be so generous in 1978.

Preston Smith won in 1968 and forged ahead with his agenda. Upon his first inauguration in 1969, he listed his priorities as water, law and order, and fairness in government. "Fairness and justice are entitlements of individuals and groups that have not necessarily received them in the past," declared Smith. "And we seek fairness to the business, industrial and professional interests, which cannot compete without access to trained and educated personnel . . ."[69] Smith reiterated these ideas in 1971. "In our haste to right the wrongs and correct the errors, we must not trample business, professional, industrial or personal enterprise. The indiscretions against nature and man did not occur overnight, and they cannot be cured instantly."[70] Despite his essentially conservative nature, Smith believed firmly in fair play for everyone, regardless of their position in society. He had often expressed a genuine sympathy for the plight of the underprivileged and efforts to reform government and society. "The poor, indeed, deserve the chance not to be poor," declared Smith at his inauguration in January 1971.[71] "The man who says America is perfect, is blind to reality," he added.

Through Smith's Goals For Texas program, he pushed for the opening of new universities and medical schools, state investment in research, increases in health services, and efforts to improve water quality across the state.[72] By the time he left office, he believed that he had largely succeeded in these goals as new schools had been built and other social services expanded. Smith realized that urbanization had created a number of new problems for the state, from growth and strained resources for growing cities to steadily diminishing resources from rural areas. "The urban population explosion had created numerous problems which involved both the local governments and the state government," noted Smith. "At the same time the smaller cities and rural areas had not only seen their people slipping away, but were lacking the opportunity for improved economic stability through industrial output."[73] In addition, the state taxation system had become very regressive as the state became increasingly dependent upon the sales tax. By the time Smith left office in 1973, Texas raised 70.1 percent of its taxes through the general and selective sales taxes, compared to the average state's 55.5 percent.[74]

Despite his understated demeanor, Smith had earned considerable respect from legislators. "He was a legislator's governor," recalled Gib Lewis. "If anyone wanted his legislative program passed, Preston Smith probably could do it more than any of the other governors."[75] Sen. Tom Creighton of Mineral Wells agreed, "Preston was an amazing fellow. He had a good sense of humor. He was a very hard worker, an early riser."[76] State Rep. Walt Parker stated, "Gov. Smith is a very ultra, ultra conservative person. I feel like he's honest in his feelings. . . . He's a person that if you don't support him he's certainly not going to support you."[77] Others, however, remained much less impressed with Smith. Oscar Mauzy commented that Smith had no leadership.[78] Despite his successes in working with the legislature, the Sharpstown stock scandal damaged his reputation and led to his defeat.

Smith made it a three-man race with his announcement in 1977. He declared that the people had lost confidence in Briscoe. "I think that this ostrich-like posture is the most tragic part of Briscoe's philosophy of government. . . . The people are left with no input . . . They have lost all confidence in state government."[79] Smith dismissed observers who claimed that Sharpstown had forever finished him politically. "I could get twenty per cent without turning a wheel," he boasted.[80] Two minor candidates, Roy Allen Mayo of San Juan and Nederland welding works owner Donald Ray Beagle, also ran but had little impact on the race.

Both Hill and Briscoe realized they had difficult races ahead. Hill believed that Smith's entry in the race would complicate his efforts and possibly divide the anti-Briscoe vote. "I thought it would hurt my chances without a runoff," he admitted years later.[81] Despite Hill's reputation as a moderate and as something of a crusader for justice, many liberals initially remained skeptical of him. Longtime Houston liberal leader Billie Carr said in November 1977, "I don't know what our people are going to do."[82]

Most expected Hill and Smith to pound away at the "ten-years-in-office issue," which would have become a record tenure in office for a Texas governor.[83] Despite his popularity in 1977, many Texans quietly expressed a weariness with Briscoe continuing as governor. But Smith and Hill instead used other issues, such as education and spending, against him. Briscoe in the meantime had developed other problems. Many Briscoe staffers became upset when Secretary of State Mark White ran for attorney general. Aides had considered White an important part of the Briscoe team. He had won his appointment as secretary of state in 1973 after Briscoe entered office. Most expected White to help with Briscoe's upcoming campaign, but when he left the post in October 1977, it was a "surprise to a lot of people that White would jump ship."[84] In the process, he absorbed many Briscoe campaign workers and sources of funding.

Briscoe, however, had what most considered one of the best political assets in the Lone Star State, his wife, Janey. As one reporter noted, "The governor may be liked and respected—but Janey is loved."[85] She had developed the reputation as the best campaigner in the state. The two rounded up his old groups of supporters in a series of rallies, receptions, and fundraisers as the campaign moved quietly across the state. Commented reporter John Bloom, "Traveling with the governor and Janey is like attending a continuous family reunion: an endless procession of barbecues, group singing (always "The Eyes of Texas"), patriotic orations, interminable introductions and small receptions among friends."[86] As Mrs. Briscoe noted happily at one reception, "We've known these people for years."[87] Briscoe found himself at his best in these informal gatherings of old friends and political allies.

His wife, perhaps the most loyal of all to the governor, fiercely defended him against critics who felt him uninspired or ineffective. "Dolph Briscoe is exactly what he appears to be," she said. "He's an honest man. People expect him to act like a politician, and he never does. It's not in him."[88]

Janey Briscoe had spent her youth in Austin, and the two had married in 1942 when she was 17.[89] After the war, the future governor decided to run for the Texas House of Representatives, and Janey Briscoe dutifully helped him in that 1948 campaign. She immediately proved a very astute campaigner. Dolph Briscoe often told the story that while he campaigned in Dimmit and Uvalde counties in his first campaign, she had spent most of her time campaigning in Medina County, adding that he had ended up doing much better in Medina.[90] She remained a constant on the campaign trail with her husband as he rose through the ranks of Texas politics and became one of his closest advisors. Briscoe claimed he owed his political success to his wife, often saying, "I never would have made it without her."[91]

Conservatives, meanwhile, bristled at the idea of John Hill as governor. Republicans especially remained deeply concerned that Briscoe would not beat back the attorney general's challenge. State Rep. Fred Agnich, a Dallas Republican, noted about Hill, "He's a brilliant lawyer; he has a fine mind, and as far as I know, is a man of total integrity and honesty . . . He's got all sorts of goofy social ideas."[92] Their concerns grew as their own polls of the other party's race showed Hill steadily gaining on Briscoe. By March, a Louis, Bowles, and Grove poll had the race at a dead heat between Hill and Briscoe. John Hill stood at 36 percent, Briscoe had 35 percent support, and Smith had 7 percent.[93]

"Inefficient too long," Hill declared the governor.[94] He argued throughout the race that the state needed new leadership, a kind of governor that could actively sell the state and create a powerful new vision for the next decade. "What this state needs," Hill told supporters, "is an articulate, persuasive, well-informed spokesman. And we don't have one now."[95]

He had won the support of union labor Democrats. Despite the negative feelings that many Texans had about organized labor and the relative weakness of unions in the South, they could prove a crucial ally in campaigns because of their tight organizations and willingness to volunteer for campaign efforts. The southern labor movement increased the political consciousness of its members and managed to win victories.[96] Southern business leaders managed to keep the union labor movement in the South small, which interested factory owners looking to relocate away from heavily unionized areas of the North. Cheap nonunion labor continued as the South's main attraction to industry, and industry seekers still took great pains to inform potential employers of their community's abundance of readily available, nonunion workers.[97]

Other important factions of the party began to drift toward Hill. Liberals threw off any reluctance they may have had for him. A straw poll of The Texas Democrats, an organization of liberal Democrats in the state picked Hill as their choice for governor.[98] The *Texas Observer* wholeheartedly embraced the attorney general in its endorsement in late March. "Ours is no reluctant endorsement, made merely because Dolph Briscoe is so bad; rather, we embrace Hill with enthusiasm, though we remain mindful of his flaws. . . . For what we've seen of John Hill as attorney general, it's a safe bet that the man would be an activist governor."[99]

Krueger asserted that the main differences between Hill and Briscoe centered on personality. He characterized the primary as "largely a case of style ... he [Hill] was considered an activist, a more vigorous campaigner, and had a more assertive style of personality."[100] Hill had structured his campaign on the premise that these differences would help him capture the nomination.

Smith, meanwhile, had difficulty gaining any traction in the polls. The race had become one between Hill and Briscoe, with Smith becoming a sideshow. Nevertheless, Smith pressed forward with his efforts against Briscoe, blasting at his spending record to anyone who would listen. Smith ran his crusade on a shoestring budget, armed only with a handful of volunteers and no campaign manager, no paid administrative aids or staff, and no money for advertising on radio or television.[101] As one report noted, "All Preston Smith has is his Nova ("I got it just for the campaign."), a tattered copy of the *Texas Almanac,* three colored charts (one equipped with a special pop-up arrow showing Dolph Briscoe's spending rising into infinity), and ... [push cards]."[102] For Smith, these simple tools would suffice. He pushed lower taxes and lower spending as his top issues in his low-key campaign.[103] Smith leveled a blistering charge against his rancher-governor opponent at a stop in Beaumont. He claimed that Briscoe had imported cattle to stock his ranch, an insult in a state with a proud ranching tradition then facing problems in some of its agricultural markets.[104]

The *Dallas Morning News* analyzed the inner workings of each campaign in March, showing sharply contrasting styles. Different automobile styles became a clever metaphor. "On a purely superficial level, Gov. Dolph Briscoe's reelection campaign is the Mercedes-Benz, challenger John Hill is the family Ford, and former Gov. Preston Smith rides the used pick-up."[105] By the middle of the campaign, the Briscoe staff had all the appearances of a veteran campaign group, used to running extensive statewide efforts and easily possessing all the resources they could ever need. Hill, by contrast, had plenty of funds available, but ran the campaign on a shoestring budget, squeezing every last cent possible. "The Briscoe effort is staffed like, even looks like, a campaign for president rather than for an incumbent governor. . . . Hill's campaign, by contrast, reflects a budget-conscious effort, [while] Preston Smith has a staff of three and travels along in a Chevy Nova, making his own calls, carrying his own bags and a chart showing increases in state spending under Dolph Briscoe."[106] Smith's underfunded, almost quixotic effort, seemed almost comically out of place.

Without a strong Republican Party to challenge the Democrats for decades, factions had begun vigorously fighting for control of the only political apparatus available, namely the Democracy. Because of this, the South for decades became Democratic for national elections and the party itself largely became a holding company of sorts for the multitude of factions.[107] Party organization atrophied with the lack of spirited opposition in the general elections.[108] The bitterest fighting in the elections usually centered on the choice for the Democratic nominee, and in Texas especially, those fights tended to be between the liberals and the conservatives. The lack of organized support and the absence of deep commitment to party therefore tended to make those who did win elections more vulnerable to pressure from influential individuals and interest groups.[109] Briscoe had openly become the leader of the conservatives, but Hill did not claim to lead any faction of the party.

As more conservatives defected to the Republican Party and the national Democratic Party became increasingly liberal into the 1970s, conservative Democrats began to see their power slip away.[110] More moderate and liberal candidates began to see their political fortunes increase as a result of the weakening opposition within their own party. In fact, studies showed that key sectors of the southern electorate, particularly whites but especially the conservatives, the college-educated, and the younger generation, had begun to realign in favor of the Republican Party.[111]

The conservative Democrats continued to maintain their dominant position from the mid-1960s through most of the 1970s.[112] With new strength from the rising minority vote, liberal Democrats threatened but failed to overturn the hegemony of the Democratic conservatives in the 1960s.[113] The strength of the conservatives nevertheless changed the makeup of the Democracy. This process continued into the late 1970s and beyond. The more moderate Hill summarily stood as a much more formidable foe than he could have a decade earlier, while Briscoe saw the strength of his conservative wing become much more anemic. Southern Democratic leaders, particularly in the state legislatures and the statewide executive offices, only had responsibility for local issues. The divisive national issues remained beyond the scope of their responsibilities, although many leaders condemned many of the more liberal developments in the national Democratic Party. These condemnations, particularly Briscoe's attacks on Carter's energy policies, helped him keep support for himself and other conservative Democratic candidates. Gubernatorial campaigns typically face fewer of the national issues, events, and personalities than senatorial campaigns or presidential campaigns, and because those national forces have generally hurt Democrats and helped Republicans, the governorship has been the greater challenge to Republican strategists.[114] Those same forces helped John Tower win handily in elections to the U.S. Senate, but had continuously frustrated Republican attempts to claim the governor's mansion for decades.

A large number of Texans retained a traditional, conservative outlook on many issues. House Speaker Billy Clayton remarked, "Texas has always been a majority conservative state," and added, "Certainly we are a two philosophy state. You still have a coalition of Republicans and conservative Democrats that work together quite well in the legislative process."[115] Or as Gib Lewis noted, "I think, more or less, the State of Texas is still in the Bible Belt. If you don't believe it, you start running those programs talking about liquor and gambling."[116]

The traditional southern governorship, in terms of its leadership potential, existed in an environment of low public expectations, and therefore the office itself often did little to provide or encourage active, dynamic leadership.[117] In the wake of Reconstruction, the reputation for corruption that many southern governments had developed disgusted the people and led to much-weakened gubernatorial powers across the region. Briscoe, with his understated style and conservative manner, embodied the expectations that many Texans had developed about their governor. More outgoing and ambitious governors than Briscoe, however, had tended to make the office more exciting and influential during their terms. Hill in particular hoped to become part of the latter tradition. In his criticisms of Briscoe, he warned of the dangers and missed opportunities that such a hands-off leadership style would have for the state. Hill often remarked, "If we continue with this drifting leadership . . . We're going to see some signs of omission that will hurt the economy."[118]

Hill believed that Briscoe's style of leadership had also caused Texas to overlook many valuable opportunities. He argued that the proper salesmanship could bring federal dollars and federal projects to the state. "The issue is who can do a better job of providing leadership, not only in Austin, but in Washington," he remarked.[119] Briscoe, however, believed that such an aggressive style would only promote controversy and what he saw as needless government programs. "There is a need for active cooperation rather than confrontation," he stated.[120]

Many of the state's public school teachers had turned against him, complaining of inadequate spending on schools and low salaries. Briscoe dismissed teacher complaints of low salaries. He pointed out that "you have to compare factors in other states such as the cost of living and the fact that we in Texas don't have a state income tax. I believe we get more in Texas for the money spent."[121] Hill rose to the defense of the teachers, quickly becoming a popular figure among the state's educators. "We must put a higher priority on human needs," he proclaimed. "Education is my number one priority, and I am committed to increasing our state expenditures on education within our available resources."[122]

Briscoe's response to education funding centered on tax relief, suggesting, "We should return at least half of the anticipated state surplus as tax relief and eliminate the sales tax on utility bills."[123] Hill, on the other hand, pounded away at the shortcomings of funding under Briscoe. He claimed that state funding fell far short of meeting the needs of students and that revenues from the state's oil and gas lands were not equally distributed to school districts. At an appearance in front of 400 students in Santa Rosa, some 80 percent of whom hovered near the poverty line, Hill declared, "I want to see to it that every youngster in this state receives a decent, quality education."[124]

By March, the depth of Briscoe's problems became apparent. New polls had shown that Hill had erased Briscoe's lead, and may have surpassed him. Hill flaunted the latest results that showed him with 36 percent of the vote, two points higher than Briscoe and far ahead of Smith's 7 percent showing.[125] This contrasted sharply with a poll just four months earlier that showed Briscoe leading by a daunting eighteen points. At a Dallas Rotary Club meeting, Briscoe dismissed the new findings, while reiterating his anti-tax push. "I don't know what good there is to be gained by polls."[126] But Briscoe had his own numbers. Three days later, he fired back at Hill, announcing that an internal poll showed him leading 38 percent to 31.6 percent.[127]

One of the governor's key constituencies stood on the edge of rebellion. Rural areas had always been Briscoe's greatest source of strength. His ranching background gave him a unique connection with Texas farmers that few urban politicians could match. Ranching had also made Briscoe one of the wealthiest men in the state. But in the 1970s, many of the smaller operators did not fare so well and feared economic ruin from imports of cheap crops. Little relief seemed forthcoming to the farmers, only adding to their sense of desperation.

Farmers in Hidalgo County decided to strike back at the cheap imports by blocking their passage into the United States, shutting off points of entry into the border county. Nearly 200 of the striking farmers were arrested for blocking the International Bridge. Briscoe stated that he understood what farmers faced, what he described as the tightest price-squeeze since the Great Depression, but added that the strike should end. The farm strike met with wide condemnation across the state. "Disgusting," snorted the *Dallas Morning News*.[128]

John Hill saw an opportunity. He quickly went to the scene and met with farmers and county officials to try to mediate a settlement to the standoff.[129] The strike soon dissipated. At Miller International Airport in McAllen on March 4, Briscoe flew in to talk with local farmers. Local farmers heckled him as he promised legislative relief for farmers hurt by the price squeeze. A Briscoe aide tried to save the day as he talked with them after the speech and reminded the Hidalgo farmers of their common agricultural heritage. "He is a farmer, just like you guys."[130] A farmer shot back, "He may be a farmer, but he ain't like us."[131]

On March 6, McAllen City Commissioners condemned both the striking farmers and John Hill's role as mediator. The city leaders declared in an official statement, "Although the attorney general apparently condones mob rule, we on the McAllen City Commission do not."[132] The prospect of making enemies had never given the attorney general much concern. Retorted Hill, "I'm proud of the role that I played."[133]

Hill would continue to pound away at Briscoe's growing unpopularity with the state's farmers. At a rally in the rural Williamson County community of Granger, he announced, "When our farmers needed help, Dolph Briscoe was nowhere around."[134]

Problems mounted in the Rio Grande Valley. Questions over the Briscoe administration's handling of federal funding for the Governor's Office of Migrant Affairs (GOMA) arose. A grand jury investigation of the office had already begun.[135] Apparently in response to the threat from the LRU, the governor's aides pushed the Carter administration to terminate a $1.5 million Community Services administration grant in Zavala County, the Zavala County Economic Development, in September 1977 after Briscoe had complained about its management.[136] The governor had set out to ruin the LRU, particularly in Zavala County, where it had control of the local government. The Migrant Affairs Office, designed to help migrant farm workers, would oversee grants going to communities across the state. The attorney general had launched an audit of GOMA to determine if the office had properly managed the distribution of funds.

Briscoe charged that Hill used the investigations "both overtly and covertly to smear my administration." Hill rejected the charges of politicizing his office. "There's just no truth to the charges. . . . This unjustified outburst is just further evidence that Dolph Briscoe is on a collision course with defeat."[137] Briscoe then stepped up his charges against Hill by demanding an audit of the attorney general's office. The governor demanded to see if Hill's office was missing any federal funds for operating the anti-crime unit. Hill denied the charges.[138] The attorney general had established a special criminal investigation unit within his office, which had caught some criticism. As Dean explains, "Hill was fascinated by the process. Hill . . . overreached. He was doing things he wasn't invited to do."[139]

At an appearance at the small airport in Vernon, Briscoe questioned Hill's response to calls for an investigation. "I don't understand what there is to hide or why someone would be fearful of such an audit. . . . I don't know why he wouldn't want to be cooperative in getting this audit of his secret police force or whatever he has." Hill charged that the audit would force him to remove investigators from his audit of GOMA.[140] On March 22, Hill shot back at Briscoe and asserted that he had "squandered" federal migrant training funds and instead used the federal grants to "buy political support."[141] Smith, watching the latest battle, concluded that the problems in the Governor's Office of Minority Affairs and prison land issues had left Briscoe "finished" in the Rio Grande Valley. "I think he's in trouble all over the state, but it's worse in the Valley," he said.[142]

Both Smith and Hill continued to use the GOMA investigation as a pointed example of Briscoe's failures. Smith cited the episode as a "typical example of the inefficiency and looseness by which the governor's office has been operating."[143] Hill similarly cited it as another example of the need for active leadership, framing the whole primary in terms of attending to the needs of the state versus a policy of neglect. "I would describe it as a contest between an attentive public official and an inattentive one, between a problem solver and a problem watcher. . . . Sins of omission do hurt. The revelations in the Governor's Office of Migrant Affairs were predictable when you reflect his inattention to the responsibilities to the job, his excessive absenteeism," said Hill.[144] Briscoe never faced any charges of malfeasance, but the GOMA scandal stung and would sap strength from his campaign.

On April 16, the *Dallas Morning News* presented a report which broadsided the Hill campaign. The paper reported that Ector County Dist. Atty. John Green had accused Assistant Atty. Gen. Dan Mano of being part of a conspiracy involving an Odessa bail bondsman and an area attorney.[145] Some time earlier, inmate Larry Lozano died in the Odessa jail under mysterious circumstances, possibly due to abuse. Green accused the attorney general's officials of trying to get the jailer to change his testimony about Lozano's death—trying to get the jailer to say Lozano did not suffer any mistreatment. The *Morning News* called the incident "an aborted attempt at witness tampering isn the Larry Lozano case and it may have exceeded its authority by applying pressure to have the Texas Rangers hand over evidence from its criminal investigation." Hill immediately called the charges "groundless" and "ridiculous."[146] Hill later would ask U.S. Atty. Gen. Griffin Bell to investigate the Lozano death.[147] The issue would ultimately play no role in the governor's contest but only marked the increasingly tense race.

Briscoe focused on his strengths to stir support among conservatives. He trumpeted what remained a successful issue for conservatives and Briscoe personally, that of taxation and government spending. He often boasted, "Mine is the first administration since World War II that has been able to call a halt to new state taxes."[148] Briscoe continued to emphasize his own fiscal restraint, charging that Hill would reverse his anti-tax policies. "The number one issue is taxes," he stated, "Whether to continue the record we have had of no new or additional taxes, living within our income or to go on the reverse of that and follow a policy that has been so disastrous to the economies of other states—a spending spree as promised by my major opponent, the attorney general."[149]

In fact, in most southern states in the 1970s tax levels remained well below the national average. Economists pointed out that this remained no accident of politics. The tax differentials simply reflect the relative income positions of the Rocky Mountain West and the South versus the industrial North.[150] Tax levels could never go too high because few resources existed to tax; in addition, the region had a traditional reluctance to engage in any broad governmental enterprise. Briscoe skewered Hill's reform proposals. On property taxes, he warned that "some so-called 'tax reform' proposals could have the effect of raising taxes," while Hill answered, "The whole system of property taxes needs to be reformed, and our expanding sales petroleum production tax revenue should be used to relieve pressures on local school taxes."[151] Hill promised to make education and tax relief a top priority. "The two go hand-in-hand," he said.[152]

Smith maintained his characteristic optimism and pushed the issues.[153] He suggested that the legislature would have to upgrade the state's educational facilities at some point but believed that the funding should come from sales taxes.[154] However, he proposed a 50 percent reduction in the state sales tax, from 4 percent to 2 percent, contingent upon the state's $1 billion budget surplus materializing.[155]

Hill left nothing to chance in the primary. He carefully scrutinized every poll and every trend in the campaign. In April, he began to tout a poll commissioned by Republican candidate Bill Clements showing Hill leading the Democratic Primary by one point. "This was no ordinary poll. . . . He [Clements] had a sampling of 1,200, which is more than most, and it cost him $30,000. This shouldn't happen to an incumbent," Hill said as the ramifications ran through his mind. "The important thing is that I've caught up to him, and he can't make it up."[156] Ironically, in the general election campaign, Hill would dismiss Clements polls showing Clements gaining on Hill.

Briscoe downplayed the discouraging poll numbers and continued to predict victory. "As was the case with my 1974 campaign, the race is not going to be as close as it seems. People are beginning to get interested in the race and they see a very clear choice."[157] Hill responded, "Briscoe took the people for granted. He made the mistake early of not taking my challenge seriously."[158]

Briscoe attacked Hill's proposed spending priorities at an Austin news conference. He used figures from Comptroller Bob Bullock's office to estimate that Hill's tax-and-spend plan would cost $3.9 billion more than the state had available. "For him to claim this amount of new spending can be financed without new taxes is sheer fantasy," declared the governor.[159] The Hill campaign fired back at both Bullock and Briscoe, deriding Bullock as "a comptroller who is an announced candidate for governor in 1982 and a self-described 'hit man' for Dolph Briscoe."[160] Hill bitterly disputed the numbers.

Bullock had a long reputation as a strong-arm politician not above moving to attack and destroy anyone who stood in his way. He had made many enemies as a result. As State Sen. Oscar Mauzy recalled, "He was Preston's political hatchet man as everybody knows. . . . The governor doesn't like Bob Bullock. Bullock is his political enemy because Bullock used to work for Preston Smith, and Briscoe is the kind of fellow that demands loyalty of people."[161] But the primary made Bullock and Briscoe odd political allies as Bullock's personal disgust at Hill prompted him to bitterly lash out at the attorney general's proposals. Bullock claimed Hill's proposed flat-rate tax on oil and natural gas would hurt state finances, stating that Texas would have lost $800 million over the previous four years if it had been in effect. Stated Bullock: "We're talking about the goose that laid the golden eggs. Hill wouldn't kill the goose but he would give away the eggs."[162] The severity of the attacks drew criticism from even the conservative *Dallas Morning News*. An editorial blasted Bullock, saying that he "came down too hard" on Hill's proposed volume tax.[163]

A reporter would later ask Bullock the source of the bad feelings between himself and Hill. Bullock thought for a moment and replied, "Well, I guess basically I don't like him."[164]

Hill critics, both well-known and unknown, continued to mount attacks on the attorney general. Most criticisms centered on the activist government that Hill proposed. Bullock called Hill "nothing more than a department store Santa Claus operating out of season."[165] A *Dallas Morning News* reader wrote, "Hill, like Carter, promises all things to all people. Like President Carter, he cannot possibly deliver. I hope the voters of Texas won't be fooled again."[166]

A Round Rock man wrote, "I have nothing against Hill personally but we don't need him as governor. . . . Gov. Briscoe has run a low-key program that appeals to most of us."[167] Hill supporters, however, continued to defend their candidate. A Tyler resident wrote, "Jefferson did say, 'He who governs least, governs best,' but all that we can say of Dolph Briscoe is that he governs not at all."[168]

By early April, political handicappers saw an exceptionally tight race developing between Hill and Briscoe. So close, in fact, Briscoe faced a real possibility of defeat. History, however, seemed to favor incumbent governors. For one analyst, the real question of the election remained simple, "Are voters ready for the activist governor that Hill would surely be, or is Briscoe really what they want?"[169]

Frustrated by his stagnating poll numbers, Briscoe lashed out, accusing Hill of manipulating the surveys. The governor claimed that university professors who actively supported Hill's campaign had conducted recent polls taken for the *Houston Post* and WFAA-TV in Dallas that showed him leading. "All polls should be suspect," explained Briscoe, "Polls shouldn't be important."[170] Nevertheless, the *Houston Post* poll showed Hill with a respectable 7-point lead, with 41 percent of the vote compared to Briscoe's 34 percent and Smith's 7 percent.[171]

A few days later, the Briscoe campaign announced its own favorable poll results. Aides explained that a survey of roughly 130,000 Texans phoned by the campaign showed that 54.7 percent favored Briscoe for reelection.[172] In most campaigns, however, calls are placed to lists of sympathizers and known voters. The results, although probably accurate from the lists his campaign called, in all likelihood did not include a random sample of voters and could not accurately be projected to the rest of the state.

Both Briscoe and Hill distanced themselves from Carter. The two steadily criticized his energy policies in an attempt to avoid being paired politically with the president. "I'm very disappointed in the energy policy that President Carter has proposed," said Briscoe. "It's the exact opposite of what he endorsed when he was in Texas in 1976. On the basis of those assurances, he carried Texas."[173] Hill called Carter's energy plan a "Trojan horse for Texas."[174] He later added, "I am disappointed in President Carter's leadership on agricultural and energy issues and his failure to treat our state fairly in rebating money to our cities. I would hope to bring about a change in those policies."[175]

Texas newspapers split their support between Hill and Briscoe. The *Abilene Reporter-News* urged Texans to stay the course and re-elect Briscoe.[176] The *San Antonio Express-News* similarly supported Briscoe.[177] Briscoe's appeal to hold the line on taxes appealed to the editors of the *Houston Chronicle* in its endorsement. "Gov. Briscoe promised no new taxes . . . he has kept that promise."[178] The *Dallas Morning News* hailed Briscoe and called for Democrats to renominate him. "The six years of Briscoe's governorship have been years of growth and prosperity for Texas. . . . The News believes that Gov. Briscoe's conservative philosophy of government—emphasizing as it does prudence, economy, and respect for local rights—is well-suited to the addressing of that state's central concerns. We particularly like his strong emphasis on holding down taxes."[179]

The more liberal *Dallas Times Herald,* contrarily, urged voters to support Hill as it considered Briscoe's leadership severely lacking in many areas. In its endorsement, the editors wrote, "In no area of state government and service is Governor Dolph Briscoe's failure of leadership more apparent than in public education. . . . While the state has had 'no new taxes' during Gov. Dolph Briscoe's term in office, property taxes have increased $1 billion, with no appreciable improvement of Texas's education standards, compared to the other states."[180] The *Times Herald* added, "[John Hill] wants to be governor, not simply wear the crown. Mr. Hill is as financially conservative as his opponent, Gov. Dolph Briscoe. . . . We believe a majority of the state's citizens will agree that a dignity is needed after six years of Gov. Briscoe's benign neglect of state government."[181]

As the campaign began to wind down, the threat of Smith tipping the balance of the race also began to falter. The question by early May essentially boiled down to whether Briscoe could force Hill into a runoff election, where conservatives almost always disposed of their more liberal challengers. Hill dismissed the threat of Smith to his victory, and proclaimed him "diminished" and estimated he would earn only 4 to 7 percent of the vote.[182] Smith, however, would not give up easily and urged Democrats to nominate him as their best chance for victory in November. The former governor darkly warned that if he lost the primary, the Republicans would win the election.[183]

The 1978 Democratic race for governor had become the most expensive election the state had ever seen. By the beginning of May, the three major candidates had spent a combined $4 million on the race. At the end of the finance report filing period on April 26, Briscoe reported that he had spent $2.7 million, borrowed $873,500, and indicated that he might borrow another $296,500 to finish the race.[184] Hill had spent $1.22 million, and reported having $174,000 on hand as of April 28 when his campaign filed a spending report. Smith had raised only $68,199, and spent a relatively paltry sum of $62,129. By contrast, Briscoe had spent only $2.3 million on the primary and general elections combined in 1972 and 1974.[185]

Late in the campaign, the Briscoe campaign emerged with a new strategy. Briscoe and his allies leveled a blistering series of attacks on Hill, charging that his would impose a state income tax. Hill bitterly denied the charges. Dean explained the source of the charge. "Hill had a number of spending proposals, but he didn't have a revenue plan, and by process of elimination, it goes down to the income tax."[186] The Briscoe campaign bought a series of full-page campaign ads in the state's most widely-read newspapers in early May. All featured the slogan, "Briscoe for Texas, John Hill for Taxes."[187]

Hill responded sharply, claiming that the tactic had backfired. On a late tour of East Texas, he claimed a five percent switch of Briscoe supporters to himself as the result of Briscoe's "last-minute smear campaign," adding, "It's a desperate tactic. . . . He has falsely represented my positions to salvage his office. . . . It is a reflection of his integrity. . . . Dolph Briscoe wants to be governor of Texas for ten years so bad he has to spend $1 million in false advertising deliberately misrepresenting my well-known opposition to a state income tax."[188] Hill explained that Briscoe had overestimated his spending by $2.2 billion, and added that he based his estimates on a projected 18.3 percent increase in revenues in the 1980–1981 biennium, close to the 20 percent increases the state had seen in recent years, compared with Comptroller Bullock's 11.3 percent projections.[189] If the current trends in revenue growth held, Hill would easily have enough funding for his proposals.

Briscoe jabbed at Hill's pledge to veto any tax bill: "John Hill has become the first political candidate in history to start vetoing promises before the election."[190] He relentlessly hammered Hill's spending plans. "He cannot escape the fact that he has over promised the state budget and cannot possibly deliver without leading Texas down the road to a state income tax." The governor also touted a poll showing him with a 40 to 36 percent lead. "I think we have the opposition on the run and on the defensive," he declared, smiling.[191]

Briscoe derided his opponent as "a captive of the spending lobby," and added, "Not in his wildest dreams can he fulfill these promises without a state income tax."[192] Hill passionately responded, "They know the only way they can prevent me from winning is to deliberately misrepresent my position on a state income tax and that's exactly what they're trying to do."[193]

Some of Hill's most prominent San Antonio backers, including campaign coordinator Sam Millsap along with State Reps. Frank Tejeda and Frank Madla, decided to call Briscoe's bluff on his state income tax tirades. Hill's backers announced a money-back guarantee on any state income tax that would be enacted during a Hill governorship. A simple contract, available at Hill's Bexar County headquarters stated that if an income tax passed the legislature in 1979 and John Hill failed to veto it, the backers promised "to pay any state income tax that may accrue against the taxpayers who sign up for the free insurance."[194] The clever strategy won the Hill campaign considerable positive coverage and placed Briscoe back on the defensive. Briscoe, however, continued to attack Hill's spending and taxation proposals, continuously repeating that Hill would enact an income tax.

The Tarrant County Coordinator for the Hill campaign, J. Clark Nowlin responded to Briscoe's attacks in an open letter in the *Fort Worth Star-Telegram*, declaring, "It is too late to try deceptive and misleading scare tactics. People know better! Your record speaks for itself. Texas needs aggressive leadership in the Governor's office."[195] In a May 5 speech, Hill pounded away at Briscoe's allegations. "I've never advocated these things and the people know it. But now they have got me trying to hang my own people. . . . Our research shows we've picked up some of Briscoe's support, people who supported him in the past but dropped him because of the cheap tactics he has used just so he can serve 10 years in office."[196]

The candidates scoured the state for every last-minute vote possible. The two both played up to their themes of leadership for the common man versus a state income tax. Hill proclaimed in an impassioned address, "Vested interests don't want me there. But the people do. And the people win every time."[197] He remained aware of the possibility that the race might go to a runoff but scoffed at any hint of concern. Hill told supporters that he had $100,000 left to wage a runoff. At a rally of 4,000 supporters at the Waco Classroom Teachers Association, he declared, "We're going to try to do it all Saturday."[198]

Briscoe continued to attack Hill as the days to the election evaporated. "Mr. Hill is a big spender, he is a big government man and he is a supporter of annual sessions of the legislature. . . . Mine is the only administration in the last 30 years not to resort to raising taxes to meet expenses."[199] In a late swing through South Texas, he stated, "I am asking for every vote."[200] He added in a May 5 speech, "My major opponent . . . has promised more than can be delivered through the current income of the state." Hill attended a cattle auction in Cuero that morning, and Briscoe followed with his own visit that afternoon.[201] Hill conceded that many analysts expected a close race with a June 3 runoff. But he added that the latest polls showed him with a strong lead. Hill touted a University of Houston Public Affairs Research Center poll showing him with a 46 percent to 40 percent lead, with 4 percent for Smith and 10 percent undecided. "If we take 40 percent of the undecided we could win without a runoff," predicted Hill.[202]

Voters flocked to the polls. Interest in the election had surged, prompting Secretary of State Steve Oaks to revise his turnout forecasts. He predicted that the Democratic Primary would now attract 50 percent of registered Texas voters, and where he had predicted a 1.2 million-vote turnout the week before, he now predicted 1.8 million voters, more than even in the 1976 presidential primary.[203] Announced Oaks, "From five working days ago until now, we've had a dramatic turnaround in absentee voting."[204]

The results shocked Briscoe and his supporters. They had expected a runoff, but the early results hinted that Hill might win without a second primary. Briscoe, who had ousted a sitting governor to win the office six years earlier, now found himself ousted. Briscoe, Janey, and their son and daughter dropped by their Uvalde campaign headquarters as the results came in. The governor announced that he would refuse to concede until election officials tabulated all the votes. The Associated Press declared Hill the winner late Sunday afternoon, but not all the votes had yet come in.[205]

Immediately, rumors swirled that many Briscoe supporters would vote Republican out of disgust for how Hill had waged his campaign against Briscoe. Hill dismissed these fears and stated that he had talked with many Briscoe supporters who had already pledged their support for him in the general election.

"A lot of people who supported Briscoe out of loyalty to him have told me that they will move over and help me in November," said Hill.[206] He immediately announced plans to meet with budget authorities and to begin preparing spending recommendations for the 1979 legislative session. Hill readily believed that history would send another Democrat to the governor's mansion in 1978. Smith congratulated Hill.[207]

Hill's 753,309 votes won the election with a clear majority, beating Briscoe by 180,000 votes.[208] Briscoe captured just over 40 percent of the vote, while Smith won only 92,202 votes. Hill won 154 of the state's 254 counties, with Briscoe taking the remainder. The other two candidates, Ray Allen Mayo and Donald Ray Beagle, placed a distant fourth and fifth with only a handful of votes.[209]

Some 256,500 more Texans participated in the 1978 primary than had voted in the 1974 contest, an increase of 14.4 percent (see appendix B). Briscoe, however, had lost more than 272,000 votes—more than one-quarter of his support—from the previous primary. He gained votes in only twenty-one counties, losing votes in all the rest. His strongest areas of vote gains lay in his native Uvalde County, where voters voiced their enthusiasm for their longtime neighbor. He gained 1,050 votes, winning the county with 86 percent of the vote. A massive increase in voter turnout in McLennan County helped Briscoe capture the county, as 14,079 more voters showed up than in 1974, with Briscoe who won 3,000 more votes, winning by 2,600 votes. He fared best in Waco and oil-rich West Texas communities as Midland, Odessa, Wichita Falls, Abilene, and San Angelo (see Map 1). The accusations from Ector County officials apparently had only a modest, local impact. Briscoe won the conservative counties of Ector and Midland by 400 votes and 600 votes, respectively. Despite the controversies with the LRU, Democrats in Zavala County overwhelmingly supported Briscoe with 627 of the 919 votes cast, or 68 percent of the vote.

But the governor had lost tremendous support, and the Hill campaign had convinced many Texans to vote who had not voted in 1974. Briscoe did not capitalize on this new voter interest in the race. Farmer discontent and Briscoe's problems with the Hispanic community became readily apparent in Hidalgo County, as Hill defeated Briscoe by more than 1,000 votes. Hill had smashed Briscoe's South Texas stronghold, winning eleven counties south of San Antonio. Where the governor had performed strongest in the Hill country and the rural counties of western and central Texas, Hill easily outpaced Briscoe in the larger metropolitan areas, east Texas, and the central Texas counties of the Austin–San Antonio area. Briscoe won only two counties in the conservative Panhandle and eight in East Texas, with the attorney general winning the rest. Hill won Harris County by 13,000 votes as Briscoe's total stood at more than 18,000 votes less than in 1974. In six counties, Briscoe lost more than 5,000 voters each. Hill won the state's largest cities with comfortable margins. The attorney general won El Paso County by 12,000 votes. In the Dallas–Fort Worth area, he again won overwhelmingly. Hill won Dallas County by more than 10,000 votes, in a county where Briscoe lost 15,601 votes from 1974 and 13,195

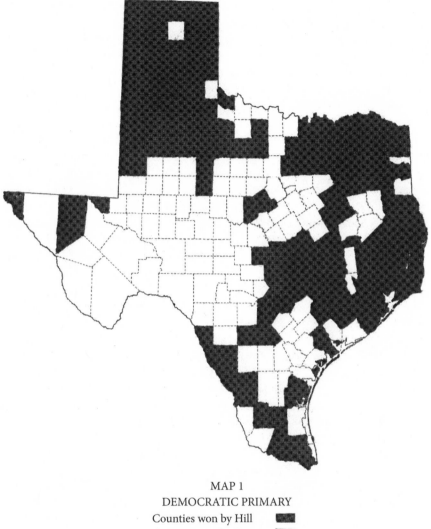

MAP 1
DEMOCRATIC PRIMARY
Counties won by Hill
Counties won by Briscoe

more Democrats participated in the primary. In Tarrant County, Hill won by 9,200 votes and 15,498 more Democrats surged to the polls. Denton, Collin, and Rockwall counties also fell into the Hill camp. Only the rural counties to the south of the Metroplex, Johnson and Ellis, went to Briscoe. Travis County went to Hill with 65 percent of the vote to Briscoe's 29 percent. Bexar County fell to Hill with a 24,000-vote victory margin.

Dallas Morning News columnist Sam Kunich Jr. recounted a number of reasons behind Briscoe's loss. Briscoe had alienated key Democratic constituencies and failed to inspire his supporters to a point that they wanted him for a third term. One anonymous Briscoe worker admitted, "Voters really didn't approve of Briscoe serving ten years. Some didn't like it because they don't like Briscoe; others just don't like the idea itself. . . . Teachers and their families were almost unanimously and actively for Hill. . . . Farmers were mad at Briscoe. . . . Mexican-Americans were antagonized at Briscoe."[210] Dave Montgomery, a reporter for the *Dallas Times Herald,* echoed these findings: "Texas voters simply didn't want to keep Gov. Dolph Briscoe in office for ten years," he wrote.[211]

Enthusiasm for Briscoe had clearly fallen by the time the 1978 primary season had dawned. Hill and Smith did not emphasize the ten years in office issue during the campaign but did not have to. The issue was in the minds of Democratic voters, most of whom ultimately did not see an advantage in extending the governor's six-year reign. By emphasizing where they believed Briscoe had failed and how they would correct these shortcomings, both Hill and Smith presented clear alternatives to Briscoe. Hill had made the strongest impression on Texas Democrats, offering a new, activist direction for the state government and the party. Voters preferred this vision over another four years of Briscoe. Briscoe had his opportunity, but Democrats decided that change represented the best course.

Hill had waged an aggressive campaign to unseat an incumbent governor. In a historic change for the Democratic Party, not only had a sitting governor lost reelection, but a moderate had defeated a conservative in the primary for the first time since the Great Depression. The discontented, from farmers to teachers to Hispanics, had flocked to Hill; but he had bruised many Democrats in the process. Hill now had to mend fences within the party to repair the damage that the difficult primary had caused. Not only did he have to see that the conservatives would stay loyal to him in the fall but also ensure that history would again favor the Democrats.

CHAPTER 3

A FAMILY AFFAIR:
THE REPUBLICAN PRIMARY

WITH EACH NEW ELECTION CYCLE, the hopes of Texas Republicans soared with the eager anticipation of a breakthrough year. But with each year, these hopes crumbled under the November election totals. Since John Tower's upset victory in the special election to the United States Senate in 1961, the party had scored few successes, save for Tower's re-elections, the occasional win of a congressional seat, or a seat in the state legislature. Somehow, 1978 seemed different to many in the party. Pres. Jimmy Carter faced increasingly bitter criticism of his policies, and at home in Texas, the Democrats presided over a lackluster administration. Reported one newspaper, "Republican chances next year are bright, but they must be measured in the context of the party's minority status."[1]

"We suspected that 1978 was going to be a breakthrough year," recalled Republican pollster Lance Tarrance.[2] To underscore the status of the party in late 1977, and despite dozens of Republican candidates running in each election by this time, Tarrance's new polling firm had the distinction of being the only Republican polling firm in the state. A significant breakthrough victory, such as winning the governor's mansion, would dramatically bolster the party's clout within the state and mark the transition from what Tarrance called a "one-and-a-half party state to a two-party state."[3]

Since the collapse of Reconstruction in the 1870s, the Republicans had remained trapped in the position of the minority party in the state. The Republicans had almost become an afterthought in Texas politics by the early twentieth century.[4] At its lowest point in the early 1900s, the party could not even manage to win second place in some elections, behind the remnants of the Populist Party or even the Socialist Party. A small core of Republican voters had remained in areas of the Hill Country and among African Americans in the early years of the century, but these voters remained hopelessly outnumbered by the Democrats. Very few Republicans even bothered to challenge the

Democrats in many elections, often leaving Republicans to choose between the available Democratic candidates in order to have a voice in the system.

The remnants of the old planter class and the upper classes controlled the politics of the state through the post-Reconstruction period, remaining firmly aligned with the Democrats. The German settlers in the Hill Country west of Austin had arrived in the 1840s and 1850s, coming to the United States with many liberal ideas and firm support for the Union.[5] As a result, the German counties sided with the Republicans and against the planter Democrats during the Civil War and Reconstruction. African Americans, when they could vote, usually stayed aligned with the Republicans. The national Republican Party remained sympathetic to civil rights issues until the 1920s, when its interest in the subject began to lag.

The long list of crushing defeats explained the reluctance by Republicans to mount a significant challenge to the Democrats. In the state's gubernatorial elections between 1900 and 1966, the average Democratic gubernatorial major-ity was 81.0 percent, while Democratic majorities in Senate races over the same period average 78.88 percent.[6] Only the existence of the Republicans on the national level allowed the state party to survive. Federal patronage provided lucrative career opportunities for the handful of the Texas Republican faith-ful. Patronage thus provided the chairman of the state Republican Party with considerable power to highlight the efforts of party supporters. R. B. Creager, a Republican National Committeeman and chairman of the Texas Republican Party from 1923 to 1950, looked upon the party in this way. Creager worked not so much for Republican votes but for Republican job-seekers who would have him to thank for their valuable appointments from victorious national Republicans.[7]

The 1928 victory of Herbert Hoover served as the only significant victory for the Texas Republican Party in the early 1900s and only the first time that the Democrats had not carried the state in a presidential election.[8] The state party soon realized, however, that the victory did not come as a sudden conversion of Democrats to the Republicans, but because of dissenting factions within the Democracy and the large number of Protestant Democrats unwilling to cast a ballot for the Roman Catholic nominee for the Democrats, Al Smith.[9]

After 1928, the Democrats resumed their unquestioned sway over Texas politics. In most elections, the state Republican Party would not even earn enough votes to stage a primary election as called for under Texas law. Even when the Republicans did hold primaries, it usually remained a wasted effort. Too few counties had Republican organizations to administer the election, and many races remained uncontested. From the inception of the primary system in 1905 to 1964, the Republicans held a primary election on the average of once a decade in the state. Many Republicans, as a result, had to vote Democratic be-cause they lacked any alternative. Analysts described this phenomenon of how the state Democratic Party had become populated by nomadic Republicans in search of candidates they could stomach:

> Indigenous to the South is a strange political schizophrenic, the
> presidential Republican. He votes in Democratic primaries to have
> a voice in state and local matters, but when the presidential elec-
> tion rolls around he casts a ballot for the Republican presidential
> nominee. Locally he is a Democrat; nationally, a Republican. Some
> presidential Republicans are genuine Republicans [often immi-
> grants from the North], who apologetically enter the Democratic
> primaries to fulfill a local civic duty. Others are genuine Democrats
> who vote Republican nationally. . . . [10]

The presidential Republican had created an unpredictable dynamic in Democratic politics, particularly after World War II as the Republican Party gained
strength. Despite their meager gains, Texas Republicans could only win on the
presidential level if they could attract enough conservative Democrats to their
cause. Presidential Republicanism got its greatest impetus from the political
changes brought about by the New Deal and its aftermath.[11] But on the state
and local level, the Democrats, conservative or otherwise, remained intensely
loyal to the Democracy. The development of a two-party state around purely
state issues remained unlikely in the 1950s and 1960s, but the motive force for
two-party politics in the South would come mostly from outside interests and
issues from the national level.[12]

The Republican Party benefited tremendously from the fierce fighting taking place within the Democratic ranks over social issues and civil rights. The
disgust of Gov. Allan Shivers with the national Democratic Party prompted
him to lead the campaign for Dwight D. Eisenhower on his march to his presidential election victory. Eisenhower would capture Texas in 1952 and 1956 by
comfortable margins. In 1956, the Republicans held most of the counties they
had won for Eisenhower four years earlier.[13] The conservatives slowly abandoned the more liberal national Democratic Party in protest of their policies.
This protest, eventually, would harden into a competitive Republican Party, but
only after many elections and the defections of uncounted Democratic voters.
The victories in the presidential elections of 1952 and 1956 nevertheless excited
the tiny group of Texas Republicans, who began to believe that their days of
obsolescence could soon end. The Republicans had become a strong protest
vote against whatever faction had gained control of the state Democratic Party.
This would prove especially dramatic in the race to fill the vacant U.S. Senate
seat of Vice-Pres. Lyndon B. Johnson. In the 1961 special Senate election, most
voters believed that a conservative Republican, John Tower, would be more
palatable than a reactionary Democrat, William Blakley.[14]

Housewives of prominent Republican businessmen became instrumental in
Tower's efforts as the Republican developed an intricate network of activists.
The work of the women's groups in the early Republican campaigns was considered crucial to their early successes, according to these early volunteers.[15] In
fact, by 1978, Republican women, represented on the state level by the Texas

Federation of Republican Women, had organized into 130 clubs with over 6,000 members on their rolls.[16]

The Texas Republican Party spared nothing in its efforts to elect Tower in 1961, efforts that paid off handsomely.[17] The liberal faction of the Democratic Party abandoned that party in the special election, either refusing to participate in the election or voting for Tower in an effort to punish the conservative leadership of the Democracy. The Republicans gladly accepted the support of the liberals and used the victory to establish their viability as an alternative party. Afterward, keeping Tower in office remained the central focus of the Texas Republican Party, and the organization grew around him. Republican State Senator Betty Andujar of Fort Worth notes that, "The John Tower campaign really was the impetus for the real formation of the Republican Party. Once we had him elected, he had to be the Republican senator for the whole state of Texas because he was our first Republican officeholder. That helped a great deal."[18]

Texas conservatives, both Democrats and Republicans, became increasingly irate at the seemingly liberal direction of the administrations of John F. Kennedy and Lyndon B. Johnson. Arizona Sen. Barry Goldwater's economic conservatism and his opposition to national intervention in racial conflicts influenced many to join the Republican Party.[19] For conservatives, their control of the various state Democratic parties in the South meant a continuing opposition to civil rights measures. With the national Democratic Party strongly supporting civil rights and the federal courts steadily chipping away at the South's Jim Crow system of white supremacy, along with the civil rights efforts of both Kennedy and Johnson, many conservatives became disillusioned with the new direction of the Democracy. By 1962, the Republicans had developed a stronger appeal to southern conservatives by remaining quiet on civil rights issues or questioning the constitutionality of some civil rights measures.[20] Republican Jack Cox scored an astounding 45.5 percent of the vote in the Texas governor's race that year against conservative Democrat John Connally, underscoring the rising strength of the Republicans.

By the late 1960s, Republicans had made inroads in the South. Moderate Republicans had some success, most notably in Arkansas. Winthrop Rockefeller had won the 1966 governor's election in the state, defeating a segregationist Democrat with a coalition of Republicans and African Americans.[21] But most of the successes that Republicans had seen in the 1960s had come from conservative candidates. In 1964, a South Carolina Democratic congressman had switched to the Republicans, and the party had won five congressional seats in Alabama, one in Georgia, and one in Mississippi.[22] In 1966, conservative Republican Claude R. Kirk Jr., had won the governor's office in Florida.[23] These successes had come at the expense of white conservatives leaving the Democratic Party and provided fertile electoral ground for the rising Republican Party.

The 1968 election season initially held great promise for Texas Republicans. The two most popular Democrats in the state, President Johnson and Governor Connally, announced that they would not seek reelection. In addition, many conservatives had become disgusted with the social activism of Johnson's Great Society programs and the excesses of the anti-Vietnam War movement, damaging the campaign of Vice-President Hubert Humphrey. Southern conservatives mounted another third-party challenge with Alabama Governor George Wallace, an avowed segregationist, while Richard Nixon received the nomination by the Republican Party. The Texas Republicans in their gubernatorial primary nominated Paul W. Eggers, a relatively unknown Wichita Falls lawyer and moderate. In the general election, Eggers seemed to vacillate between a strategic desire to reach out for "kamikaze" Texas liberals on the one hand, who had become disgusted with Democratic nominee Preston Smith, and to appease the conservative Goldwater Republicans in his own ranks on the other. In a bitter campaign, Humphrey edged Nixon in the presidential contest and Smith defeated Eggers to capture the governor's mansion.[24] But Eggers scored 43 percent of the vote in his under-funded effort.

Despite some degree of success, the Republican Party faced an uphill climb across the South. The party had won only six states of the old Confederacy in the 1968 presidential election, largely unable to crack the states it had lost in 1928. To become a viable alternative, the Texas Republican Party needed the ability to send its message across the wide expanse of the state. The very size of Texas made it even more difficult for the party to compete than it did in the other, smaller southern states. Expenses overwhelmed the resources of the small party. However, a number of wealthy conservatives who had made a fortune in the state's oil industry happily provided those financial means.[25] Analysts expected that it would take many years for the southern Republican parties to gain any significant traction against the Democrats. One noted that the wealthy in and out of the South had the means to sustain the Republican organization in a long struggle for victory, and that the development of the southern urban middle class would give the Republicans a potential source of votes in those states where it could achieve some kind of competitive equality.

The Republicans would gain strength from the fallout from the Democratic infighting, and the influx of Republicans from the North, coupled with a strengthening middle and upper class, would give them the voters needed to maintain their momentum. Liberal Democrats would tear away from the party in protest of conservative candidates, as they did with the candidates who opposed John Tower in 1961 and 1966. Conservatives would break away in protest of liberal candidates, as the 1960, 1968, and 1972 presidential election results in the state testify.[26] In addition, the state's new arrivals had very little invested in the tradition of Democratic supremacy. But as time progressed, an increasing number of the conservative Democrats joined the Republican ranks permanently. Liberal Democrats and Republicans from all ends of the political spectrum were ecstatic by John Connally's defection to the Republicans in 1973, but conservative Democrats remained much more concerned, as one of their greatest champions within the party left.[27]

By the 1970s, with a few notable exceptions, most Democratic statewide organizations in the South were so atrophied and splintered that they were unable to cope with a substantial Republican challenge. Thus, party machinery proved ineffective when it appeared, breaking down or fragmenting sufficiently so that the party literally handed elections to the Republicans.[28] This same phenomenon that elected Tower to the U.S. Senate would help Bill Clements tremendously in his gubernatorial campaigns. Although many conservative Democrats and conservative Republicans remained close ideologically, conservative Democrats remained with their party out of tradition or personal appreciation for an elected conservative Democrat. As long as the conservatives maintained control of the state Democratic Party, local leaders could easily separate themselves from the more liberal direction of the national party and conservative Democrats could still find a place within the Democratic Party, basing their support on local issues. By the late 1970s, the increasing strength of the moderates and liberals within the party began to push many Texas conservatives, already alienated by the national party, into the Republican Party. Bill Clements suspected this trend when he began his run for governor in 1977.

The 1976 Texas Republican Primary proved that the Watergate scandal had not shaken the faith of the party stalwarts. The strength of the party had grown to such an extent that Texas Republicans had held primary elections in every election year since 1962, but could never muster much more than 100,000 voters in any individual contest. Only the die-hard Republicans would bother participating in the primary, which gave most Republican voters a familiarity with one another in a throng of Democrats. From 1965 to 1982, the Republican primary vote in Texas represented an average of 11.9 percent of the total Republican vote in the general election as independents and many dissatisfied Democratic primary voters would turn to the Republican candidates.[29]

Gerald Ford, a moderate who became president after Nixon's resignation, began a run for a full term and filed to run in the 1976 Texas Primary en route to the party nomination. California governor and former actor Ronald Reagan had become an outspoken conservative activist and had gained a strong following. In fact, by March 1976, the Reagan movement not only had a considerable grassroots following among Republicans, but it also began to pick up adherents from outside Republican ranks as well, including conservative Democrats and former Wallace supporters.[30] The repositioning of the Republican and Democratic parties on racial issues had played a significant role in enabling the Republicans to attract the landslide white vote needed for victory in the biracial electorate as Republican presidential nominees and Republican presidents have consistently taken significant positions in opposition to the wishes of most African Americans.[31]

John Tower, as the lone elected statewide Republican, would have a decisive role to play, many believed. The Republican Party had steadily made the election and reelection of Tower its priority. He had long identified himself with the most controversial of the conservative policies. He had been involved with efforts to thwart the 1954 school desegregation decision, fought to dismantle the 1960 and 1964 Republican national platforms of their strong civil rights planks, and had even sponsored a proposed constitutional amendment barring what he called "forced busing" to deftly defeat his 1972 senatorial opponent, Democratic moderate Barefoot Sanders.[32] He had backed Reagan in his ill-fated effort to capture the nomination in 1968 against Nixon. Tower decided not to repeat that failure in 1976 and back the sitting Republican president. Interestingly, despite his talk between 1964 and 1976 of the party capturing the political center, Tower had a Senate voting record that placed him at the right edge of his own party.[33] This move to Ford disappointed many conservatives, but they would not back away from Reagan, causing a firestorm in the primary. The Ford campaign spent $1 million—one-tenth of its entire primary budget—on Texas, but Reagan nevertheless carried every congressional district.[34] A record of more than 400,000 voters cast ballots in the Republican contest, six times as many as had participated in 1974.[35] Reagan beat Ford by a two-to-one margin, taking all of the delegates and handing Tower a stunning defeat.

The Reagan forces would not be very forgiving to Tower for his support of Ford, despite the senator's service for the Texas Republican effort. Tower, Ford's designated floor manager at the national convention, found himself cut from the list of Texas delegates and facing the possibility of real trouble for his reelection in 1978.[36] Conservatives had long dominated the Texas Republican Party, but moderates suddenly found themselves at odds with an increasing number of party members. A new Republican Party had emerged in Texas by the mid-1970s, with conservatives in the ascendancy.[37] It had become clear how strongly they controlled the party in 1978. A study of Republican delegates to the state convention that year found that 90 percent considered themselves conservative, while 5 percent considered themselves moderates, and liberals comprised the remaining 5 percent.[38] The Republicans' southern strategy brought new types into the party, quite different from its urban and Appalachian-Ozark mountain base of years past, forcing a sharp swing to the right and, in some cases, purging moderates and alienating many African American voters.[39] The Republicans lost the state to Democratic nominee Jimmy Carter in 1976, but they began to look to the 1978 state elections with renewed hope.

Jack Orr, the new Executive Director of the Texas Republican Party, dismissed concerns about the party's factionalism in 1977, describing it as "Almost zero. We're about 90 percent unified, but we do have some growing pains."[40]

For conservatives, the election and subsequent administration of Jimmy Carter was the last straw in what for them was an intolerable streak of progressivism and activism. Inflation, the energy crisis, the explosive issue of court-ordered busing, the Panama Canal turnover, and other troubles added to the criticisms of his presidency. Jimmy Carter's popularity faltered as the nation's economic problems and foreign policy crises mounted, fueling Republican electoral hopes. In a Louis, Bowles, and Grove poll in March 1978, 57 percent of Texas Democrats rated Carter as fair to poor and 61 percent of all Texans rated Carter's performance as fair to poor.[41] Carter, the nominal head of the Democratic Party, had become the focal point of the nation's frustrations.

Other demographic shifts would begin to reveal potential weaknesses in the Democracy. The Democratic agricultural base had begun to fade. Working-class whites, particularly in rural areas, constituted a diminishing portion of the southern population as the region's increasing prosperity elevated many into middle-class urban occupations or mid-level incomes.[42] The South's shift away from an agricultural economy toward a service-oriented economy heavily rooted in professional, managerial, and commercial sectors, coupled with increased urbanization, had become expected to foster growth in the Republican Party.[43]

The rapid rise of relatively affluent suburbs also added Republican voters, adding to the party's new base. By 1950, more than 62 percent of Texans lived in urban areas, a figure that would top 79 percent by the 1970s.[44] The population of Houston would increase by 44 percent in the 1970s and climbed from seventy-sixth to sixteenth place in national per-capita income ranking.[45] Fort Worth, however, had lost population in the 1970s to its suburbs, and Galveston gained only 96 residents.[46] The major thrust of growth in the Dallas-Fort Worth area, particularly after the opening of Dallas–Fort Worth Regional Airport in 1974, had begun to shift to the suburbs in northern Dallas and Tarrant counties as well as the suburban counties of Collin and Denton. The old, rural Texas continued to disappear. Although the Panhandle and the German counties of the Hill Country comprised a significant portion of the higher-ranking Republican counties, they did not provide the majority of votes cast for the Republican nominees but rather the state's seven most populous counties, with populations each exceeding 200,000, normally supplied around half of all the Republican votes cast in Texas.[47]

Tower would seek reelection in 1978, but no obvious candidate for governor had appeared. A number of names circulated in late 1977. The *Texas Observer* rated three of the most powerful Texas Republicans of the day on the possibilities that they may seek the office. Anne Armstrong, a South Texas rancher, former ambassador, and former advisor to Presidents Nixon and Ford, had little interest, despite her influence in the party. George Bush had served as a Republican congressman from Houston in the late 1960s and had lost two statewide runs for the U.S. Senate in 1964 and 1970 but had never expressed much interest in state government and had become more interested in a potential presidential run in 1980. John Connally, former Democratic governor, conservative champion, former Secretary of the Treasury, and Republican convert also seemed more interested in a presidential run, but often found himself criticized by leaders of his newly adopted party. The *Observer* concluded that there remained "no prospect for any of them running for statewide office."[48]

Congressman Jim Collins of Dallas, who had a very enthusiastic following among Dallas-area Republicans, openly pursued the possibility of a run for governor. The volunteer base of the party in Dallas had become dominated by women, many of whom had gotten their start as political activists by working for Collins, according to former volunteers.[49] The Republican community in Dallas brimmed with excitement over the speculation in late 1977. Collins sized up a race with the presumed Democratic nominee, Dolph Briscoe, calling him "a formidable opponent."[50] He clearly understood what a Republican victory would mean. "A one-party government is just not good for Texas," mused the congressman.[51]

Many Republicans lacked confidence in his chances and believed his re-election to a strongly Republican congressional district would best serve the Republican cause. As one commentator phrased the situation, "Almost to man they told Collins not to give up a cinch congressional seat for a cinch whipping in the governor's race."[52]

Rumors also swirled that the party's 1972 nominee, Hank Grover, would run. Grover would ultimately decide against running in 1978. Former Dallas state representative and state party chairman Ray Hutchison also gained consideration.[53] Hutchison had gone around the state looking for candidates. He had even sent a letter to Bill Clements, asking him to run.[54] He could not find any willing candidates. He finally dived into the contest in October 1977. "He was running because he was state chairman, and we didn't have anybody else," Tarrance noted.[55] Despite this almost default nature of his candidacy, Hutchison had many avid admirers who boasted of his chances in the general election. Republican State Representative Fred Agnich of Dallas commented in September, "I think Ray will make a real race . . . It's going to depend on how bitter the fight is in the Democratic Primary."[56]

Hutchison had become a well-known and fairly popular leader for Texas Republicans. The tight-knit nature of the Texas Republican Party in the 1970s had become a strength for Hutchison's candidacy. Recalled Tarrance, "I grew up in the Texas Republican Party. Everybody knew everybody. The people who helped me set this [polling firm] up were in Texas. . . . My market area was always Texas. It was a relatively small club—we'd all known each other 10 years, 20 years."[57] In many ways, the Texas Republican Primary had always been something of a private affair among an extended family of partisans. The Clements candidacy, however, would change it.

Bill Clements was born in Dallas and grew up in University Park, an affluent suburb nestled in northern Dallas. He later attended nearby Southern Methodist University. He became involved in the oil industry, eventually establishing his own oil drilling contracting corporation, SEDCO. Already coming from a well-to-do family, SEDCO made Clements a multimillionaire. He maintained an active interest in politics, working as a fundraiser, advisor to candidates, and eventually became deputy secretary of defense. Despite calls from prominent Texans to run for office, he had always resisted the call. As he evaluated the seemingly precarious position of the nation in the global energy market, he decided to take action.

The series of energy crises the nation experienced during the decade had increasingly concerned him. Like most Republicans, the wealthy Dallas oilman had almost no confidence in President Carter's abilities to address the problem of energy. Clements once stated that he agreed with Carter on only one thing on the energy crisis: It was the moral equivalent of war.[58] The *Dallas Morning News* in a series of editorials blasted Carter's energy program. "Though Texans are admittedly biased in the matter, we find it increasingly hard to understand what President Carter is trying to accomplish with his 'energy' plan."[59]

Oil remained a hugely important commodity for Texas. Severance taxes from oil provided a great deal of tax revenue for the state. The share of gas and oil severance taxes fell from a high of 31.3 percent of all state tax revenue collected in 1957 to 13.0 percent in 1973.[60] The rate would see a brief period of modest recovery in the middle of the decade. In 1977, gas and oil severance taxes contributed 20.3 percent of state tax revenues, but would fall to 18.9 percent in 1978.[61] High energy demands, however, forced Texas and the rest of the nation to begin importing an increasing amount of oil. By 1975 the state began to import more crude oil than it exported, and between 1972 and 1982 oil and natural gas production declined 21 percent and 26 percent, respectively.[62] Texas oilmen grew concerned for the future of their industry, and the prospect of relying on a foreign power for the nation's oil supply struck fear into many as they saw an increasingly anti-American world. National security and consumer concerns grew during the second wave oil crisis that occurred in the fall of 1977.[63] In West Texas, a region that depended on oil production, problems in the oil industry rattled the economy of many communities and their confidence in Carter.[64]

Bill Clements had made a fortune as an oil-drilling contractor. His company, SEDCO, had expanded from its modest beginnings in Texas to having operations around the world by the 1970s. He had developed an impressive resume. In the late 1970s, estimates of Clements personal worth ranged from $29.4 million to $75 million.[65] He had become a noted advisor to Richard Nixon on defense policy. Nixon appointed him to a blue-ribbon committee to study Pentagon defense policies in 1969, and he became Texas co-chairman of the Committee to Re-elect the President in 1972 before becoming deputy secretary of defense from 1973 until the end of Ford's term in January 1977.[66] Despite this, Clements had very little name recognition even among Republicans and had never expressed an interest in running for any office. As far back as 1964, Clements had been approached about running for the U.S. Senate, but considering himself an independent at that time, he declined in order to concentrate on his business enterprises. In 1968, Clements was approached about running for governor as either a Democrat or a Republican.[67] He again declined.

Clements had also served on the board of regents for Southern Methodist University. He moderated a symposium at the university on oil and America's energy future in November 1977, which was attended by U.S. Senator Harrison Schmitt, a New Mexico Republican. More than 2,000 people attended the event at the university. After the symposium, Schmitt talked with Clements about the possibility of running for governor of Texas. As it turned out, Clements would not need much convincing. Clements's wife of just over two years, Rita Crocker Bass Clements, had served as a Republican National Committeewoman and was deeply interested in the Republican cause in Texas. They had discussed how close the Republicans had come to wresting the governorship away from the Democrats in recent elections. With the exception of the disastrous Watergate-tainted election of 1974, each Republican gubernatorial candidate had garnered at least 43 percent of the vote, and two had come within 200,000 votes of victory since 1968. Mrs. Clements believed that her husband could push the party over the top and urged him to run, believing, as did most Republicans at the time, that Texas would never be a two-party state until it elected a Republican governor.[68]

The fact that Hutchison had already announced his candidacy mattered little. Clements wanted a Republican victory in November. Clements and many others believed that Hutchison could not break the Democratic hold on the office of governor. Clements believed the traditional Republican money sources would quickly go into Tower's reelection bid, and Hutchison's Dallas lawyer image did not fit the idea that many average Texans had about their governor.[69] A successful candidate had to have a large amount of money that he could depend on to spread his message, independent of the traditional political system. In other words, that candidate had to want to spend millions of dollars of his own money. Once Clements made up his mind, almost invariably he would do whatever the job demanded.

"Let's do it," Clements decided.[70]

Word of the impending run by Clements spread quickly. He announced, "I am a Republican and I will be running as an independent, conservative Republican."[71] Jim Collins voiced his support for a potential Clements run. "It would be very difficult for me to have any enthusiasm at all to oppose him," added Collins.[72]

On November 16, 1977, Clements announced his candidacy, declaring that he would win. "I am convinced that I can win, and I can assure you that if I didn't feel that way and have good reasons to believe that, I wouldn't be declaring and wouldn't be in the race."[73] He realized that the state did not yet have enough Republicans to win the election outright but knew that Texas long had a large population of sympathetic independents and conservative Democrats.

Perhaps in 1978 he could find enough to win. His announcement included pointed appeals to "independents and Democrats as well as Republicans," to convince them that he was the best choice for the job.[74]

The almost-impulsive decision to run for governor caught many by surprise. When asked in 2004 why he decided to run in 1978 after resisting years of calls to run, he replied, "I don't have any idea. I just decided it."[75] Added Clements, "I had been asked half a dozen times. Both Democrats and Republicans asked me to run. I was a declared independent. John Connally and Allan Shivers asked me to run for the Democrats. Republicans asked the same thing."[76] The time seemed right for Clements. Once he decided, he threw all of his energy into the effort.

Clements quickly contacted Republican leaders across the state to solicit their support. Hutchison, however, had worked the trenches with the state committee members and precinct chairman and others, developing a close relationship with many. Clements, though respected and experienced in Republican politics, had not built the close ties that Hutchison had in his years as state chairman. He brushed these concerns aside and hammered home the belief that he alone could win the general election.

Clarence G. Thompson of Fort Worth, a machine operator, also made the race.[77] He had little impact on the contest, however, and garnered only a few thousand votes.

Hutchison commented years later about Clements: "He was going to set a new pattern in Texas politics; he was going to spend wealth without restraint. . . . the first thing he pulled out of his bag of tricks was that letter from me [asking him to run for governor], waving it around."[78] The letter had embarrassed Hutchison, but the former party chairman pressed forward with his own candidacy. He believed that his vision and years of experience would best serve the Republican Party in the general election.

In the primary, Clements pounded away at the idea that he alone could unseat the Democrats in 1978. He had both the will and the financial means to do so. He carefully presented a plan in which he would locate the votes for winning the general election. Up to this time, the large metropolitan areas, particularly the Dallas–Fort Worth metroplex and Houston provided most Republican votes in any general election. These areas also contained most of the Republican organizational facilities. In fact, in 1978, Harris and four surrounding counties would contribute 22 percent of the vote for Clements, while Dallas and Tarrant counties would contribute 18.1 percent of his votes, while for Hill, the Houston area would contribute 18.5 percent and the Dallas–Fort Worth area would contribute 14.5 percent of his votes.[79] Though these areas remained rich in votes, Clements had to expand into territory unfamiliar to Republicans to win the general election. Without some indication of how he could defeat an incumbent governor or a popular attorney general, he would have difficulty in even winning the primary.

By February 1978, he unveiled to the state the strategy he would use. Chris-

tened "Plan 254," he would go across the state after the summer and busily organize Republican organizations, or at least Clements-friendly organizations,
in all 254 of the state's counties.[80] Dozens of counties had no Republican organization at all, and as a result, would not even participate in the Republican
Primary. These counties, however, would participate in the general election,
and Clements believed many of these isolated communities contained many
conservative Democrats who could sympathize with the Republican Party. "I
was the first Republican in Texas to campaign in the rural areas," Clements explained. "I campaigned on the basis of those many years of voting, I had been
an independent. I just decided to run as a Republican."[81]

With his vast financial resources, he emphasized to voters, he could essentially buy the organization that he needed to win. He could thus spread the
message of victory and organize potential voters and not drain the limited
resources of the state party. In previous elections, the financing and organizational structure that Republican candidates needed to organize and com-
municate with their voters did not exist or had evaporated before the election.
Clements insisted that he would not have that problem. Declared Clements,
"Every one of them [previous GOP gubernatorial candidates] ran out of gas in
the fourth quarter . . . I'm not going to fold."[82]

The fight between Hutchison and Clements became increasingly tense. At
a Dallas Republican Women's meeting between the two candidates, Hutchison
made an attempt to show party unity under any circumstances. He announced
that he would back Bill Clements if he won the nomination and would give 1
percent of his personal wealth to the Bill Clements campaign. Clements replied
in his usual dry manner: "Well, you know Ray, without being facetious, one
percent of zero is zero."[83]

Hutchison attempted to reach out across the state to find Republican voters wherever he could, hoping that many of these voters would remain with
the party in November. Plan 254 called for Clements to begin these massive
statewide outreach efforts after the May primary. Realizing the limited reach
of the party at this stage, Clements concentrated on the party's traditional base
of voters. Winning the primary had to come first. As he explained, "If you're
going to hunt birds, you have to hunt where the birds are, and in the primary
we're talking about 20 counties. In the general election, we're talking about 254
counties."[84]

D Magazine, a local magazine highlighting life in Dallas, published its article, "The Abrasive Candidacy of Bill Clements," in March 1978. The subtitle
neatly encapsulated the feelings that many had about his sharp-edged nature:
"If nice guys finish last, Bill Clements will win walking away."[85] The article
took a tongue-in-cheek jab at Clements's initial lack of visibility in Republican
Party circles and his seemingly sudden decision to run for governor. "In Houston and San Antonio, people asked 'Who is Bill Clements?' In Dallas, at least
some Republicans knew him, but found themselves wondering, 'Who asked
Bill Clements to run?'"[86]

It quickly became clear that Clements had taken the initiative in the race and built a steady groundswell of support. Clements had resources that Hutchison could not access, and Clements quickly overcame his lack of name identification. Again and again, Clements emphasized the same message to victory-starved Republicans: Bill Clements can win. The *Texas Observer* emphasized this point and the problems it presented for Hutchison. "Clements is reaching the Republican primary voter far more efficiently than Hutchison; he is able to do so because he has the money to run a textbook campaign. 'Electability' has been Clements' selling point."[87]

As the Clements campaign soared, Hutchison's problems mounted. Barbara Gardner, a long-time Republican leader in Houston and Hutchison campaign coordinator resigned from the Hutchison campaign. Gardner claimed that she took the job according to an approved Hutchison campaign plan. She quit, complaining of interference from Hutchison's new wife, former Republican State Rep. Kay Bailey of Houston. Announced Gardner, "Through a comedy of errors or whatever, I was not able to adhere to that game plan. Maybe somebody else can make it work."[88] Privately, the Hutchison campaign tried to reorganize and redirect its efforts in the face of the unstoppable Clements onslaught.

Hutchison's campaign manager, Irving State Rep. Bob Davis, downplayed Gardner's criticisms and welcomed Hutchison's new wife to the team, adding, "As far as I'm concerned, she's not meddling. She is participating, and I hope that she continues."[89]

A Hutchison mass-mailing to Houston Republicans faced infuriating delays. Davis blamed bad weather in the mailing's Dallas production area. One Hutchison source said that the campaign lacked $12,000 to pay for the mailing, originally due for release in February. Davis admitted that the delay hurt the Hutchison effort.[90] The whole episode emphasized the serious problems that Hutchison faced. Hutchison had based an inordinate amount of his mass advertising efforts to Houston Republicans on one mailing. And he could barely afford it. Clements, on the other hand, used several mailings, newspaper ads, and broadcast ads—all of which trumped Hutchison's efforts.

In any election, the race becomes a contest of name identification. Advertising aimed at a specific audience becomes the means by which candidates attract that identification and gain support from the voting public. Clements had the means to reach all Republican voters repeatedly and win their confidence. By March 1978, it had become apparent that Hutchison faced serious problems in even reaching the same Republican voters he once led.

The hard-edged conservative message of Clements resonated among Republicans. As an oil executive, Clements seemed to have the expertise and the answers for the problems of energy security. In previous elections, the issues that had alienated many conservatives from the national Democratic Party had little to do with the local governance. Local politicians did not decide civil rights issues such as busing, fair housing policies, affirmative action, and voting rights issues, and other volatile national issues that Republican candidates used effectively in the South during presidential elections, such as foreign policy and national defense, and did not have as much relevance at the state and local level.[91] Oil, a key state industry, had become a powerful issue. With the nation's energy supply threatened in the 1970s, those issues hit Texas hard. Voters began looking for candidates who would address the threat to America as well as their own economic interests.

The causes of right-wing growth in Texas politics have stemmed largely from psychological and social factors, national events, and problems of international affairs.[92] The shock of the changes and trends taking place in society prompted some to react in very defensive ways and often to become very suspicious of anyone proposing a change in the status quo. Americans have long enjoyed a history of security and success that has made many conscious of the nation's strength and superiority, and that impression has become magnified in Texas, the only state that ever really stood as a viable, independent republic.[93] The adventurous image of the frontier, particularly the more notorious lawless and violent days of the late 1800s, long since became ingrained in the imagination of Texans. Many still saw themselves as an extension of the traditional frontier figure, a solitary figure fighting the elements to build a life for themselves. The environment and the frontier and vigilante memories seem to help spawn a certain amount of political extremism as a result.[94] As State Sen. Tom Creighton, a Mineral Wells Democrat, explained his feelings on government, "I believe in the principle that government does not give you what it does not first take from you. I think that's what the majority of the people that I represent believe."[95] Although Clements remained far removed from the more extremist political elements, his seemingly abrasive nature fit this traditional image that many Texans looked for. By addressing oil concerns, he sought to remove a threat to Texas.

Hutchison would not give in to Clements easily. He fought back with a series of fierce accusations. In April 1978, Hutchison charged that SEDCO Maritime, Inc., a subsidiary of Clements's SEDCO, received a $100 million federally-guaranteed bond backing in 1975 while Clements served as Deputy Secretary of Defense for offshore drilling rights. Hutchison did not charge Clements with corruption but with relying on the government to help his business. "It raises an ethical question," declared Hutchison, "He says he's a free enterpriser at the same time he engages in corporate welfare."[96] The charges fell flat, however, when Hutchison admitted accepting government assistance for himself, "a form of welfare," as he derisively called it, by attempting to collect on benefits promised through the GI Bill.[97]

Hutchison also raised questions about Clements's loyalty to the Republican Party. He sharply pointed out that Clements supported Johnson over Goldwater in the 1964 election.[98] While at a rally in the panhandle, he charged that

Clements's lack of experience in an elected position posed a grave risk to the state. He declared that his opponent had "absolutely no experience, no knowledge, whatsoever, of the office of governor."[99]

The Clements tenure as deputy secretary of defense also came under fire. At the same time, Hutchison questioned his opponent's electability. While in San Antonio, Hutchison berated Clements for the closure of Webb Air Force Base in Big Spring and for cutbacks at Kelly Air Force Base in San Antonio. "Republicans are beginning to realize that Clements's spending matches the historical image of Republicans in Texas and that's the image of a loser not a winner in November," said Hutchison. "When I win, the Republicans will be in a position of being the party that beat the big money and that will be to our advantage in November."[100]

Since so many communities depended on military bases for their community's livelihood, Hutchison had found a potential weakness in his adversary. He exploited these defense cutbacks while Clements served in the Nixon and Ford administrations. While raising questions about cuts to the naval air station in Corpus Christi and elsewhere, Hutchison lectured, "Right or wrong, whether or not it was in the national interest, in the state's interest, or in the taxpayer's interest, the simple truth is that people in Big Spring, the people in San Antonio, the people in Laredo where unemployment in now running 15 percent—the people connected with military installations—are going to vote against the person they perceive did them wrong."[101]

Clements responded to Hutchison's newest round of attacks. He defended the closure of Webb AFB. "It was surplus. It was redundant. . . . All of these things are done to protect the taxpayer."[102]

The *Austin American-Statesman* remained pleased with Hutchison's overall strengths and more diplomatic style. Hutchison had entered the race as an accomplished former legislator and an effective leader of the Texas Republican Party. He seemed to fit the mold of the typical party nominee. As the *Statesman* editors mused, "As a state legislator, Hutchison twice was selected as one of the ten best members. He has a generally sensible conservative approach to state government but also comes across as a man who has genuine concern for people and their problems."[103] The splash and comparative extravagance of the Clements campaign failed to impress them or a number of other voters, however. "Clements, who has no legislative experience, might be the sort of fellow would not get along with the Democratic majority in the legislature. He intends to spend his way to nomination and into the mansion, and he may do it. That doesn't make him the better candidate."[104]

Hutchison strived to expand the base of the Republican Party during the primary, fighting for every possible vote. "We're trying to get the Republican Party out of the country club and black ties and into the parks and playgrounds with the people," he explained.[105] He campaigned in the Democratic stronghold of Harlingen, speaking at the mostly Democratic Harlingen Rotary Club. "The party regulars notice when you are down there. . . . And they want you to be down there," declared Hutchison.[106] Hutchison told his supporters in late April that he believed Clements had peaked three or four weeks earlier. He predicted that he would win the primary with a comfortable majority of 55 percent of the vote.[107] Clements, in contrast, declared that he would get the nomination, and he cited polls such as the one taken by a Dallas radio station giving him 85.7 percent over Hutchison's 14.7 percent in Dallas and Tarrant counties—the stomping grounds of both candidates.[108]

Clements announced that he expected to win the primary with 60 percent of the vote. Again, he carefully explained why this was not an empty boast. "If the election [turnout] is down, then our percentage goes up because we know our voters and he doesn't know his."[109] He credited phone banks for much of his success in the race. "It gives us the tools by which we can gauge the election and the momentum of the election."[110] At a campaign stop in Fort Worth, he declared the city as important to the election as any because of its concentration of Republican voters.[111]

The *Houston Post* contrasted the dramatic differences that had emerged between the two campaigns. Hutchison traveled about the state in a motor home and conducted a door-to-door campaign, while the better-financed Clements campaign used private airplanes and hosted free barbecues for potential voters.[112] Hutchison clearly relied on the down-home personal touch, while Clements used his wealth to dazzle Republicans. Hutchison could not match Clements dollar-for-dollar, but hoped his leadership in the Texas Republican Party and popularity within the Republican grass-roots system, which comprised the majority of the primary voters, would carry the day. He dismissed the Clements spending spree.

"There's no question he's going to be famous," Hutchison said. "He's just not going to get nominated."[113]

The events taking place in the Democratic Primary did not escape the notice of the Republican candidates. Hutchison had belittled Dolph Briscoe as "inept."[114] At a campaign breakfast in Houston, Bill Clements announced that he expected John Hill to beat Dolph Briscoe for the Democratic nomination, deriding Hill as "the liberal, lawyer politician."[115] He confidently declared that against the moderate Hill, "I'll have Briscoe supporters coming to my side in droves."[116]

As the fight between Briscoe and John Hill became more intense, the Democratic contest began to draw more attention from anxious Republicans. Painfully aware of the record of Republican near-misses in the general elections, many conservatives wanted to ensure that one of their own, either Republican or Democratic, would win the general election. Many political observers believed that Hutchison, a former Republican state chairman, would benefit from a low Republican turnout because of his greater familiarity among Republican activists—those most likely to vote in the primary.

Hutchison grew concerned as some Republicans peeled away to back Briscoe in the Democratic Primary. "Briscoe's latest television blitz against his opponent, Atty. Gen. John Hill, is like applying a blotter to the Republican Primary, sending voters out," noted Hutchison.[117] He added, "I'm concerned about Hill and the cost of all of his programs myself."[118]

He recalled an encounter at an Austin event in which a woman told him that she usually voted Republican, "But I've got to vote in the Democratic Primary this time," she insisted. "We've got to stop that John Hill."[119]

Despite the acrimony between the Democrats, the Republican Primary had drawn more excitement for a statewide contest than at any other time in state history. Secretary of State Steve Oaks predicted a Republican turnout of 100,000 to 110,000, second only to the 1976 primary.[120]

At a joint appearance late in the campaign, Hutchison and Clements clashed at the Dallas Press Club. Hutchison said he would unequivocally support Clements in a general election race but wanted to see a full disclosure of Clements's finances before making such an endorsement. Clements responded that Hutchison was using "lawyer-like innuendos" to imply that he had conflicts of interest in his business, SEDCO. Clements says he would congratulate Hutchison "in good grace" and back him financially.[121] Ultimately, Hutchison weakly offered that he would support Clements if he won. "I don't support Democrats," he said.[122]

Hutchison took a last swipe at the experience of Clements and even suggesting he supported the treaty turning the Panama Canal over to Panama, stating that he "knows absolutely nothing about the State of Texas. . . . I've tried to make the point that it would be sheer folly to nominate and then attempt to elect a person who participated in the drafting of the Panama Canal treaty, as Mr. Clements did."[123] The Clements campaign denied the charge, pointing out that Clements served as deputy defense secretary when the original treaties were drafted, but according to a staff member of the U.S. Senate Armed Services Committee, Clements testified against the final product.[124]

Clements himself scoffed at Hutchison's attacks. "Part of his problem is frustration."[125]

In the final newspaper endorsements of the primary, the *Austin American-Statesman* and the *San Antonio Express* backed Hutchison.[126] But both Dallas newspapers, the *Dallas Times Herald* and the *Dallas Morning News* endorsed Clements. The *Times Herald* declared, "Bill Clements offers a record of administrative skills, a dedication to high performance, and an outspoken commitment to lean, streamlined government. Mr. Clements, a highly successful businessman, understands fully the importance of solving the nation's energy problems and he had the drive and the intelligence to analyze the issues facing state government."[127] The *Morning News* echoed these sentiments, stating, "By almost any measure, Clements is a remarkable man. . . . What energy means to Texas, Clements understands as well as any man."[128]

Both candidates began a last swing through Texas to shore up support. Clements, on a swing through Austin, brought former Republican gubernatorial candidates Paul Eggers and Jim Granberry to reinforce the depth of his party appeal.[129] Both voiced their enthusiastic support for Clements. "We're going to win by a very comfortable margin," Clements reassured his supporters as they headed to the polls.[130] He also unveiled a full-page newspaper ad in major newspapers across the state. The ad included a stirring slogan from Clements, "I believe the future of Texas is the challenge of today."[131]

Clements went to San Antonio to thank his phone bank volunteers. He told supporters that in the general election, he would be unrelenting in his criticisms of Jimmy Carter and any of his fellow Democrats who supported him. "I will remind him [the Democratic nominee] how proud he was for electing that peanut farmer from Georgia."[132] He also urged his staffers to keep working hard in the last days of the campaign to get their voters to the polls. "We're in the last two minutes of the fourth quarter and we've got to play hard-nosed ball," he said.

Stormy weather forced Hutchison to cancel late campaign appearances in Beaumont and Nacogdoches.[133] As it turned out, it would matter little.

Clements won the primary easily, overpowering Hutchison in all regions of the state. He garnered nearly 73 percent of the vote.[134] The 115,000 votes cast for Clements by themselves were more than Republicans had ever cast in a gubernatorial primary in Texas. Hutchison earned only 38,000 votes. The scale of the Clements victory left many observers speechless.

After the campaign, Hutchison offered to support Clements. He gladly accepted the support and immediately began bearing down on his next opponent, Atty. Gen. John Hill.

Clements had spent an estimated $2 million on his campaign in the primary.[135] The finance reports showed the scale of the Clements advantage over Hutchison. The *Houston Post* declared that Clements had set a record for spending in the primary campaign, far exceeding the $400,000 spent by Albert Fay in his unsuccessful bid for the nomination in 1972.[136] The Clements finance report to the secretary of state showed that through April 26, the eleven different Clements campaign committees had raised $398,775 in contributions, and had loans of $1,335,000 (mostly from Clements himself), and had spent $1,473,778. Hutchison, meanwhile, could manage only a tenth of the Clements financial effort, with $138,617 in contributions, $22,500 in loans, and spending a paltry $161,500.[137]

Solid finances and a conservative ideology directed the outcome of the Republican Primary. With his victory, Clements overcame the personalism that had dominated the small party and established himself as a viable contender, establishing a pattern of professional organization within the party able to appeal to a much broader base of donors and voters than in the past. Clements had come from obscurity to trounce the Republican establishment with an effective message and a towering amount of funds.

The Republican voter that propelled Clements forward in the primary still came from a narrow demographic. Conservative white voters controlled the contest. In fact, a study of the Texas Republican gubernatorial primary electorate in 1978 revealed that blacks and Hispanics made up less than one percent of the voters.[138] In decades past, white conservatives had controlled Texas and would not give up that control easily in spite of increased civil rights and voting rights for minorities. For the time being, the Republicans basked in the success of their primary and turned to the general election.

"Most people were surprised that Bill Clements won the primary," recalled David Dean, "If not more so than Hill defeating Briscoe."[139] For Clements, however, wining the primary was only a minor obstacle to a much more formidable goal—winning in November.

CHAPTER 4

EYE OF THE STORM

"JOHN HILL WILL BE governor of Texas," boasted the *Texas Observer* after Hill's primary victory.[1] Liberals and progressives across the state leaped for joy over the election results. Their champion, though an avowed moderate, seemed poised to reclaim the governor's mansion from the conservatives for the first time since the Great Depression. From the time the state held its earliest primary elections at the beginning of the twentieth century, winning the Democratic contest essentially meant winning the election. Only twice before in any statewide race did the Democratic Primary winner not win the general election: Waggoner Carr in 1966 and Barefoot Sanders in 1972—both losing Senate races to John Tower.

After the exhausting campaign, Hill had little reason to believe history would not repeat itself. He had over a century of Democratic tradition and a huge lead in statewide polls working in his favor. A poll released by the firm of Louis, Broyles, and Grove in early June showed him leading Clements by a margin of 62 percent to 16 percent, with 16 percent undecided.[2] In addition, the poll showed that nearly 75 percent of Briscoe supporters planned to stay true to the Democracy and support Hill. After a bitter fight, the party seemed to begin to repair its divisions in preparation for the fall contest.

Hill had never faced a Republican opponent before. His experience in state government began when then-Gov. John Connally appointed him secretary of state in 1966. His first run for governor in 1968 met with defeat in the primary. In 1972, he defeated Atty. Gen. Crawford Martin in a bitter primary fight to win the attorney general position for himself and faced no Republican opposition in the fall campaign. Similarly, when Hill ran for re-election in 1974, he again faced no Republican opposition. "I was elected as a Democrat with no Republican opposition and that is something I honor in terms of the way I look at life," he would later recall.[3]

Politicians usually suspended campaigning for the summer once the primaries ended and resumed around Labor Day. The intense heat of a Texas summer often made campaigning impractical. And the usual lack of Republican opposition in the fall made it unnecessary.

The primary fight had exhausted Hill and his staff. Hill believed that his staff had earned a break, and he did little campaigning in the first weeks after his victory. Certainly the long summer months would afford his staff an opportunity to reenergize their spirits. "My people were all worn out," Hill said, reminiscing on the long-ago campaign. "Looking back on it, it was a mistake, we should have kept campaigning."[4] Despite the incredibly high poll numbers, Hill faced a number of potential problems. These included lingering resentment from the Briscoe camp and the political baggage from the unpopularity of Jimmy Carter.

The outgoing governor, Dolph Briscoe, still stung from the defeat. His family had become furious with Hill for the years of feuding with Briscoe and the intensity of the campaign against him. In the initial days after the campaign, the governor made a statement to the state's political writers. He announced that he accepted the decision of his party. But he offered only a tepid endorsement of Hill. "I support every person on the Democratic ticket, as I have every time. . . . I was born a Democrat and I'll die a Democrat."[5] He expressed confidence in the Democratic ticket. "Texas is a Democratic state, and I expect Texas to remain a Democratic state."[6]

Briscoe's comments had considerable importance for Hill. Despite the loss, Briscoe had a very large number of supporters who would prove crucial in the general election. The governor had made a strong statement of support for the Democratic Party and his hopes for its continued success—but without naming his opponent in the primary. Hill immediately thanked Briscoe for his comments and added that his support "assures a unified Democratic Party in the general election [guaranteeing] Texas a continuation of the century of Democratic officeholders in the State Capitol."[7]

Although Carter had won Texas in the 1976 election, he had enraged many during the election; and his standing in the state deteriorated during his term. Carter had faced a popular Texan, Sen. Lloyd Bentsen in the Democratic Primary in 1976, but Bentsen had ended his national campaign long before the May primary and Carter won easily.[8] In an interview later that year, Carter had accused Lyndon Johnson, still a beloved figure among many Texas Democrats, of being a liar, mortifying many Johnson supporters in Texas and forcing Carter to issue an apology to the Johnson family.[9] Nevertheless, some of Johnson's old supporters remained cool to Carter during the 1976 election.[10]

Carter and his supporters faced a stream of vicious, biting comments from conservatives. His critics remained unremitting in their criticism of Carter, even years after his presidency ended. John Connally wrote in 1993, "I thought the people had lost confidence in Jimmy Carter, not in themselves. . . . I disagreed with his handling of the economy and felt he was incapable of inspiring confidence. But I also recognize that he suffered from almost unending bad luck."[11]

John Tower commented on Carter in 1991, "Guerilla warfare between Congress and the White House . . . badly damaged Jimmy Carter's presidency."[12]

As the 1978 mid-term elections approached, Democrats had become vulnerable because of Carter's performance. Jimmy Carter had helped reconstitute the Roosevelt coalition in 1976 that had brought the Democrats so much success, but he would become a spent force by 1980 and neared that point in 1978.[13] In the primary, Hill had fought off charges that he supported Carter's energy plans. During the general election, his opponents promised they would not stop trying to tie him to Carter. Especially Bill Clements.

Hill prepared for an ambitious legislative agenda for 1979, assuming leadership of the party. After his past primary victories, he took advantage of the lack of general election opposition to outline an agenda for his tenure as attorney general. "One thing that helped me in trying to be a good attorney general was that I didn't have a Republican opponent," he pointed out.[14] "So, I had six months to contemplate and plan how I would handle that office." Hill hoped that the same strategy would help him prepare for the governor's office. His campaign manager, John Rogers, had worked for Hill in his race for attorney general in the 1972 Democratic Primary and then served as press aide to Democratic Senate candidate Barefoot Sanders in the general election that year.[15]

Hill basked in the glory of his primary triumph. The towering personal wealth and tenacity of Republican nominee Bill Clements did not faze Hill in the least. "I spent about $1.3 million in the primary, and I'll spend about the same amount in the general election. I've already been tested in one 'checkbook' campaign, and I'm not worried about another," the new Democratic nominee said dismissively.[16]

At a meeting of state Democratic leaders on May 16, he trumpeted party unity and declared that he would meet the Clements threat head on. "The nominating process is over and now we're going to war," fired Hill in an address to the State Democratic Executive Committee.[17] "We're not only going to preach party unity but practice it." He asserted that he had received unanimous backing from the 100 former Briscoe backers with whom he had communicated so far. "I've had no refusals at all, from anyone."[18] Coupled with Briscoe's earlier comments, the party seemed to repair its divisions, at least in public. Clements, on the other hand, countered that Briscoe backers continued to move into his camp in droves.

Shortly after the primary, Hill went to Washington to meet with President Carter.[19] But the meeting enraged many Briscoe supporters. Briscoe also went to Washington to meet with Carter, but Hill and Briscoe had separate meetings with the president and did not see each other.[20] To Briscoe supporters, Hill seemed to act as if he had already become governor, trumping the visit by the governor. It insulted many in the state who still had warm feelings for a governor who still had eight months remaining in his term. Democratic Senate nominee Bob Krueger noted, "There were a lot of bad feelings after the

Briscoe loss. . . . Hill, as I recall, did not make much of an effort to reach out to Briscoe."[21] As Briscoe's general counsel, David Dean, remembered, "Shortly after the primary, Hill started acting like he had won the election." He quickly added, "He forgot there was a man named Bill Clements between him and the election."[22] Clements also worked to remind voters that he would not go away quietly.

Not only did the incident alienate many Briscoe voters, but it added to the criticisms many already had of Carter and the Democratic Party. As one Dallas woman wrote, "John Hill recently stated that he did not need Jimmy Carter. Let's not be tricked by this politician's statement. After receiving the Democratic Party's gubernatorial nomination, the first thing he did was high-tail it to Washington to see Jimmy Carter."[23]

Another Dallas resident attacked Hill, writing, "[John Hill] is a talker, not a doer . . . We don't need another like Carter in Austin."[24] These sentiments did not go unnoticed by the campaign. Hill forces remained conscious of the problems of being in the same party with Carter in 1978. The campaign's association with the Carter administration remained sparse. Hill announced that he would reject help from the national party and rely strictly on the state Democratic organization to win the campaign. "I'm going to win on my own . . . I think it's important that I address the issues in the campaign and speak for myself," he declared.[25] Democratic National Committee Chairman John White, a fellow Texan, agreed with the decision. He derided national Democratic interference in Texas as "stupid."[26]

Carter bristled at these comments but nevertheless launched a brief tour of the state on June 23 and 24, attempting to rally the Democratic faithful. He visited a number of military bases, speaking on issues of defense, jobs, inflation, and energy. He also appeared at a Democratic fundraiser in Houston. Carter spoke warmly of Hill at the gala: ". . . The two national parties have always been divided: one, the party of memory, and the other one, the party of hope. Our party, the oldest in the world, is still the party of hope, of youth and of vitality. That's why I'm convinced that John Hill will be Texas' next governor."[27]

The Democratic Senate nominee, Congressman Bob Krueger of New Braunfels, did accept help from the national party, with campaign appearances by Vice-President Walter Mondale and First Lady Rosalyn Carter.[28] Krueger commented in a 2004 interview, "How could I run against a Democratic president in the White House? I would have felt like a traitor. I was dating Jimmy Carter's personal secretary. John Hill, on the other hand, not only kept his distance, he was not willing to say that he could support Carter."[29] He added from his own recollections that Carter quietly fumed at Hill's decision to distance himself from the president. Noting a gathering of Democratic leaders that summer, "Jimmy Carter came down to Austin, and he stopped and talked to me. He looked at John Hill and turned and walked away. Hill was sort of groping after him, chasing after him."[30]

"When the election was over, it was very bitter," noted Dean, "No love lost between John Hill and Dolph Briscoe, spouses, and staff."[31] Despite the public statements to the contrary, relations between the two factions remained tense. Briscoe allies still attempted to undermine Hill. Briscoe's Criminal Justice Division had audited Hill's organized crime unit and released a report on May 17 stating that the Organized Crime Task Force operated as an intelligence agency illegally. Hill denied the charges.[32] No charges against Hill or his staff ever appeared, but the brief incident only served to embarrass Hill and lead more voters to question him.

Hill insisted that he worked to convince the governor's supporters to help him in the general election and to try to smooth over relations between the two factions. "The largest part of the Briscoe forces voted for me, but we lost enough to hurt me. I should have gotten on the phone and talked to more of them. I got on the phone and talked to many," he said. Years after the election, he maintained that it had become a misconception that he ignored the Briscoe voters, but added in retrospect that he should have worked harder for them.[33] The efforts that he had made to reach out to Briscoe Democrats apparently failed to impress a significant number of them.

Hill's forceful, ambitious nature had earned him many enemies, even within the Democratic Party. The family of Hill's 1972 opponent for attorney general, the incumbent Crawford Martin, became very vocal in their opposition to Hill. He had drawn their ire when he announced that he would challenge the sitting attorney general for his position. "I waited and I thought Crawford Martin would retire in 1972," explained Hill. "He had three terms. I was very disappointed when he didn't, and he and I were friends. And I think he knew that I did want very much to have an opportunity to run. I did not enjoy for a minute running against Crawford, but that was the way the cards dealt, and I went ahead and ran and was fortunate enough to win."[34]

Martin died following the primary. The strain of the race had worn him out. His widow, Margaret Martin, would angrily endorse Clements over Hill. "I am not surprised by John Hill's dirty campaign tactics this year because I know from firsthand experience that he waged the same kind of negative and divisive campaign against my husband, Crawford Martin, in the 1972 attorney general's race . . ."[35] Comptroller Bob Bullock had publicly expressed his dislike for Hill on a number of occasions.[36]

Other candidates attempted to join the fray. One civil servant, Ricardo Lopez, announced his intentions to run as an independent candidate for governor, describing himself as a Hispanic dissatisfied from La Raza Unida as well as the Democrats and Republicans. His proposed platform included mandating that nobody in state or federal employment be paid more than $75,000 per year.[37] His effort collapsed, however, and he did not run. Two minor-party candidates did run. Sara Jean Johnston ran for governor for the Socialist Worker's Party, and Mario C. Compean served as the candidate for the La Raza Unida Party.[38] The LRU, however, stood on the brink of collapse and no longer represented near the force in Texas politics that it had a few years earlier. The publicity accompanying the denunciations of the group by the Briscoe administration and others had a disquieting effect on conservative Hispanic supporters of the LRU. The death blow for the party, however, came from the arrest of key party leaders on marijuana smuggling charges.[39] By 1978, the LRU's only real impact remained in South Texas, and even there its power had steadily faded.

The increases in the number of voting minorities had helped the Democratic Party compensate for the loss of conservative voters to the Republican Party. The number of registered Hispanic voters had reached 591,950 by 1978.[40] Even more encouraging for the future of the party, the population of voting-age Hispanics in Texas rose 82 percent between 1970 and 1980.[41] In addition, more than two million African Americans had signed onto the voter registration rolls by 1978.[42]

Hill, however, had developed some enmity within the Hispanic community as he continued his high-profile investigations of Zavala County government. A ten-month investigation resulted, with much media fanfare, in the indictment of three officials on charges of corruption and misuse of public funds. The charges, although later dropped or found baseless, caused considerable damage to the organization and placed the LRU on the defensive.[43] Hill's image in the eyes of many Hispanics and LRU sympathizers diminished as a result.

Turnout in southern gubernatorial elections had skyrocketed over the previous few decades, from less than 20 percent in the 1940s and 1950s, to almost 40 percent by the 1970s.[44] Ten million whites had newly registered in the 1970s. This increase in white voting strength also meant that Republicans and conservatives who previously had no interest in voting had begun to register and vote in increasing numbers, counteracting the increases in the numbers of minority Democrats. Because of the overpowering strength of the Democrats, Texas politics had largely become unorganized, in the sense of block-by-block, precinct-by-precinct partisan activities to turn out voters. The small, tightly-organized Republican organizations that emerged in the 1950s had put together small grassroots volunteer operations that expanded with their growing electoral strength.

Increasingly, voters became aware that heightening competition between the parties meant that their individual votes became a more valuable commodity for ambitious office seekers. Participation increased as a result. More campaign worker contacts from activists in both parties also increased turnout. Thus, stronger partisanship meant increased turnout, but only African Americans acquired stronger partisan ties after the mid-1960s, namely in favor of the Democrats, while whites loosened their partisan allegiances.[45] In addition, urbanization also changed the character of southern politics. The massive migration in the state would cause individuals to reconsider many of their political beliefs as their lifestyle and occupations changed with a move from a small town or countryside to a large city. Particularly for the many who have migrated from small towns and farms to the cities, the new urban life necessarily results in some severance of old customs, practices, and beliefs. Clever politicians take advantage of this indecision and absorb new voters into their ranks of supporters.

Nationally, 39 percent of the nation's voters identified themselves as Democrats in 1978, with an additional 21 percent identifying themselves as Republicans, and 38 percent labeling themselves as independents. This made the independent vote an increasingly powerful swing constituency. In 1972 and 1976, 49 percent of southern voters identified themselves as Democrats, while the proportion of self-proclaimed Republicans hovered just below 20 percent and independents numbered near 30 percent for both elections.[46] Independents and disaffected Democrats had the numbers to tilt the balance of southern elections in favor of the Republicans, and already had in a number of instances. Since many of these new independents had left the Democratic Party, they remained skeptical of Democratic overtures, leading them to vote more often for Republicans. Even more troubling for the Democrats, the Republicans had captured the independent vote in every presidential election from 1968 to 1976.[47]

In the bitter intraparty war earlier that spring, the Democrats had paid little attention to the unfolding events in the Republican Primary. "I really didn't pay much attention," Hill commented, "Maybe that was one of the things I did wrong. I was too busy trying to win the Democratic Primary."[48] He indicated that Ray Hutchison would have served as a preferable opponent because his elected experience provided an opportunity to contrast the two. Like many others, he did not initially expect Clements to win the Republican nomination because of his low name-identification within the party. "Hutchison had more of a record to run on than Clements," recalled Hill.[49]

The Clements–Hill match-up fascinated political observers, but many believed that Hill would win, as Democrats had for a century. Clements nevertheless would present a strong challenge to the Democrats, much stronger than they had previously faced in a governor's race. One columnist noted that Hill would have to tread carefully not to anger either the liberal or conservative wings of the party. An issue that appealed to one side could repulse the other. If Hill could keep the fractious Democratic constituency intact, he should win. If either the moderate-conservatives or the liberals "sit on the sidelines in the fall, Hill's chances are nil."[50] Hill seemed to have the charisma that 1970s politicians needed for success, compared to Clements, Briscoe, and Hutchison. "Clements, the fighter, was sincere but abrasive," noted another writer, "Hutchison too scholarly; Briscoe vague and inarticulate. . . . John Hill may not be as conservative as Bill Clements. But Hill is no flaming liberal."[51] Clearly, Texas voters both Democratic and Republican hoped for something new, a break from the past to some extent. But the question remained what direction voters ultimately wanted to take the state. "The Democrats' choice of John Hill and the Republican choice of Bill Clements as their gubernatorial candidate ensures a sharp clash of personalities and parties. In rejecting Gov. Dolph Briscoe for a third term, most Democratic voters were clearly unenthusiastic about his effort to stay in office for ten years," noted the *Dallas Times Herald*.[52]

Democratic leaders remained confident of Hill's chances. Despite his personal dislike for Hill, Bob Bullock nevertheless stated his belief that Hill would carry the election in November, avowing that it would require a "massive effort" by Bill Clements and a "massive foul-up" by Hill for Clements to win the general election.[53] Liberal state senator Oscar Mauzy proudly predicted, "We're going to have an activist governor for the first time, in my opinion, since Jimmy Allred. . . . He is aware of problems; he is a problem-solver; he is the kind of fellow who is not afraid to butt heads with you."[54]

Hill had the support of the labor unions. This support did not mean much, given the small numbers of union supporters in the state and the low opinion of unions that many Texans had. On July 4, the AFL-CIO union endorsed Hill. Clements dismissed the show of support and said that the endorsement "proves . . . that my opponent has indeed cut a political deal with labor to keep quiet about the [right-to-work] issue."[55] But the union's ability to mobilize often counterbalanced the wealth and organization that anti-union candidates, particularly Republicans, could provide. By the 1970s, however, unions had come under increasing attack nationwide, and union opponents had redoubled their efforts against the organizations in the South.

Texas union membership had long remained among the lowest, proportionally, of any state in the union. Decline set in during the 1960s, and by 1982, only 13 percent of the industrial work force belonged to unions in the state.[56] The agricultural, frontier tradition of individualism had led many Texans to question the need for unions, and the seemingly radical nature of unions led many to question not only their motives but their patriotism. For decades Texas conservatives tried to link desegregation and unionism in the public mind, and union foes often accused unions of having communist ties.[57] In fact, even the AFL leadership itself in the 1940s was not above alleging that the CIO was communist-led.[58] These alleged radical links made allying with unions dangerous in the South, but their strength made them increasingly indispensable to the campaigns of moderates and liberals.

Despite the low numbers in the South, many sympathized with the goals of unions. According to surveys of workers in the late 1970s, while northern blue-collar workers remained far more industrialized than southern blue-collar workers, many unorganized southern workers wanted to belong to a union. The combined percentages of union workers and those wanting unionization in the South remained comparable to the industrial Northeast.[59]

The Republicans saw real opportunities. Hill's support seemed weak among many traditionally Democratic constituencies and the conservative and liberal Democrats remained divided. Clements had the wealth necessary to mobilize his base and spread his message. By contrast, the Hill campaign did not have quite the wealth that Clements possessed. This, however, did not bother Hill much. Briscoe, a two-term governor with his own almost inexhaustible supply of funds, had spent nearly twice the amount that Hill had in the primary. Hill beat him by 180,000 votes. Fundraising thus did not seem as much of a priority. "I didn't put in hardly any of my own money," noted Hill, "Didn't raise that much money."[60]

Clements realized that the fallout from the primary had provided a vital opening for him. "The Democratic Primary was very hotly contested," he explained, "Those three had a very hot, tough race that was really unpleasant. There were really hard feelings between all three of them."[61] Clements tried to exploit the bitter feelings between the Democratic camps. He averred that key Briscoe supporters had flocked to him. Conservative voters supported the conservative Clements, because regardless of party, conservative Democrats and conservative Republicans saw the biggest threat as the liberal Democrats and the agenda they championed.[62] Clements derided Hill's experience as attorney general and leadership abilities. "He's a liberal lawyer-politician who doesn't understand the management of a big operation," said Clements with his usual verbal swagger. "If he thinks this race is going to be some kind of cakewalk, I can assure you he has hold of a hot enchilada."[63]

The Republicans would spare no effort in their attempts to capture the governor's mansion in 1978. Ray Barnhart, the state Republican chairman, promised an "unprecedented team effort" in the fall campaign.[64] Clements also would use Carter against Hill at every opportunity. It would gain him important visibility but would drown out his own agenda for Texas. The *Dallas Morning News* admitted that it posed benefits and potential risks. "As a campaign ploy, it's not a bad idea. President Carter isn't popular in Texas. He'll be hard-pressed to carry the state again in 1980 without a definite change in public opinion. But the strategy of running against Carter can obscure state issues that need discussion."[65] Everything from energy to national defense to farm policy came under attack by Clements. At one appearance in June, he criticized Carter's decision to increase beef imports as a "direct and dramatic effect on the economy of rural Texas."[66] These issues played well to the traditionally conservative rural population anxious about farm imports and their own economic viability.

John Hill had difficulty reaching the Briscoe voters. As David Dean noted, "Almost everything he did caused offense to the Briscoe administration and appointees."[67] As a result, many Democrats initially supported Hill, but without any enthusiasm. Many waited to see what Hill would offer or if a candidate for whom they had a stronger preference would emerge. "For a while everyone sat and watched," recalled Dean, "Then along came Clements, and the more they saw, the more they liked. Clements was his own man and presented a vision for Texas. He had personal integrity and could win."[68]

The Clements campaign dismissed the early polls showing Hill with such daunting leads. The public would largely forget about politics until the November election day approached. Lance Tarrance's experience as a pollster told him not to rely on these early polls. "Polls before October 1 are kind of futile," he stated in a 2002 interview.[69] The pollster for the Clements campaign would not pay attention to other polls, questioning their methodology and accuracy. "[We] were always trying to see where we were with real turnout. . . . We didn't pay much attention to other polls—they were generalizations, not very precise," explained Tarrance.[70] The heavily publicized polls reported by newspapers and even commissioned by large media outlets had inaccurate polling methods, concluded Tarrance. "No likely turnout voter modeling, they poll only registered voters," he mused.

Tarrance's firm used the latest polling techniques to get the best sample possible and to get the most information from poll participants as possible. This would prove crucial in trying to win over independents or conservative Democrats hesitant about supporting a Republican. His firm used the new technique of tracking polls to see how a specific group responded to the unfolding events of the campaign over a successive series of days. "My firm was famous for looking at ticket-splitters," Tarrance said.[71]

"We had a lot of open-ended verbatim questions," he explained further. They would try to ascertain why the voter stood for or against that candidate and pollsters would write down everything the participant told them. In this way, the campaign could learn not only how well an advertising strategy worked but why it worked and what issues most strongly affected potential voters. The comments from voters proved revealing. "Clements . . . came in as larger than life, tough as nails. The rural areas liked his straightforward talk."[72]

Even the most ardent Republicans remained uncertain if Clements could win, but they still got swept up in the excitement of his campaign. "I knew there was a chance—there always is a chance—and I thought he had a little better chance than we've had in the past largely due to the exposure that he had because of the money he'd spent," recalled Republican State Sen. Ike Harris of Dallas, "If I were betting money I sure wouldn't have bet it on Clements."[73] By mid-summer of 1978, polls were indicating that Clements was developing a good deal of respect among Democrats. One Democrat had described Clements as "one tough dude" to Clements pollsters.[74] "Clements captured people's imaginations. . . . His enthusiasm was contagious," said Dean.[75]

The Republicans, however, had numerous problems of their own. Despite the apparent weaknesses developing in the behemoth Democratic organization, no one could consider the much smaller Texas Republicans as invulnerable. John Tower, long the focus of the state party's efforts, faced a difficult reelection campaign. His support of Ford in the 1976 primary and his own personal issues added to his problems. Democrats considered his victories in 1961, 1966, and 1972 as simply a matter of luck against a string of weak candidates. "[My] divorce and the lingering bad blood generated in the 1976 Ford-Reagan primary battle put me at a disadvantage," Tower wrote of the 1978 campaign.[76] He would need all the resources of the Texas Republican Party to win again, drawing on a still shallow pool of campaign donors and volunteers.

Despite the growing strength of the Republican Party in Texas and the efficiency of its organizations in the larger cities, the party had very little organization outside the metropolitan areas. The party had built its strength in the cities and had yet to break into the more rural communities, still Democratic strongholds. Despite efforts at organization, Republicans still lacked an effective voice in many areas of the state. According to the Tower campaign, 64 counties had no Republican county chairmen as late as October.[77]

To help solve the organization problem, Clements had unveiled "Plan 230" to organize Republican or Clements organizations in the 230 least-populated counties.[78] The Republicans had strong organizations in the 24 largest counties in the state, but the Democrats also had effective organizations in the large cities and overpowering strength from the courthouse crowds of the rural communities. This usually cost the Republicans the election. Throughout the summer months, Clements quietly moved across the state, mobilizing support in these smaller counties. The campaign steadily picked up supporters. The campaign considered the winning the support of more rural voters as indispensable any chance of the campaign succeeding.

The Clements campaign spared no expense in hiring the best political talent available to run the campaign. He hired Nola Smith Heale as campaign manager, a veteran of numerous Republican campaigns, including Tower's re-election bid in 1972. She became the first woman to direct a statewide campaign in Texas.[79] The Clements team also included Stuart Spencer and former Air Force Secretary Tom Reed, former strategists for Gerald Ford. Heale analyzed the dynamics of the campaign and concluded that the campaign must portray Clements as a conservative businessman, as opposed to a career politician, and bring his name identification up to a competitive position primarily through media, polling, and the hiring of Nancy Brataas of Minnesota to organize phone banks that would attract 25,000 volunteers to get out the Clements vote.[80]

"One of the early-on problems of the Tower campaign was to shore up holes left in the dike when prior Tower workers flooded over to the Clements campaign," Tower officials explained after the election.[81] The two campaigns worked closely together, coordinating strategies, appearances, and voter turn-out programs. Correspondence flowed freely between Clements staff members and Tower staff members. Tower prided himself on what he considered his rapport with the Hispanic community, suggesting ways to win over more minority voters to the Republican cause. These suggestions included the "Nosotros Con Tower" (We are with Tower) campaign.[82] Bob Krueger, however, pointed out that these efforts represented more of a media distraction and a way to deny votes to Democrats rather than win the confidence of the minority community. "He [Tower] had no rapport with the Hispanic community. The Hispanic community gave me my strongest area of support."[83] He added that Hispanics remained conscious of the voting records of both men, with Tower against civil rights initiatives and Krueger strongly in favor of them.

On June 15, Billy Clayton had a 30-minute meeting with John Hill, telling him that a tax-related special session of the state legislature might be coming.[84]

Hill had served in the often-cutthroat political world for many years and could read the handwriting on the walls. He knew that many Briscoe supporters and members of the Briscoe family had lined up against him and would enjoy nothing more than to see him go down to defeat just as Briscoe had. Even in the years since the race, he remained uncertain of their exact activities but knew their ultimate goal and knew prominent Briscoe officials worked feverishly to undermine him. "Yes—headed by Mrs. Briscoe," pointed out Hill in 2002. "I can't say that exactly. She was very active on the telephone. Dolph Briscoe called the special session to hurt me."[85]

Hill tried to get ahead of the issue as the session approached, delivering a series of speeches on economic issues. He declared economic growth the top issue facing the state. "In its broader aspect, it's how do we protect the economic base of this state and enhance it."[86]

On June 20, Briscoe and House Speaker Billy Clayton met to discuss the possibility of a special session for tax relief. A two-week session would come during the summer months to avoid interfering with legislative elections, which would give the legislature very little time to study and prepare any proposals. The state had a considerable budget surplus, and Briscoe and Clayton believed that the state should cut taxes accordingly. California simmered in the midst of a property tax rebellion, the notorious "Proposition 13" debate, and many conservative Texas politicians had decided to get ahead of the popular anti-tax movement before they too became lost in a swirl of voter rage. In addition, an activist reformer seemed poised to take the governor's office and unveil new social spending programs.

A number of Texans doubted the wisdom of an election-year special session put together so quickly but accepted it nonetheless. "It is questionable whether the legislature should meet in the emotion-charged atmosphere created by California actions in an election year [property tax debate]," declared the *Dallas Morning News*. "Governor Briscoe has never liked to call a special session of the Legislature. So it is curious that he would seriously consider this one."[87]

Clements immediately applauded the idea of a special session: "Now's the time to provide meaningful tax relief to the taxpayers of Texas," he crowed.[88]

On the last day of June, Briscoe called a special session of the state legislature to begin on July 10.[89] He announced, "I have concluded that our best hope for tax relief for the citizens of our state requires action now."[90] Dallas Democrats remained skeptical of the session. Oscar Mauzy called the session "ill-timed and ill-advised." Rep. John Bryant added, "Hasty legislation makes for bad laws and we're in real danger of having that."[91] Senator Harris pointed out that the session had no planning at all.[92] Hill, however, applauded idea of a special session and endorsed a popular bill by Rep. Wayne Peveto, D-Orange, to require a single tax assessor to set tax valuations in each county, with governmental units approving their own tax rates to the single value, removing inequalities from the property tax system.[93] The session opened on July 10, despite the questionable planning or motives of the session.

Briscoe favored an increase in the residential homestead exemption for school tax purposes to $10,000, while Texans over 65 would receive an extra $10,000 exemption from school districts.[94] The state would pick up the $600 million tab over the following two to three years. The tax cuts would be funded from the estimated $600 million to $750 million state budget surplus from the biennial cycle, which would end August 31, 1979. Even the conservative *Dallas Morning News* editorial board warned against any hasty decisions. "But the lawmakers should be cautious about launching another major tax or spending limitation in a special session. Most proposals have had too little study."[95]

Sen. Oscar Mauzy theorized that Clayton planned the session to embarrass Hill and give Briscoe one last triumph before he left office. In an October 1978 interview, he stated, "Now, what I'm getting ready to tell you is nothing but surmise and suspicion and gossip and rumor on my part. I think Billy Clayton talked Dolph Briscoe into doing it. At first, he talked Janey into it, and then Janey talked Dolph into it on the basis that this would make Briscoe the hero of the hour in Texas. . . . I think it backfired."[96] Harris echoed these suspicions. "One of the stories around—and I imagine there's some credibility to it—is that Janey Briscoe wanted him to leave a legacy for the state."[97]

The session did not go well. Clayton warned of a possible second special session if the first did not produce substantial cuts. "I don't know what it would take to satisfy him [Briscoe], but he wants substantial relief," announced the speaker as he pressed legislators to pass more aggressive tax cuts. The Legislative Budget Board warned of possible deficits by 1979 through Briscoe's proposal, erasing the stream of budget surpluses.[98] By the end of July, the House had twice failed to pass a tax relief amendment.

The resulting tax bill affected sales taxes on utilities, inheritance taxes, and property taxes. It would repeal the 4 percent state sales tax on utility bills and give cities the option to repeal the 1 percent levy on gas and electric bills. In addition, it increased to $200,000 the size of an estate exempt from state inheritance taxes. The amendment would also allow agricultural land taxation based on the production value rather than through the market value and also announced new homestead exemptions for home owners and senior citizens from property taxes. The broad-ranging tax-cut proposal would appear on the November ballot for voter approval.[99]

"I'm very pleased with the overall product of the session," boasted Briscoe.[100] Clements, on the other hand, called the results "woefully inadequate" but announced that he would support it.[101]

Briscoe received little credit for the resulting tax relief proposal. But the results had a clear message for Hill: He would receive no funding for his new programs. "I don't think there's any question about that," noted a disappointed Mauzy, "When Hill comes to office in January, he won't have available to him sufficient resources to carry out his campaign promises."[102] Observers noted that the whole session had embarrassed Hill, stating that the attorney general had been "outmaneuvered."[103] Although not fatal, the session only emphasized the problems Hill had in reaching out to the conservative faction of the party and the mistrust they had of him.

In the days after the election, Billy Clayton tried to deflect the suggestion that conservative leaders had designed the special session to embarrass Hill. "I don't think that this was the case," remarked Clayton, "There might have been some thought along the lines of there being less monies available for some of the many promises that Hill had made in the primary race."[104]

The Hill campaign moved into the waning days of summer still possessing a commanding lead. Many forces worked against him to deny him the governor's mansion and the bold, idealistic agenda he proposed. He knew he would face an energetic challenge from Clements, and he also knew he faced a challenge from conservative Democrats bent on sabotaging his agenda, fiscally or electorally. Such fights had occurred before, and the Democrats had almost always emerged victorious, regardless of internal battles. Despite the challenges, both Hill and Clements knew the real general election fight had yet to begin.

Gov. Preston Smith poses in the governor's office in 1969. Smith's unpretentious, grandfatherly demeanor won him many supporters during his four years as governor.

Gov. Dolph Briscoe and his wife, Janey, appear at his inaugural parade in January 1973. Briscoe often credited his wife with his political success and relied on her advice and support throughout his career.

Gov. Briscoe and his wife, Janey, host the Southern Governors' Conference in San Antonio in August 1978. In spite of his bitter loss to Atty. Gen. John Hill in the Democratic primary, the Briscoes tried to keep a positive face in public.

Gov. Briscoe at a press conference, circa 1976.

In a proud family moment, Atty. Gen. John Hill swears in his daughter, Melinda Hill, to the state bar in 1978, as wife Elizabeth "Bitsy" Hill looks on. Though Hill would fall short in his quest to become governor that year, he served as Chief Justice of the Texas Supreme Court from 1985 to 1988.

In January 1979, the newly inaugurated Gov. Bill Clements and his wife, Rita, walk through the traditional saber arch provided by the Ross Volunteers of the Texas A&M University Corps of Cadets.

Portrait of four Texas governors, circa 1981. From left to right, Gov. Preston Smith (1969–73), Gov. Bill Clements (1979–83, 1987–91), Gov. John Connally (1963–69), and Gov. Allan Shivers (1949–57).

CHAPTER 5

THE BEST-LAID PLANS

BILL CLEMENTS HAD SEEN the early poll numbers circulating around the state. The first polls in late May showed Hill over Clements by 52 points. Clements laughed at the numbers and brushed them aside. Clements believed he would win by a comfortable margin that he repeated at every opportunity: "I'll beat him about 53 percent to 47 percent."[1] The statement did not represent an empty boast. Research by the Clements campaign showed that such a victory margin remained possible, and it served his larger strategy of building up support during the campaign.

Explained Clements campaign aide David Dean, "No one wants to back a loser. He [Clements] tirelessly explained the numbers. He would produce the money, they would produce support."[2] If he repeated it often enough, with enough conviction and just enough facts to support it, people would believe it. As fall approached, the numbers began to prove his theory.

As the primary season ended, Clements immediately dived into an aggressive plan of organizing in the most remote corners of Texas and trying to win as many Democratic converts as possible. "Summertime was usually a time off. No one told Bill Clements—he couldn't rest," David Dean recalled.[3] Given the considerable disadvantages he faced, he could not afford to rest.

The entire general election strategy of Clements rested on a narrow set of variables. The combined strength of the conservatives, both Democratic and Republican, would easily win an election in Texas into the late 1970s. The problem for Republicans lay in convincing enough of those conservative Democrats to bolt from their own party. The party did not yet have the strength to win on its own without the defection of Democrats. Although conservative Democrats and conservative Republicans agreed on many issues, the Democrats remained in their party, either out of loyalty to the organization or a particular official, pride in identifying themselves as part of the Democracy, tradition, or disgust at some Republican issue or candidate. Liberals had sometimes broken away in enough numbers out of disgust at a conservative Democratic candidate to elect

Republicans, namely Sen. John Tower. Enough conservatives had also broken away in the past in enough numbers to allow Republican presidential candidates to win statewide, namely with Dwight D. Eisenhower in 1952 and 1956 and Richard M. Nixon in 1972. But such revolts in the Democratic ranks had only occurred with federal elections, not state elections. Since the Republicans had won statewide federal elections before, they believed they could muster the strength to win a state-level office. The question remained whether Clements could make that theory a reality. The recent history of the Texas Republican Party revealed a list of near-misses in gubernatorial contests.

Clements recognized during the primary that the bitter contest would leave many Democrats willing to consider an alternative to the eventual nominee. Either for dislike of John Hill's tenacious style or moderate policies, many Briscoe voters would not support Hill with much enthusiasm. "Bill Clements immediately reached out. The real challenge was with the Democrats. There were not enough Republican voters," said Dean.[4] Although Dean was a trusted ally to Gov. Dolph Briscoe, mutual friends of both Dean and Clements had reached out to Dean, urging him to join the Clements team. Clements still seemed a long-shot in May with very little name-identification, and Dean had worked closely with Democrats for years. He considered the offer. "It was one of the hardest decisions of my life. . . . I knew Hill really well—we had to toe-to-toe a number of times. I didn't think John was the right temperament to be governor at that time."[5]

Weighing his options, he made his decision. "I signed on with Bill Clements on June 1." Dean became deputy campaign manager and chairman of the Democrats and Independents for Clements Committee.[6] Immediately, the campaign began working to secure the support of other Democrats and curious independents. It remained no small effort and consumed considerable attention by the Clements campaign. By July, the Clements campaign had a full-time staff of three working to win the votes of Democrats and independents.[7]

To dramatically symbolize the attempt to reach out to Briscoe voters, the Clements staff moved into the old Briscoe campaign headquarters in Austin. With the permission of the governor's primary staff, the Clements campaign took up the remainder of the lease on the office space. "The Bill Clements people were very anxious, very excited," said Dean.[8] This excitement energized their efforts.

Clements touted Democratic support at every opportunity, claiming that Briscoe voters continued to pour into his camp. In the days after the primary, Briscoe commented that he remained unaware of any defection of his top supporters to Clements and added that he discouraged any such defections.[9] However, he remained quiet on the defection of Dean to the Clements camp. In a powerful move to lure away conservative Democrats, Clements had a reception in Uvalde—at the bank owned by Dolph Briscoe. Obviously, Briscoe knew that Clements would appear at such a highly publicized campaign event on his own property. For Briscoe supporters looking for an alternative to Hill, the governor did not need to say anything else. "The first stop on the Clements fall campaign—very pointedly at Uvalde, Texas—was a reception at Dolph Briscoe's First State Bank," noted Dean.[10] "He [Clements] encouraged Briscoe Democrats that they were released to do what they wanted. . . . Most weren't even thinking about supporting Republicans." Although Hill may well have had success with his sporadic contacts with Briscoe supporters, the Clements campaign steadily scooped up an increasing number of Briscoe voters. The efforts to attract Briscoe supporters steadily gained momentum. Dean declared that "For every public backer, there were five or six in private."[11]

Voters do not always vote solely for one party in an election. Ticket-splitting, as political scientists refer to the phenomenon, had long since become a common fixture in Texas politics and elsewhere. This phenomenon, for example, allowed Richard M. Nixon and John Tower to carry the state in 1972 while for various reasons Dolph Briscoe and the other statewide Democratic candidates won their contests simultaneously.[12] Studies have shown for decades that victory for a party at one level in a community does not necessarily mean that their fellow partisans will do so well.[13] In an election where the Republicans would not challenge the Democrats for many local offices, ticket-splitting became indispensable to Republican chances, toward which Clements worked feverishly.

The shift of voters from one party to the next usually happens over a period of time. Some series of events, issues, or candidates upsets members of a particular party, and they then begin to look for alternatives. Over a period of time in which the disenchanted vote for members of other parties, that traditional loyalty fades and a loyalty to a new party often emerges. Race issues had become a major factor in the Republican upsurge in Texas as many turned away from the civil rights agenda of the national Democratic Party, further exacerbated by the socially liberal ideology of many candidates, which also contributed to the emergence of the Republican Party in Texas.[14] Demographic patterns have also spurred Republican growth in the state as many new Texans come from traditionally Republican states and had little sense of loyalty to the established political traditions of the Lone Star State.[15]

Clements did not hide his strategy for defeating Hill. He highlighted it at every opportunity, carefully explaining how he would defeat a century of Democratic entrenchment and decisively capture the governor's mansion. As a businessman, he had built a multi-million dollar corporation by carefully selling his proposals to potential investors and partners. For Clements, selling himself as the state's next governor did not seem so totally foreign to his experience. At an appearance at the University of Texas at Arlington in late June, he declared that he would spend $3.5 million in the general election, with three-fifths on media advertising, and would spend the summer organizing support in the rural areas and would then return to the urban areas, the more traditional sources of Texas Republican support, after Labor Day.[16]

Despite the sympathy that many Texans had developed for Republican issues and the immense financial resources of the party, Republicans had very little organization outside the major cities. In fact, the low level of Republican voting below the presidential level had emerged largely as a result of the organizational weaknesses of the party, as the organization could convince very few Republicans to run for state, local, or congressional offices.[17] As one observer sized up the race, "Republicans will run well in the urban areas and in medium-sized cities. But the rural vote will eat them alive."[18] Clements had to run well in rural areas to win. For a statewide victory, analysts concluded that the party must have at least 52 percent of the vote in the major cities, a break-even showing in the next 28 urban counties, and at least 46 percent of the vote in the remaining rural counties.[19]

Pundits concurred, "With the strong statewide ticket that includes Sen. John Tower, Republicans will turn out in the cities. If Clements can make a favorable impression on rural Texans, he can run John Hill a close race. If not, all bets are off."[20] Clements continued his efforts to organize the rural areas and launched a series of ten-second radio and television spots to increase his name identification, while Hill settled into Austin to rest for the summer.[21]

"Never have the Republican gubernatorial candidates organized the rural areas . . . the concentration has been in the urban areas," Clements stated.[22] He also claimed that Plan 230 had already met with success in organizing support and netting important defections from Briscoe Democrats. The Republican boasted that the campaign had already covered 11 counties in the panhandle and had picked up in some 90 counties the names of county chairmen and regional chairmen who personally worked for Governor Briscoe and other Democratic candidates willing to help Clements.[23] He again predicted that he would win with 53 percent of the vote.

The novelty of a Republican campaigning in the rural areas in the late 1970s impressed many. "It was a brilliant move to do it in the summer, when the Democratic guard was down and people weren't watching," Lance Tarrance said.[24] The resources that Clements had allowed him to spend more time campaigning in areas uncertain about supporting a Republican. As State Sen. Betty Andujar of Fort Worth noted, "His money enabled him to do something that I don't think Republicans had ever done before. He deliberately set out to organize the rural counties. The Republicans would win in the metropolitan areas but always lose out in the rural counties. I think that the Briscoe people probably helped in that very greatly."[25] Republicans had begun to see evidence that rural residents did not seem as nearly intractable as once assumed. Observers pointed to a substantial increase in Republican voting in the deep rural South in 1976 from even the party's national landslide in 1972.[26] In effect, Clements had the money to rewrite the rules of Texas campaigning and now needed to prove that he had the message and the charisma to bring his ideas to fruition.

Clements would spare no resources. He announced in mid-July that he had convinced the two most prominent figures in the national Republican

Party in 1978, Ronald Reagan and Gerald Ford, to campaign on his behalf. The two would also headline a September 12 fundraiser, at $1,000 per plate, for Clements. To further consolidate support, Clements said he would use telephone banks, rows of volunteers to contact potential voters and steer them to their polling sites. He boasted that he would have 50,000 volunteers on the phones on Election Day to mobilize his supporters.[27]

At a joint appearance between Hill and Clements in Amarillo, Clements decided to use a stage prop to illustrate how he would tie John Hill to the faltering Carter administration. At the head table, Clements sat with Hill and Hill's wife, Bitsy, his own wife, Rita, host Amarillo Mayor Jerry Hodge, and the mayor's wife. When Clements stood to speak, he pulled out a rubber chicken to symbolize Carter and promised to hang "this dead chicken around Hill's neck."[28] Clements fumbled with the rubber chicken and it landed in Mrs. Hodge's lap, horrifying the audience who believed the chicken was real. The audience's disgusted reaction perplexed Clements, and the incident created a stir across the state.

Clements explained his thinking behind the rubber chicken episode to an aide, "Farmers in Texas, when a dog got into a chicken coop, would hang a dead chicken around the dog's neck and after a couple of weeks, the dog wouldn't go into the chicken coop anymore and get after the chickens."[29] Clements, whose family had owned a ranch in Kaufman County for years, knew this old farm trick and expected anyone else who grew up in rural Texas to immediately understand the reference. Urban newspaper writers and political analysts who grew up in the cities may not have understood the reference or become offended by it. "There was nothing wrong with it," recalled Clements. "In rural Texas, it was a standard distraction."[30]

While the incident may have crippled other campaigns, it became an example of how "everything turned to gold for Clements," as Dean explained.[31] Dean had known Mayor Hodge for some time and quickly moved to smooth over any strained relations between Hodge and Clements. "I finally persuaded Hodge to back Bill Clements," recounted Dean. He had found the now infamous rubber chicken and handed it to Hodge. At an appearance announcing Hodge's endorsement, "He embraces Bill Clements and urges Briscoe Democrats to back Bill Clements. Hodge gives the chicken back to Bill Clements. The prop became larger than life," remembered Dean.[32]

Since the Republican organization remained small, both the Tower re-election campaigns and the Clements campaign worked closely together on many issues, often sharing staff and information. The two campaigns corresponded with each other often, compared issues, arranged for periodic joint appearances, and helped organize get-out-the-vote efforts. Lance Tarrance served as pollster for both campaigns. As the two races tightened, they began to affect each other as many of they depended on many of the same voters.

In previous campaigns, some Republican candidates accused Tower of hogging the available Republican volunteers. The 1972 Republican gubernatorial

nominee, Henry Grover, had blamed Tower for his defeat because of the senator's use of so many volunteers.[33] He considered running against him to avenge
his loss. With the encouragement of friends among the ranks of Reagan supporters in 1978, Grover decided to enter the Senate race. In fact, as late as June
1978, polls showed Grover to have a following of 2 to 3 percent of respondents;
but Reagan forces, wishing to keep Grover supporters within Republican ranks
and to demonstrate leadership clout, proceeded to dry up his financial and
volunteer support, forcing him to drop out of the running.[34]

Senate nominee Bob Krueger, like other Democrats, saw Tower as vulnerable. A moderate like Hill, the two appeared together at Democratic rallies
across the state, filling Texas moderates and liberals with the hope that they
could oust two conservatives from office and replace them with thoughtful activists in one election. Krueger campaigned exhaustively. While Tower worked
in Washington, the "New Braunfels Flash," as journalists dubbed the New
Braunfels congressman, appeared at scores of small-town rallies with the slogan, "We need more than a vote—we need a voice."[35] Krueger gained steadily,
running strongest in San Antonio and South Texas and briefly appeared to
overtake Tower, while Tower's staff responded with highly targeted and local-
ized media expenditures and campaign appearances to counteract the energy
and enthusiasm of the Democrat.[36]

On August 3, John Connally announced that he would endorse Bill Clements,
carefully disavowing his past connections to Hill and the Democratic Party. "I
appointed John Hill as secretary of state. But John Hill as governor would have
no choice but to support President Carter, his national program, and his national party leaders," explained Connally.[37] "Some people say my friend Bill
Clements comes on too strong. And I say that's good because what we need
is a strong governor. Strong enough to fight for what we Texans believe in
and strong enough to assure that the federal government doesn't dictate every part of our lives," he added.[38] Although Connally had appointed Hill as
secretary of state and bore him no ill will, the announcement did not surprise
many. Connally had switched to the Republican Party earlier in the decade and
now prepared to run for the Republican presidential nomination in 1980. If he
had any hope of capturing the nomination, he could not possibly endorse the
Democrat.

Clements secured another important defection. He announced that the
campaign had hired Bill Lyon, former Harris County campaign manager for
Dolph Briscoe, as assistant campaign manager in charge of coordinating African American support for Clements. Clements hoped that such a defection
would draw more minority voters away from the Democrats. Lyon stated, "For
too long the Democratic Party has taken the black vote for granted . . . Bill
Clements is not writing off the black vote."[39] African Americans had become
a vital Democratic constituency, indispensable to any chance of success statewide. If enough African Americans defected to Clements, it would prove fatal
to Hill's campaign. "If we get any percentage above 18 percent, Bill Clements

will be your next governor," Lyons predicted.[40] James Baker, the Republican candidate for attorney general, also announced his intentions to help the party make inroads into the African American vote to aid the party's efforts.

Labor Day weekend marked the traditional beginning of the general election season. Clements began with a series of high-profile appearances and rallies. "I want a new president in 1980," he declared at a September 4 rally at his Forney ranch.[41] As promised, he continued to pound away at the Carter administration, using the president's unpopularity to build support. To some observers, he ran more against Carter than against John Hill. Every aspect of the Republican's campaign revolved around defeating the president for reelection. In fact, an excerpt from his campaign materials regarding how Clements promised to help the medical profession answered with the statement that he "promises to do everything in his power to prevent Jimmy Carter from carrying Texas in 1980."[42]

The Clements campaign had hyped the rally in Forney for some time. Hundreds of supporters drove out from nearby Dallas and Fort Worth to enjoy barbecue, politics, and Clements's hospitality. One report indicated that perhaps one thousand had attended.[43] He announced his plan for what he called the "Taxpayers Bill of Rights," which included a system of initiative and referendum, calls for public votes on all taxation matters, opposition to any corporate or personal income tax, and requiring a two-thirds legislative vote to impose taxes.[44] He continued to pound away at his themes of low taxation and energy policy. He reiterated his opposition to Carter energy plan and called for immediate oil and gas deregulation, declaring, "The United States energy shortage . . . has now built into a crisis . . . when the crisis explodes into a national emergency, our Texas assets are likely to be seized unless we supply some national leadership now."[45]

He spoke at length on the problems of the industrial Northeast, hinting that a liberal social agenda and labor unions had caused the decline of the industrial states. He tried to tie Hill to the same ideology, hinting that his election would lead to the same problems for Texas. "For many reasons, Texas is at a crossroads. The industrial base of the Northeast is obsolete. The people there have voted themselves more services than they can afford. As a result, they are not competitive producers, in either domestic or world markets."[46] Clements called Hill a captive of the "teaching establishment."[47] He also warned that unless districts forced teachers to become more accountable and challenged teachers' unions, the state could not educate students. "By 1983, we will have schools that produce educated children . . . Or the school system will have been captured by the education establishment, with collective bargaining and ironclad tenure as an absolute roadblock to local school board control."[48] His anti-union sentiments and pro-industry stands played well with his audience.

A few days later, Clements repeated these ideas at the Texas Republican Convention. He reemphasized his intentions to win, spelling out once again his plan of attack and emphasizing that the party had the numbers to win if it could properly organize its support. "I plan to win . . . Neither of these men [1968 and 1970 nominee Paul Eggers and 1972 nominee Hank Grover] had the organization or enjoyed the support that we do today. . . . We are going to win on this third time at bat with 53 percent of the vote."[49] He noted that he had received support from sources that he described as "close to Governor Briscoe," but did not elaborate.[50] Clements added that the traditionally Democratic rural areas would not go uncontested and emphasized the unprecedented success of Plan 230 and pulling together an effective campaign team. "We have paid close attention to rural Texas . . . as of today, 90 percent of the counties have Clements campaign chairmen in place . . . We have sown the seeds of organization this summer. . . . As a result of his [David Dean's] efforts, the Briscoe political organizers in over 130 counties are publicly aboard my campaign."[51] The Hill campaign had taken note of the energy and strength of the Clements effort. Hill campaign manager John Rogers noted in a November 1978 interview, "By September, we knew the Clements campaign was formidable. We all knew what they were doing. They used tremendous amounts of money very astutely."[52]

Hill realized that Clements would outspend him, but worked to raise enough funds to have the resources to wage an effective campaign. The spending gap did not worry Democrats, since Republican candidates had outspent the Democrats before, only to lose their races. On August 1, Hill collected $320,000 in donations at a Houston fundraiser attended by some 45 people.[53] Lowell Leberman, Hill's finance chairman, noted that a Briscoe backer gave Hill $10,000 and promised to hold fundraisers for him that would raise $50,000 to $70,000 each. Hill told supporters, "The only way we can offset a 3-to-1 spending margin is to work our people three times as hard."[54] Hill called his $1.25 million campaign budget "comfortable" and "competitive" with the $3.5 million Clements would spend in the general election and added that 95 percent of all those active in the Briscoe campaign were actively and publicly for Hill.[55] A few days later, he raised $725,000 at an Austin fundraiser attended by 2,500.

On September 12, Ford and Reagan arrived in Texas to campaign for Clements. Clements had high hopes from their appearance in the state and had trumpeted their impending arrival for some time. Their three appearances in Dallas, Austin, and Houston brought out large numbers of the Republican faithful to see the party's two most visible national leaders. The *Houston Post* ran with the headline "GOP's big guns in state" to underscore the hopes that Republicans had for the success of the appearances.[56] In Austin, a crowd of 5,000 met at the Clements rally at the University of Texas. Ford and Reagan hammered away at President Carter, while praising Clements. Ford hailed him as "the best general manager of the Pentagon," while calling the 1978 election a referendum on Carter's economic, energy, and national security programs.[57] Reagan echoed these same themes, lauding Clements.

The state press howled at the verbal gaffes of both Ford and Reagan. Ford urged crowds to help Clements get elected "governor of the great state of California." Reagan had commented, "So far the crowds have been enthusiastic and I think it looks great for Hill." The *Austin American-Statesman,* the *Houston Post,* and other newspapers had highlighted these comments but almost buried that evening's Dallas fundraiser where 1,300 Republicans, including such major state party leaders as Anne Armstrong, George Bush, and John Connally, raised $1.3 million for Clements.[58] Clements, basking in the success of the Dallas fundraiser, stated that Texas Republicans for sixteen years "have been knocking at the door" of the governor's mansion. "I'm ready to go in," he said to wild applause.[59]

The Democrats held their state convention in Fort Worth the week after the Republican meeting. The convention's 3,000 delegates and supporters in attendance wildly applauded Hill. Hill attacked Clements, declaring that he "has no experience in state government and . . . is divisive in his approach."[60] Hill announced his spending plans to the convention, calling for one-third of the state's budget surplus to education, one-third to other human needs, and the last third to tax relief from property and utility taxes.[61] A few days later, he issued a six-point anti-inflation program for the state, which included a freeze on state taxes, careful budget management, limitations on state spending, and utility bill relief.[62] Reporters described Hill's performance at the convention as lackluster. "Hill didn't hurt himself much but didn't help himself much at the convention," wrote one reporter.[63]

The Clements camp stepped up the pressure on Hill, refusing to yield an inch to the Democrat. Clements released the names of more Briscoe Democrats who had switched to his side, bringing the total claimed by the Republicans to 433, with 93 having served as county chairmen of the Briscoe reelection efforts.[64] While in Fort Worth, Clements announced "Operation Observation" to follow Hill and correct misstatements. The Republicans hoped to increase the pressure on Hill by responding to his statements immediately and not to let a charge or a pledge go unchallenged. Hill rejected the Clements self-proclaimed truth squad, declaring, "I'm not going to say anything incorrect. I deal in fact."[65] Hill further dismissed the whole Clements operation as "a publicity stunt."[66] As the polls still showed Clements behind, observers noted that for Clements, "For every plus, he seems to pick up a minus."[67]

In late September, Governor Briscoe's wife, Janey, made an explosive statement that again put Hill on the defensive. In a telephone conversation with the *Austin American-Statesman,* she said that she would vote for John Hill "because of loyalty to Dolph," but she thought that Clements would make a more responsible governor in fiscal matters and also commented that her two daughters and son leaned toward the Republican.[68] Mrs. Briscoe reportedly laughed when asked if she would "hold her nose" while voting for Hill, stating, "That might be an appropriate way to put it. . . . Bill Clements is a more conservative man. I think he would be more responsible in knowing the value of a dollar. Dolph and I are very conservative in our thinking."[69]

Briscoe's son, two daughters, and one son-in-law now openly backed

Clements. Janey Briscoe further added that the Hill campaign had not sought the support of the governor. Cele Briscoe, the governor's daughter, confirmed her mother's claims, declaring that she "can't support someone like Hill. It's not because he beat my father, but because of his beliefs and philosophy."[70] Dean responded to Cele Briscoe's comments, "I guess you could take that as an endorsement."[71] The fact that Briscoe's children would openly support Clements over the man who defeated their father did not surprise Dean. "They knew Hill well," he said. "They had a pretty good perspective on his character. They'd seen what'd happened between John Hill and their dad over six years."[72]

Dean doubted that Dolph Briscoe directly aided Clements. The almost-legendary loyalty his supporters had for him came in part from his loyalty to them. "He is loyal. He was not about to endorse publicly a Republican. If he voted in the general election, I imagine he would've voted for Hill. He might have secretly hoped that Bill Clements would win. He's very committed, very loyal to the Democratic Party."[73] State Rep. Fred Agnich supported this contention. "In the off the record conversations with many of his [Briscoe] supporters—I'm informed, at least—he did say he would prefer Clements. Now, Janey Briscoe worked avidly for Mr. Clements. She really did. She went out in the line for him and worked just as hard as she could, and she was a factor in the race."[74] Krueger stated that had heard of no direct aid from Briscoe to Clements. He noted, "I think there was a certain annoyance to John Hill in that election. Briscoe himself is still a Democrat. He is still a very decent man, and he supported [Democratic President Bill] Clinton."[75] Briscoe himself probably maintained a nominal allegiance to the party, but many members of his family and closest advisors openly supported Clements. Clearly, the governor did not discourage this and did nothing to support Hill. No evidence has emerged, however, that he personally aided Clements.

Clements himself contended that he did not seek any endorsements from the Briscoe family. "That they 'offered' support is a misnomer," he reminisced in 2004. "They held a press conference and said they supported me. They never contacted me. It was a complete surprise. . . ."[76] The tension between Briscoe and Hill was well-known, but this comment broadsided Hill and underscored the problems Hill faced and the momentum that Clements continued to build. Clements happily pocketed the invaluable words of praise and pressed forward. "I really appreciated their endorsement," he added.[77]

Janey Briscoe's words haunted Hill, who continued to insist that most Briscoe voters continued to support him. At a campaign appearance in Waco, he dismissed the reports that Briscoe Democrats continued to hemorrhage out of the party. "There's a lot of misrepresentation going on about this so-called Briscoe support for the other side," pointed out Hill.[78] "The truth is the other way. If we started playing the release-the-name-game of Briscoe supporters, I could start around this room and give you quite a few you can see and recognize were key supporters of Governor Briscoe that are now openly for me, and I very much appreciate that." Hill said he did not plan to ask Briscoe to actively campaign for him. He believed that he did not need his active support. Hill took Briscoe at his word. "He said he intends to vote for me and support the ticket. . . . That is keeping with the tradition of our Democratic Party. Once we pick our nominees . . . we normally—most Democrats—unite, and I think that's what's happening here."[79]

For the remainder of the campaign, he would exhaustively appeal to party unity. "I still say 95 percent of the key Briscoe organizers and workers are for me," he maintained.[80] He also responded to the comments that he never asked the governor for his personal support. "There's just a misunderstanding," explained Hill at a later appearance. "I have never asked the governor to support me, but I take him at his word he will vote for the Democratic ticket."[81] The lingering hard feelings between the two from the primary prevented them from repairing their political relationship that year. Krueger stated in 2004, "A lot of Briscoe supporters went to Clements. If Hill had more modesty or magnanimity, he might have prevented that."[82]

Mrs. Briscoe had wielded considerable political influence, and the governor often listened to her advice. As a veteran campaigner, she knew how to work the campaign system, and she also knew how much attention her comments would receive. State Rep. Gib Lewis noted, "She had a great deal of influence, a great deal of influence. Many times I've been in his office, and Janey would be there with him."[83] State Senator Oscar Mauzy agreed. "I think Mrs. Briscoe played a significant role in influencing the governor. And I'm not saying that's necessarily bad. He trusts her; he confides in her. I think that's fine, but I think she plays an inordinately heavy role at this time. By that, I mean, since Briscoe was defeated in the Democratic Primary, she has taken Briscoe's defeat as a personal insult to her, to her family."[84]

On October 1, accusations of misconduct hit the Hill campaign. A Webb County man, Joe M. Guerra, told the *Dallas Morning News* that he was fired by Webb County Commissioners in November 1975 after he reported widespread irregularities in the county's finances, with up to $900,000 unaccounted for.[85] He claimed that Hill and Webb County Dist. Atty. Charles Borchers refused to push for an investigation even after he showed them an audit. The charges stung the Hill camp. The Democratic nominee had prided himself on his aggressive record as attorney general. His greatest critics had never before criticized him for avoiding an investigation but for going outside his jurisdiction to conduct investigations and his unyielding stances on legal issues. A Hill spokesman dismissed the charge as "the type of claim you get in a political season. . . . I think John's track record on investigations all over the state would prove that [allegation] a fallacy."[86] On the same day the story broke, the *Dallas Morning News* editorial page featured a glowing endorsement of Clements, not mentioning the Webb County issue at all:

Other men might be hobbled by seeking the governorship first
without first holding other political office. Not Clements, we believe. His whole life shows that he is up to any job he cares to take
on. . . . There seems little doubt that the dynamic Clements would
galvanize the governor's mansion as it has not been since the John
Connally years.[87]

Hill blasted the *Dallas Morning News* and launched a counteroffensive against
the charges. "The story is 180 degrees from what actually happened," he declared.[88] At a series of news conferences in Dallas, Austin, and Houston, Hill
angrily denied the charges, claiming that a 1976 investigation resulted in the indictment of a county employee. He added that the claims were "totally false."[89]
Hill said that the paper omitted any mention of the efforts of his office and how
local leaders had praised his efforts. The paper defended its story.[90] An *Austin
American-Statesman* editorial on the Webb County allegations largely exoner-
ated Hill, but chastised the increasingly negative tone of the race:

> Hill said the story was false, that he did send an investigation, and
> local officials praised the Attorney General's role in the investiga-
> tion, which was pursued about as far as probes of corruption ever
> are. That did not stop Clements from accusing Hill of a "violation
> of the public trust," nor Hill from trying to hang Richard Nixon and
> 'dirty tricks' around Clements's neck.[91]

Within a week, the allegations had faded. Observers realized that this election
would have more allegations hurled between the two candidates. As one editorial noted on the scandal, "It appears Hill has emerged relatively unscathed, but
he can't be sure when the next nuke is going to fall—not with his Republican
opponent, Bill Clements, manning the bombsight. . . . Clements strategists hint
they have a lot more ammunition to fire."[92]

The Clements campaign remained relentless in its assault. The Republican
ridiculed Hill at every opportunity. He also proceeded with hard-punching issues commercials on radio and television across the state, targeted with a finely
tuned interlock of careful polling and media budgeting, while discouraging
poll numbers showing him still behind prompted him to redouble his efforts.[93]
Nearly a million phone calls were made from mid-October to early November,
with half of on Election Day.[94] Clements had utilized all of the modern campaign techniques that his resources could produce, but still had yet to break
ahead of Hill in any poll. In the meantime, Hill and Krueger announced a joint
fifteen-city helicopter tour of Texas for October 20 and 21, where they met with
enthusiastic crowds.[95]

Hill had seen enough elections in Texas to know how bruising elections can
become. He fully expected the Clements campaign to unveil a series of blistering attacks, but did not yet know what shape they would take. He believed that

the "tax-and-spend" charges that Clements hurled would allow the Republican to close the gap as he promised to cut state government by 25,000 employees and return $1 billion to the voters, simultaneously portraying the Democrat as a governor who would keep big spending programs.[96] At an appearance in Dallas, Hill predicted that the race would become a "vicious, mean, and ugly campaign." He accused Clements of practicing "dirty tricks," an allusion to his work with Richard Nixon's 1972 reelection campaign. "Since he was co-chairman of CREEP in Texas, it is no surprise he would pick up some of the aspects of that campaign," cried the Democrat.[97] He also claimed that Clements campaign workers identified themselves as radio-station employees to gain access to Hill's media schedule and blasted the Clements campaign for a series of vicious anti-Democratic mailings.

Hill could make no moves without finding himself the subject of another Clements attack. He announced that he would join Oklahoma and Louisiana in a coordinated attack on gas-pricing features of the new federal energy bill. The attorney generals of those states had begun to organize a federal lawsuit against portions of the new national energy plan. Texans had roundly criticized the natural gas price controls portion of Carter's energy plan, but Clements scoffed at the move as politically motivated. "If John Hill was sincere in his claimed opposition, he would have begun working long ago."[98] An incredulous Hill retorted, "Bill Clements is out of step, not only with the rest of the Republican ticket in Texas, but also with the rest of the state when he criticizes me for filing suit on behalf of the energy bill."[99]

The polls continued to give the Hill campaign a degree of comfort. In a widely publicized poll commissioned by *Texas Monthly* and the *Austin American-Statesman,* taken September 29 through October 7 showed Hill with an eleven-point lead.[100] The poll had encouraging news for Hill across the state with one month before the election. Since the poll did not appear publicly for another two weeks, it presented an inaccurate picture of public opinion in late October as opinions continued to shift. Nevertheless, the poll revealed that statewide, Hill led with 44.8 percent, with 33.7 percent for Clements, and 21 percent undecided. Ticket-splitters seemed to break almost evenly between Hill and Clements, with 21.4 percent of Democrats for Clements and 20.2 percent of Republicans for Hill. Some 57.4 percent of Democratic Primary voters supported Hill, while 69.5 percent of Republican Primary voters indicated their support for Clements, near their final percentages in the primaries. Apparently, both Hill and Clements had yet to energize support within their own parties much beyond their supporters in the primary, and the bulk of their own partisans had yet to concentrate on the election. Hill especially seemed to have problems exciting his Democratic base, despite his statewide lead.

The poll also revealed that Harris County remained the only major urban area with a Clements lead.[101] Only 33.2 percent of Harris residents favored Hill, with 38 percent for Clements, and 28.8 percent undecided. Hill maintained a narrow lead of 2.4 percent in the home base of Clements, the Dallas–Fort Worth metroplex, with 26.2 percent undecided. In Bexar County, 46.1 percent of voters backed Hill, with 35.3 percent for Clements, and 18.6 percent undecided. In Travis County, home to a strong and outspoken body of Democratic voters, 52.1 percent supported Hill, 29.6 percent supported Clements, and 18.3 percent remained undecided. In the remainder of the state, 49.3 of Texans backed Hill, with 32 percent for Clements and the remaining 18.7 percent undecided. Hill took 47.2 percent of the men's vote, with 33.7 percent for Clements. Just over 42 percent of women supported Hill and 31.3 percent backed Clements. The two remained almost even among whites, with 38.4 percent of whites for Hill and 39.4 percent for Clements.

Among minority voters, Hill had a commanding lead, not unexpected for a Democratic candidate. More than 72 percent of Hispanics and 67.9 percent of African Americans supported Hill.[102] Clements could only manage 17 percent support from Hispanics and 8.6 percent from African Americans. Among La Raza Unida Party members, 55.1 percent preferred Hill as at least a second choice, none backed Clements despite Republican efforts to reach out to Hispanics, and 44.9 percent remained undecided. Overall, the poll showed that in most major areas, Clements had yet to break out of the 30 to 40 percent range. But a large portion of the public remained undecided as to whom they would support.

On the same day the *Texas Monthly* poll became public, Hill released the results of his own campaign poll, which showed him with an even wider lead than before. The poll showed Hill with 52 percent of the vote, Clements with 30 percent, and 18 percent undecided. "It's all over," Hill declared to supporters across the state.[103] "We think we have enough votes to win regardless of the turnout. . . . The polls show I'm going straight up." The Clements campaign bitterly disputed the results and pointed to a September Clements poll that showed the race in a dead heat with Hill at 33 percent, Clements at 31 percent, and an astounding 35 percent undecided.[104] The polls reflected the uncertainty the electorate had about Hill. Many voters preferred Hill but had not ruled out giving Clements a second look. In both polls, however, Clements remained in the same narrow range. Clements dismissed the *Texas Monthly–Austin American-Statesman* poll, declaring that in the primaries, "every candidate they said was going to win lost."[105]

Clements later noted that the poll numbers showing him behind did not discourage him at all. "I don't have that much confidence in the polls. I still don't."[106]

Late in the campaign, Tower realized his own reelection efforts remained in jeopardy. Key areas had not yet yielded the support he needed. "My campaign tracking polls out, nightly telephone surveys, showed that our support had grown soft in West Texas and in the Dallas–Fort Worth area," wrote Tower. "My pollster, Lance Tarrance, warned that we would have to prevent Krueger from making inroads in the southwest Houston area; otherwise I would not be able to win statewide."[107] Clements understood what the numbers meant for his own campaign. Although the senatorial and the gubernatorial contests had their own dynamics and own issues, the closeness of both races linked the two. Turning out Republican voters had become vital to the survival of both candidates. At a Houston campaign appearance, Clements had called Harris County the key to the election.[108]

The race for both Senate and governor remained uncomfortably close for Republicans, despite their outward confidence. A Tarrance tracking poll showed Bob Krueger with a five-point lead over Tower by the week of October 12–19.[109] Texas Republicans faced the prospect of losing their senator and possibly gaining a governor—or losing both. Since Tower would appear at the top of the ballot, observers expected much of his electoral strength to transfer to down-ballot races, such as governor. Clements theoretically could win with a Tower loss, but it would prove an additional burden to a campaign still trailing John Hill.

By October 24, Tower had retaken the lead, but had lost it again to Krueger two days later.[110] This see-saw frustrated both the Tower and Clements campaigns. By the week of October 20–27, Tower had 43 percent of the independent voters to 29 percent for Krueger. Tower had 32 percent of the conservative Democrat vote, compared to 55 percent for Krueger. Throughout October, Tower's polls showed he had only a quarter of the Hispanic vote, compared to 53 percent for Krueger. Tower had one-sixth of the African American vote, compared to a 51 to 59 percent vote range for Krueger.[111]

The campaign could not explain why Tower's efforts seemed to falter. Tarrance had written to Tower campaign manager Ken Towery, highlighting the problem areas for the campaign. "For some odd reason, West Texas and the Dallas–Fort Worth area are not spilling out their guts for Tower. If that trend persists, we cannot make up the vote deficiencies caused by South, Central, and Eastern rural Texas. . . . If Krueger can cut up the vote-rich Southwest Houston area, Tower will not be able to win statewide."[112] In other areas, support for Clements became clear. Campaign officials now could predict Clements victories in some counties. Cooke County, once a Democratic stronghold, now seemed to lean heavily toward the Republicans, prompting one aide to scribble, "This area should go for Clements."[113]

Clements had tried to engage Hill in a series of debates. The debates would give voters a chance to compare both candidates at the same time. Hill remained reluctant to debate, unwilling to give Clements any further publicity or openings to attack him. In early September, Clements had reiterated his call for a debate with Hill; Hill demurred.[114] By October, the two had agreed to a series of joint appearances. At one such appearance on October 24, Clements blasted the increases in Hill's staff and budget at the Attorney General's Office. The Republican called for more debates, and Hill refused. The Democrat stated that he had no apologies to make for not debating Bill Clements on Dallas public television station KERA, citing three upcoming press conferences with Clements on commercial stations in Houston, Dallas, and Amarillo.[115]

At their Amarillo debate on October 31, Clements blasted Hill as "a liberal claims lawyer who has made a career out of government service in Austin."[116] During the televised debate, the attorney general threw doubts on Clements's business activities. As criticism of the ruthless Shah of Iran increased across the globe, Hill attempted to tie Clements to the increasingly fragile regime. Hill accused Clements of having a partnership with the Shah of Iran, alleging that Clements had used his position as Deputy Secretary of Defense under Nixon and Ford to enhance his oil holdings in Iran for SEDCO.[117] SEDCO had formed a subsidiary to drill oil wells and dig pipelines in Iran, with the shah's government as partners. Clements retorted, "I am not a partner with the Shah, and I never have been."[118]

Hill waged a pointed defense of his own performance as attorney general. He defended his record of fiscal responsibility as attorney general against Clements's charge that his number of personnel increased 300 percent and his budget increased 600 percent since 1973. Hill pointed out that a new worker's compensation program for state employees had increased the number of employees in his office and because of his office's efficient enforcement of the law, his staff took in $25 for every $1 spent.[119] To Hill, these exchanges exemplified the type of discourse of the election, one based on accusation rather than substantive debate on the issues affecting the future of the state and proposed solutions. "The race ultimately was not fought out on issues," recalled Hill. "Most of our debates were largely over perceptions."[120]

"I will not run out of gas in the fourth quarter," Clements had said repeatedly throughout the campaign.[121] The fourth quarter issue had haunted Texas Republicans for years. Several times before they had come within striking distance of victory, only to see their candidacies fade in the last days of the election. In these cases, the Republicans had spent all of their money trying to keep up with the Democrats in the weeks leading up to election day, leaving them without sufficient funds to organize Republican voter turnout or to counter a wave of late advertising by the Democrats. The Republicans would run out of money and enthusiasm late in the campaign; the Democrats did not.

Clements borrowed and spent heavily to overturn the curse of the fourth-quarter fade. By mid-October, he had announced that he had pumped an additional $1,775,000 of borrowed money into his campaign for governor, obtaining the loans from three Dallas banks. On Clements's campaign finance report, he took in $3,077,692 including loans and spent $3,100,627 in a massive flood of advertising.[122] The campaign finance report also revealed that while Clements may have picked up Briscoe voters, he had not convinced many of them to donate to his campaign, as few of the names of contributors on his reports were traditionally associated with Democratic politics.[123] By comparison, Democrat John Hill reported revenues of $1.5 million and expenditures that left him with a modest surplus, without borrowing funds.[124]

Expensive campaigns had long been a feature of Texas politics. The immense expanse of Texas forced statewide candidates to travel large distances in the course of a campaign.[125] The large, rural congressional and legislative districts of many areas demanded similar travel for seekers of those offices. In order to spread their message, statewide candidates had to advertise in more than a dozen media markets for television, radio, and newspapers.

Analyses of political campaigns have revealed that the biggest spenders do not always win and even when they do, money alone not always acts as the most decisive factor.[126] Candidates do not normally have the funds to spend unless they have an energized base of supporters willing to donate these funds. Texas conservatives, controlling most of the industry and finances of the state, provided much more money to campaigns than the state's liberals, who typically appealed to Texans with far more modest incomes. A Republican outspending a Democrat in a campaign in Texas was not unheard of by the late 1970s. Hill's spending efforts remained in line with the traditional political tactics of Texas. The attorney general blasted the spending of Clements, accusing him of trying to buy the election. "It is going to be in the $7 million range in an attempt to buy this election. That isn't going to work."[127]

The *Dallas Morning News* described Hill's outlays as "more traditional," though by spending nearly $2.6 million by the end of October, he had spent more than all candidates combined in either the 1972 or 1974 general elections.[128] Late finance reports showed record spending for the two candidates. Bill Clements had spent $6.4 million, $4.2 million of which he loaned to himself, compared to $2.54 million spent by Hill.[129] The *Dallas Times Herald* pointed out that the two had spent a combined $9 million for a post that paid only $66,800.[130] Clements poured his cash into advertising and the phone bank. The phone bank itself would cost roughly $500,000.[131] Hill also spent lavish amounts on organization and advertising, but not as much as Clements. Hill had long since known that he could not match the spending strength of Clements. "Clements spent $4 or $5 million of his own money—very few people can do that," Hill recalled. "I didn't spend too much of my own."[132] Newspapers noted that he must make up in enthusiasm what he lacks in money for a media blitz.[133] At repeated opportunities in the last weeks of the campaign, Hill urged supporters to vote and not to believe that they had the election won before they had cast the ballots.

By the late 1970s, religious conservatives had become increasingly strident in their opposition to the Democrats and government activism. Many had come to identify conservative political stands as synonymous with faith. The gubernatorial election became embroiled in this intensifying movement against the Democrats.

In Hill's crusades to protect children and nursing home patients from abuse, he won both praise and scorn. Lester Roloff, a Corpus Christi radio evangelist, in particular had become a vocal opponent of Hill. The fight between the two began after Roloff started a home for wayward children, and the attorney general believed that the homes should come under state oversight and regulation to ensure the safety of the children. Roloff fought this as state infringement on church activities and denounced Hill. Clements aligned himself with Roloff, and the preacher began distributing pro-Clements literature at churches and parking lots across the state.[134] Roloff's message, financed by Clements, accused Hill of being a liberal and "anti-church and anti-Christian" because of his attempts to enforce state law.[135]

In addition, Republicans distributed a tabloid newspaper across the state, the *Texas Spectator.* This paper roundly criticized Democrats and featured articles lauding Republicans with advertising from Republican candidates.[136] The *Spectator* repeated the most vicious allegations of the Republicans, many false, to the rage of Hill. Among the misrepresentations, the paper charged that Hill favored a bill that would let state government set local property tax assessments and rates, which, in reality, the bill would not permit. The paper reached one million Texans at a critically short time before the election.[137] Hill prepared for a relentless attack against Clements in response to the incident. He planned to shoot a television commercial in San Antonio and saturate the state with a $500,000 purchase of air time.[138] His campaign manager, John Rogers, however, talked him out of the plan, urging him to take the high road and stay positive.

The effort to portray the Democratic nominee in such a negative light and distort his record troubled Hill, even years after the election. Noted Hill in a 1999 interview, "I still consider myself a moderately conservative Democrat, which is what I have been all of my life, although Mr. Clements spent an awful lot of money trying to prove I was a wild-eyed liberal. People that know me know that what I just said is the truth."[139]

Ballot security became a major concern for Republicans late in the campaign. A number of elections in years past had become notorious for ballot fraud, tipping the balance of the election one way or another. In a tight election, even small-scale fraud could give the election to one candidate or another, depending on who controlled access to the ballot boxes. In 1978, the Democrats controlled access in most areas, with Republicans controlling the others. Ballot fraud accusations had tainted a number of elections in years past, particularly the 1941 and 1948 U.S. Senate elections and the 1960 presidential election.[140] Republican state chairman Ray Barnhart wrote party leaders across the state, emphasizing the importance of ensuring that the election would remain free of irregularities. "Ballot Security must be of prime importance to the Republican Party of Texas," he declared.[141]

As a result, the state party launched Project LEAP, or "Legal Elections in All Precincts." Armed with a $15,000 budget, the party planned to train poll-watchers at twenty locations across Texas. By October, the Republicans had established a committee to organize ballot security and sent lists of attorneys to contact in case of ballot problems.[142] In early November, the Bexar County Republican Party announced that they had six attorneys on standby and claimed that they would go to court on Election Day to halt voting at places where voting irregularities emerged.[143]

Secretary of State Steve Oaks responded to the concerns of Republican officials that ineligible voters might vote or eligible Republican voters might be
denied access to the ballot. "Any candidate who satisfies you that his name
should appear on the list of registered voters should be permitted to vote under the 'challenge' procedure by filling out the proper affidavit."[144] Barnhart
pointed out that the election code stated that no one could vote without a
voter registration card unless it had become lost, mislaid, or left at home. "I
believe that the secretary's instructions can create serious misunderstandings
that could inadvertently result in massive voter fraud," he announced to reporters.[145] Oaks responded that he would release another statement to clear
up any misunderstandings.[146] Internal memos, however, only added to Republican worries. "Ballot security problems are starting to come in statewide,"
stated one report.[147]

The traditional habits of Democrats, used to having no significant fall opposition, had led many to neglect the general election. For years, only a handful could vote and still claim an easy victory. A *Dallas Times Herald* columnist
noted the perilous position that this apathy had placed the Hill campaign:

> The Democratic gubernatorial candidate believes he will win, but
> he also knows he can lose. Apathy is dangerously high among
> Democrats this year and a low turnout could throw what seems a
> cinch victory into the hands of Hill's Republican opponent . . . as
> State Democratic Executive Committee member Josephine Miller
> put it, 'Democrats think the election is over when they vote in the
> primary.'[148]

As Clements gained in the polls in October, Hill began to realize how much
more important Democratic turnout had become to his cause. Hill tried to
fight any apathy within the party and to energize his supporters to vote. He reiterated the fact the polls still showed solidly him ahead and that they needed
to vote, citing a Krueger campaign poll that put him at 54 percent.[149] He continued to host rallies across the state, receiving warm welcomes wherever he
went.

On November 2, Hill hosted a rally of state and local Democratic candidates in Houston, attracting 6,500 Democratic faithful for politics as well as
25-cent beer and tacos.[150] Hill also tried to emphasize fiscal responsibility in
his speeches. He called for auditing the performance and efficiency of all state
agencies spending federal dollars. "Our approach will be to get every ounce of
productivity from every state tax dollar that's spent," said the Democrat.[151]

The Clements campaign searched exhaustively for new opportunities
to divide Hill and the Briscoe Democrats. In late October, he accused Hill
of retaliation in an incident that resulted in the removal of two Galveston
County Democratic Party precinct chairmen from their posts for supporting

Clements. The Republican charged that Hill was "directly responsible."[152] The chairmen had indeed admitted that they would support Clements over Hill. The Democratic Party required that any individual who held an office within the party itself, whether a county chairman, state executive committeeman, or local precinct chair must support the party's candidate, the very reason the posts originated. The two men had taken oaths to support their party's nominees. To waver in the slightest would undermine party discipline and efforts to clinch victory.[153] The announcement of the two left Galveston Democratic officials with no choice but to remove them.

Clements, on the other hand, made the incident look like a wholesale purge of dissenting Democrats and corrupt, strong-arm politics. At appearances in Houston and Galveston, Clements blasted the removal of the two precinct chairmen and charged that the county had discriminated against his party by printing the Republican candidates' names in a different type-face. "It's the old game, right here in the shadow of downtown Houston. But the game can be over if you want it to be."[154]

Former Gov. John Connally accompanied Clements on a late swing through the state. He joined the attacks on Hill and the Democratic Party ideology. In Houston, he said to a crowd of 600, "I know my old friend John Hill said he's not a liberal and he may not intend to be. But he can't help himself, he just has to be."[155] Clements followed up with a rallying call to area voters. "The election will be decided by what happens here in Harris County," he declared to supporters.[156] The Houston area had long served as a powerful source of Republican strength in the state. The September *Texas Monthly* poll showed Harris County as the only major metropolitan area with a Clements lead. The Democrats, however, had thousands of voters in the area and could easily entice independent voters to vote for Hill. If the Democrats performed well in Houston, the Republicans had almost no other comparable area to compensate with votes.

Hill crisscrossed the state, shoring up his support. To a gathering of fifty in Abilene, he announced that while his campaign surged ahead, Clements had peaked. "He ran out of gas almost three weeks ago," said Hill.[157] He discussed a new Krueger poll, taken October 25–28, which showed Hill leading by a 51 to 35 margin. The poll also showed Clements leading in only two metropolitan areas: Houston by one and Midland–Odessa by nine. Hill led by 10 percent in Dallas–Fort Worth, Corpus Christi, and Beaumont-Port Arthur, and had even larger leads in Austin and South Texas. "We have the potential to carry every county in this state. We have the votes and the momentum to do it," declared Hill, but at appearances in Fort Worth and Plainview, he warned supporters not to become too complacent.[158]

The Midland-Odessa area, dependent on the oil industry for its livelihood served as another major Republican stronghold. Briscoe had won the area in 1974 in the wake of the Watergate scandal and a weak opponent, but Hill had a much more difficult race. The wide Hill lead in the Clements stronghold of the

Dallas area came as a surprise. While in Austin, he boasted that the Democrats had devised the best get-out-the-vote campaign in years and predicted a higher turnout than that predicted by the secretary of state.[159] The encouraging polls meant nothing if his supporters did not vote.

Dean himself leveled a series of blistering attacks on Hill late in the campaign in an attempt to drive disaffected conservatives into the Clements camp. He repeated the charges from family and supporters of former attorney general Crawford Martin, accusing Hill of causing his death. "He died after John Hill leveled a dirty, bitter campaign on him."[160] Hill's hard-charging reputation had helped him succeed in many instances, but his opponents now tried to use that reputation against him. As State Sen. Betty Andujar pointed out, "I think that John Hill would be surprised at the people who were afraid of him as governor because he'd been pretty tough to work with as the attorney general. . . . I think there was a feeling that there would be a great sweep of change and that many people who'd worked in the bureaucracy would be moved out and a liberal group would come in."[161]

Hill worked feverishly to energize minority support. He had hired three statewide minority coordinators and boasted that minorities had become a part of the top leadership of his campaign in the big cities. In contrast, Clements's "Estamos de Acuerdo" (We are in Accord) program attempted to garner Hispanic support through billboards, radio and television ads.[162] Meanwhile, the Mexican-American Legislative Caucus, a group of 13 Democratic state representatives and senators, campaigned actively across the state for Hill and Krueger, hoping to rally Hispanics to the Democracy and block whatever sympathy remained for the LRU. State Rep. Matt Garcia of San Antonio remarked on Hill's civil rights efforts, "[Hill] has done much to afford us protection in the courts."[163]

Similarly, African American legislators worked to inspire more African Americans to vote for the party. In late October, six African American Democratic legislators spoke at a rally in Dallas on behalf of the attorney general. They argued that Hill was more sensitive and more responsive to the needs of the African American community. State Rep. Al Edwards of Houston blasted Clements and the Republican Party, declaring, "The Republican Party has done nothing for black people since Lincoln, and he was shot."[164]

Clements continued to bear down, calling his election a chance not only to break the Democratic monopoly of statewide offices but also to stop the tide of liberalism in the state and break with what he derided as corrupt machine politics. Said Clements, "We certainly owe it to generations yet unborn to make 1979 the year the last vestiges of machine politics in Texas were destroyed."[165] He continued to portray Hill as a radical out of touch with average Texans. "I believe in those who produce something useful, not in those who talk, complain, and regulate," he averred.[166]

Nearly a month after the initial Webb County allegations surfaced, a new round of allegations emerged—this time against the Republicans. Joe Guerra, at the center of the initial accusations against Hill in a sworn affidavit to the *Dallas Morning News,* had now become accused of possible collusion with the Republicans. According to the paper, the new accusations came from "un-named sources who claim they monitored telephone conversations between Clements aides and a Laredo city official 'suggesting Republican campaign in-terests promised as much as $200,000' to the official."[167]

The Republicans denied the charges and immediately tried to place the blame on the Democrats. David Dean angrily rejected the charges against the Republicans as "absolutely and categorically false . . . There is no doubt in my mind that these scurrilous comments came directly from John Hill."[168] The charge that Hill had somehow engineered this latest accusation dumbfounded Hill. "It's a totally new allegation I've never heard before."[169] The charges would fester through the election, with both sides finding themselves accused of wrongdoing.

The brutal politics of accusation easily spiral out of control, often with each accusation becoming more vicious than the one before. In the quest for power, the frenzy and emotion of a campaign can tempt supporters and opponents of a particular candidate to twist and exaggerate facts, or lie outright. The true facts often become lost in such an exchange, but not before the reputations of candidates and innocent bystanders become tarnished. The 1978 campaign, typical of many Texas elections, had already seen several such instances.

Newspapers across the state began to issue endorsements of Hill. The *Texas Observer* enthusiastically called on its readers to vote for Hill. "This is a his-toric election—it marks the first November ballot in 42 years to be headed by a Democratic nominee who can be supported with enthusiasm—rather than nose-holding—by the state's little people."[170] Two of the three major news-papers in the Dallas-Fort Worth area, the *Fort Worth Star-Telegram* and the *Dallas Times Herald* endorsed the attorney general. Wrote the *Times Herald* editors, "He [Hill] offers Texas a dynamism which has been lacking in the ex-ecutive branch of state government and a deep understanding of the problems of a growing and changing population. . . . A man of performance."[171] The *Star-Telegram* agreed, arguing that the state needed Hill's leadership. "He has a solid record of public service and will offer decisive, progressive leadership. He is committed to a freeze on state taxes, a limit on state spending, improving state budget management and utility bill relief."[172] The *Austin American-Statesman* similarly lauded Hill. "John Hill may be the best candidate for governor in decades. Judging from his record, he should win easily over his Republican opponent, whose chief qualification is money . . . He is moderate politically. His record proves it. That Bill Clements considers Hill a 'liberal' says more about Clements than Hill. . . . He has a fine record of fighting corruption."[173] The *Statesman* criticized Clements on further occasions. At one point, the pa-per stated that he had "no grasp of the issues or the office."[174]

While in San Antonio, Clements predicted victory in Bexar County. He pounded away at Hill, touting his campaign's latest polls showing a tight race statewide and in the San Antonio area. "We have caught him and he knows it," he beamed.[175] He spoke of the large percentage of undecided voters in many polls and added, "That's where the election is."[176] A number of late polls indicated that Hill had fallen below the 50 percent line, but still held the lead. The campaign announced a tireless effort in the last days of the race to claim the undecided voters. Clements boasted that he had drawn even in the summer months, working hard, and added with emphasis to the dejected Briscoe Democrats, "While the opponent playacted as governor."[177]

Hill again attempted to counter Clements's strengths on energy issues and his criticisms of the Carter administration's energy policies. He announced a plan to free Texas oil prices from all federal controls. And he again tried to rally his supporters, attacking the tone of the Clements effort and trying to convince voters that Clements had lost momentum. "Bill Clements ran out of gas three weeks ago. His effort to buy the election with a negative campaign attacking me has failed. He doesn't have a program of his own," cried Hill.[178] Clements, in response, again raised questions about the attorney general's conduct in Webb County. On November 2 and November 3, he again accused Hill of failing to fully investigate corruption accusations in Laredo. Hill retorted, "I never ducked an investigation in my life. I have done more than any attorney general in the history of the state to deal with corruption."[179]

La Raza Unida candidate Mario C. Compean, who co-founded the LRU in 1970, declared that he had "become probably the most unlikely campaigner that Republican Bill Clements has ever had."[180] He added, "It's not my goal to elect Mr. Clements, but if that happens, it's probably the next best thing to my being elected. . . . We need to break up the monopoly hold in state politics by the Democratic Party. The election of a Republican would mean from now on the Democrats and no one else will be able to take the Mexican American vote for granted. . . . We need to sacrifice Hill and Krueger for our own good."[181] The LRU realized they would not win, but hoped that they could spoil the election for the Democrats in what had become a tight race. Compean did not encourage his supporters to vote Republican but to vote for the La Raza Unida and deny much-needed votes to the Democrats.

Hill dismissed the anemic LRU and claimed that they no longer remained a factor in the race.[182] Compean demanded that the major parties treat Hispanic voters with respect. "We [Hispanic voters] are no longer in anybody's back pocket." he said.[183] "If I weren't in the race, Hill would be just as reactionary as Clements." But for LRU stalwarts, survival became the most important goal of the election. With its leadership and reputation in tatters, Compean fought for the group to maintain regular ballot status. La Raza Unida needed 2 percent of the statewide vote to maintain regular party status.[184] In the waning days of the campaign, even that remained uncertain.

Clements still trailed in statewide polls in the week before the election. For the Republicans to claim victory on November 7, they still relied heavily on massive turnouts of Republicans in Houston and Dallas. The early November numbers for the party had not produced encouraging results in Dallas County. The independent voters seemed to lean toward the Democrats. A Dallas commentator wrote that both Tower and Clements "seem to be in trouble and their margin of victory in Dallas County may not be much to brag about if they do not make inroads among independent voters here."[185]

Clements responded with a massive advertising campaign in Dallas. One full-page advertisement in the *Dallas Times Herald* cited his experience in civic affairs and government service. "Bill Clements is the Difference Texas Needs," read the headline.[186] The ad also blasted away at Hill's credentials as a public servant. "John Hill received a teachers' union endorsement in return for promises to raise all teachers' salaries regardless of performance. . . . Bill Clements is a businessman and a manager. . . . John Hill is a professional politician. . . . Bill Clements is a conservative. . . . John Hill is a liberal."[187]

Clements responded to criticisms that his campaign had taken too negative of a tone and concentrated too much on personal attacks on Hill. His abrasiveness had repulsed many voters, but fascinated others at the same time. "He is waging a campaign of innuendo and dirty tricks against me and I am just meeting him head on," Clements told a gathering of the Houston Rotary Club.[188]

As the last weekend of the campaign approached, a bombshell hit the Clements campaign. An Iowa man sued his corporation, SEDCO, for $42 million, alleging that SEDCO swindled him out of $16.9 million in a Persian Gulf oil deal. SEDCO officials angrily denied the accusations and stated that they had previously sued him for debts against the company. Clements dismissed the suit, claiming that the lawsuit "doesn't amount to a hill of beans."[189] The Republicans, however, saw more sinister forces behind the timing of the lawsuit, just days before the election. The Clements campaign called the timing of the suit "amusing" and aides claimed that the story was planted by Hill campaign.[190] Hill had attempted to make Clements's business dealings an issue, but no evidence has ever surfaced connecting him with the Iowa suit or any unethical business activities.

Clements exhorted the Briscoe Democrats and independent voters to support him at last-minute appearances around the state. "The ticket splitters hold the outcome of the election in their hands," he cried.[191]

At an appearance in Houston, Hill touted a local KPRC-TV poll showing him with a 46 to 35 lead, with 19 percent undecided.[192] The same poll had accurately forecast that Hill would win the primary and was dismissed by Briscoe as biased. Hill warned supporters of the dangers of low voter turnout, claiming that the Republicans hoped for it. He followed up with a confident prediction of victory. "All the hurricanes in South Texas, dust storms in West Texas, hail storms in the Panhandle and torrential rains in East Texas can't keep us from winning."[193] Hill reiterated that Clements had run out of gas. "Hurricane Bill Clements is stalled off the coast. . . . and is just spinning around."[194] Hill released another poll taken the previous week that showed him with a comfortable 51 to 35 lead. Most polls showed Hill comfortably ahead. The Clements polls, however, continued to show the race extremely close.[195]

Polls, however, have a built-in margin of error of three to five percentage points. This can throw the percentages of either candidate up or down that many percentage points, changing the shape of the race considerably. Given these margins, Tarrance believed that his polls showing the race much closer remained technically consistent with the other results and stood by them.[196] The wild fluctuations in Hill's numbers hinted that some portion of Hill's support remained uncertain about their candidate.

While in Midland, Clements touted a late October poll conducted by Staples & Staff that showed the race a statistical dead heat, with Hill leading only by four points and 14 percent undecided.[197] This poll showed that Clements had closed a deficit of 32 points in three months. Hill ignored the numbers and pressed on. "My opponent's support is like Galveston Bay, 25 miles wide but only 4 feet deep."[198] Hill later explained that despite the wide discrepancy in results with different polls, his supporters would find encouragement in polls showing him with a comfortable lead. "I felt my polls were accurate," he said. "I thought it would help my campaign to show that we were ahead. I picked up a lot of support. I didn't base my campaign on polls. It wasn't that. I thought it was better to release favorable polls."[199]

Dallas-area polls had produced discouraging news for Clements. "The Clements campaign felt they would do well in Dallas without a lot of work. Hill was stronger than they expected."[200] To counter Hill's unexpected strength in the last days of the campaign, Clements unveiled an advertisement aimed at Dallas local pride. The area had become a critical area for both campaigns, and Clements remained determined to win the metroplex, his home. "Dallas needs a Governor," read the ad, "The State of Texas has never had a governor from the D/FW area, but with your help, Bill Clements can be the first. Bill Clements has worked to help make the Metroplex what it is today. As governor, he will work for the Metroplex of tomorrow."[201]

Early voting reports provided mixed information on the state of the campaigns. The Clements campaign had energized Republicans, with traditionally Republican precincts showing heavy turnout. Secretary of State Steve Oaks commented, "Absentee voting in metropolitan areas and traditional Republican strongholds is unusually heavy this year, indicating GOP candidates may make strong bids to capture some statewide offices and retain a Texas Senator Saturday."[202]

At such late stages in elections, campaigns concentrate on getting their voters to the polls. A lighter turnout usually favored Republicans and their tight-knit and mobilized organizations, while heavy turnout usually favored Democratic candidates. In fact, a majority of the total voting-age Texans had never gone to polls in a single election. In off-year general elections and important statewide primaries, blue-collar turnout—which leans Democratic—probably averages between 5 and 15 percent.[203] Oaks revealed the emerging early turnout numbers. "The information we have now, based on a comprehensive survey of absentee voting, indicates absentee voting in metropolitan areas and traditional Republican areas is extremely heavy and ahead of 1976 levels."[204]

Regardless of the final results, Oaks believed that the election had produced important changes in the nature of Texas politics. "I think this shows Texas definitely is a two-party state, and I think it portends that we are going to see some close races on election night," explained Oaks. "Being nominated as a Democrat in the May primary is no longer tantamount to election as it used to be in Texas."[205] Other election officials announced their final turnout projections. They expected turnout to materialize as light to moderate with an estimated 37 percent, or about 2.3 million voters, reporting to polling sites.[206]

Some Democratic areas apparently also had early success in turning out their voters. Dallas County Clerk Larry Murdoch told reporters that he had forecast about 48 percent of the county's 602,000 voters would participate.[207] For Dallas County, this represented a fairly strong turnout. The Bexar County Clerk predicted a near-record turnout of 140,000 votes in the county.[208] San Antonio remained a vital area for Hill.

The Clements campaign worked diligently to identify and energize supporters and remind them to vote on Election Day. These efforts included telephone banks and tracking polls. Pollster Lance Tarrance explained that in the 1960s and 1970s, "Republicans generally believed in a lot of research—very business-oriented. . . . We did an awful lot of research, generally twice that of the Democrats."[209] His firm used the new method of tracking polls, nightly mini-samples of 125 voters, which could determine within 24 hours the effects of an event or media buy. "Today, they are standard-operating procedure, but fairly unique to us in those days. I'm not sure if the Democrats did that," said Tarrance.[210] Once the campaign had essentially identified their voters, volunteers would telephone them to direct them to their proper polling locations. "It was a matter of understanding our subset—people who were going to turn up. . . . Clements hired a tremendous force of people to turn the vote out."[211]

"The Democratic Party was starting to move more urban and west," said Tarrance.[212] "Because Hill was considered a moderate, he probably had a soft underbelly." The Democratic lock on East Texas, he believed, "was beginning to break apart in 1978." Hill faced some vulnerabilities in the region, but retained a clear lead. The strength of the party in the region had begun to falter slightly, and Democrats now had to work harder for votes. An internal Carter campaign memorandum in October 1976, for example, noted slipping support in East Texas, but Carter carried the region with ease.[213] "Dallas and Houston were putting together a lot of demographic pressure on East Texas," Tarrance explained. Growth of the two areas, coupled with their media reach, had begun to affect the region. The upsurge in Republican strength in these metropolitan areas pressed Democrats to squeeze their strongest areas to compensate for the difference. The Republicans could draw on areas ready to question their traditional allegiance to the Democrats, while the Democrats could find no comparable Republican area. In addition, "there was quite a bit of nationalization."[214] Clements had found more favorable ground to attract support by attacking the unpopular Carter and what he seemed to represent to conservatives against the moderate and much more popular attorney general. He had slowly succeeded in making the election a referendum on Carter among many Texas voters.

The energy of the Clements volunteers had impressed the Republican. At a stop in the Midland–Odessa area, he thanked his volunteers for their efforts. He announced to a modest gathering of seventy-five supporters that the telephone banks had contacted 1.1 million Texans.[215] In the meantime, Hill supporters refused to yield to Clements. "John Hill is conducting a personal campaign. People who know him will vote for him," supporters had emphasized in an attempt to dispel the negativity of the Clements charges.[216] Hill had continued to emphasize fiscal issues, reiterating his plans for the projected $3 billion state budget surplus: "We should use one-third for property tax relief, one-third for education and one-third for other needs."[217]

Hill had time to visit his mother in East Texas while the campaign traveled through the region. She had told him about the attacks that the Clements campaign had waged against him. Mrs. Hill told him that Clements was making him sound like "not just a liberal but a bad, bad ol' liberal."[218] The attorney general had seen the dynamics of the race and privately remained uncertain of his chances. He confessed his fears of losing the race to his mother, who replied, "If the Lord doesn't intend for you to win he'll have something else waiting for you."[219]

Commented Hill in 2002, "People who know me know I'm not a flaming liberal. It was just a big lie."[220] Hill had based his support on the same coalition of minorities, teachers, farmers, lawyers, and establishment Democrats who had brought him through the primary, while Clements mounted a saturation campaign, buying all the media time and space that he could, ultimately borrowing about two-thirds of the money to finance his campaign and Hill strived to avoid campaign debts.[221]

Republican officials remained uncertain about their chances in the last days. It seemed possible to some that Clements would win and Tower lose.[222] Both Democratic and Republican officials conceded that the Tower–Krueger race remained a statistical tie. "It's a turnout race," said Richard Perkins, secretary of the Texas Democratic Executive Committee. "Flip a coin," admitted Ray Barnhart. "It depends on who goes to vote."[223] Clements remained behind in the polls, but with the combination of his momentum and the soft support for Hill, a Clements victory remained quite possible, filling Hill supporters with dread.

Hill condemned the sentiment among some Republicans wanting as few voters, or as few Democrats, as possible to vote. In his last-minute appeals to the voters, he declared, "The Republicans are saying, 'low voter turnout, low voter turnout, low voter turnout. . . .' They say if the people don't vote, we still have a chance."[224] He urged Democrats to show up and vote to turn back the Clements tide.

The Clements campaign had decided to exert its resources in a last-ditch bid to flood the media market with his message. Previous Republican campaigns had usually exhausted their resources by this point and tried to coast into Election Day. The millions of dollars that Clements had personally pumped into the campaign meant that he indeed had not run out of gas. He still had the resources to go on the offensive, and given that the polls still showed him at best slightly behind, he had no choice.

Across the state, Clements saturated the markets with television and radio ads. The mass of advertisements caught the Hill camp by surprise. "I didn't foresee the force of his finish. I just didn't see it coming. When it hit, it was too late to do anything about it."[225] He added that the ads had all broken into an us-versus-them argument, portraying Hill as an untrustworthy radical. No matter what Hill said or did, Clements continued to bear down on the same theme. "Texas is still a very conservative state," said Hill, "Even if you are well-known in the state, there are still an awful lot of people who don't know you. He portrayed me as good-guy, bad-guy."[226] Hill did not unveil a grand finale of advertising to rally his voters or even expect a late buy from Clements.

Most observers at the time judged Hill as over-confident and badly underestimating the strength of Clements.[227] "John Hill had underestimated Bill Clements and greatly overestimated his own abilities," recalled David Dean. "Very late in the campaign he had cranked up his own campaign. After September, he realized he had a horse race with Bill Clements suddenly within striking distance. The momentum had clearly shifted to Clements."[228] Hill had run a very traditional campaign. Voters, however, had become hesitant about supporting the attorney general and had become increasingly interested in Clements. The Republican had organized a totally modern campaign, fully utilizing all of the latest polling and voter turnout techniques as well as his own impressive resources and the national Republican Party. Conversely, the Hill campaign had made serious miscalculations in the face of the Clements onslaught. As Dean pointed out, "Hill did it exactly perfect for us. Super-confident, carefree. Claimed it before his time—not disrespecting his opponent but disrespecting the voters. He refused to debate. They were taking the voters for granted. . . . As Clements seemingly did everything right, Hill did everything wrong."[229] Krueger recalled that his staffers had told him that "they felt that they [the Hill campaign] did not have much of a voter turnout effort."[230] By Election Day, the Clements campaign had more than a thousand Democrats working for the Republican, while other conservative Democrats, particularly courthouse leaders, assured Clements they would not work against him, even if they could not offer any public support.[231]

One of the wildest gubernatorial campaigns in recent memory wound to a close. Voters surged to the polls to select their next governor, either the first activist since the Great Depression or the first Republican since Reconstruction. The Democrats hoped that history would repeat itself once more and enough Democratic voters would show up at voting sites to elect Hill. The Clements campaign hoped their aggressive spending and careful planning would produce a victory. At best for Clements, the polls showed the race a dead heat. "There was never a poll that showed us ahead," said Tarrance.[232]

CHAPTER 6

"AND THE PEOPLE WIN EVERY TIME"

November 7, 1978

VOTERS SURGED TO THE POLLS on that fateful Tuesday. Newspapers across the state exhorted Texas residents to vote. As the *Houston Post* argued, "If you do not vote today, you are handing your vote to the candidates you do not want to see in office."[1] Strong voter interest had become obvious during the early voting period and as long lines of voters grew at the state's polling sites. By the time the polls closed that evening, voters had turned out in numbers well ahead of predictions, with a turnout rate of 47.7 percent.[2] And the decisions of those voters would change Texas politics forever.

Nearly 2.37 million voters cast ballots in the 1978 fall election, some 715,000 more Texans than in the 1974 election (see appendix G). In Bexar County, for example, the county clerk's initial prediction of 140,000 voters proved a considerable understatement when more than 170,000 turned out on Election Day. Independent voters showed a special interest, with nearly 400,000 more voters casting ballots in the November election than in the Democratic and Republican primaries combined. These numbers remained short of the record 4 million who voted in the 1976 presidential contest. The turnout demonstrated that a competitive two-party race in the state could produce intense voter interest.

The initial returns showed incredibly close contests for both governor and for the Senate. The numbers that emerged, however, proved discouraging for both Democratic nominees, John Hill and Bob Krueger. Bill Clements and John Tower led, though slightly. The results became a foreboding echo of 1972 in which Tower won reelection and Republican gubernatorial candidate Henry Grover led briefly on election night. Results remained mixed in the counties considered vital to Hill's victory. Of those fifteen counties identified by the Democrat, he remained ahead of his vote projections in seven and behind in three.[3]

Election officials were unable to count all of the ballots on Tuesday night.

The Texas Election Bureau discontinued counting at 1:30 A.M. and announced that it would resume later in the morning. The last numbers released in the early hours of November 8 showed Clements with a narrow 28,000-vote lead, with 931,600 votes, or 50.3 percent, and Hill with 903,826 votes, or 48.8 percent.[4] One-third of the votes, thousands of ballots, remained uncounted. Texans remained unsure who would win the election. The tide favored Clements, but history favored Hill. Hill could still win the election, but Clements appeared to stand on the brink of victory.

Some Texas newspaper writers, unsure of how the election would end, simply shrugged their shoulders, bowed to tradition, and declared Hill the victor. Although Clements had won Potter County by some 300 votes, the *Amarillo Daily News* trumpeted the headline "Hill edges Clements" for its November 8 morning editions.[5]

Hill told supporters as the hours wore on, "We may have to have a victory breakfast." Clements, hearing the comments at his own election watch party, replied, "I'll damned sure be there."[6]

Within hours after the counting resumed Wednesday morning, it became clear that Bill Clements and John Tower had won their respective elections, but by the narrowest of margins. Clements had a lead of 18,612 votes, or less than .08 percent over Hill; Tower had a lead of 12,088 votes, or just over one-half of one percent.[7] Clements immediately declared victory, flashing the mistaken *Amarillo Daily News* headline in a manner reminiscent of Harry S. Truman's brandishing a similar headline from the *Chicago Daily Tribune* in his upset victory thirty years earlier.[8] Realizing that the narrow margin would likely prompt a recount, the Republicans, fearful of any attempts by Democrats to tamper with the returns, immediately leapt into a defensive position to protect the ballots. David Dean recalled how the Republicans nervously realized that the election had not yet finished. "We didn't even have a victory celebration. Bill Clements had to claim victory the next day. We immediately went into ballot security mode. We knew that 14,000 votes could disappear overnight."[9]

Dallas Morning News editors, who had championed the Clements effort, wrote that the Clements victory represented "one of the biggest political upsets in Texas history."[10] Another newspaper called the vote "the surprise of the political year," and noted the historic implications of the election as it wrote the election served as a "harbinger of the two-party system in Texas."[11] The missed projections and later shock of many media observers at the results bemused many Clements supporters. As pollster Lance Tarrance commented, "The media wasn't prepared for a Republican victory."[12]

"The political climate of Texas will never be the same again," confidently declared Clements.[13] Hill, however, took an entirely different tone after watching his hopes dashed. "It hurts too much to laugh, but I'm too old to cry," said a disappointed Hill, who added, "I'll be watching for any errors in the count that may change the result."[14] The closeness of the results prompted Secretary of

State Steve Oaks to conduct an informal recount. By Friday, Oaks announced that his staff had made an unofficial telephone poll of county clerks in an effort to get a more accurate unofficial count of the results. The poll showed a change of slightly less than 3,000 votes of the 2.3 million total ballots cast in the Senate contest and a change of less than 200 votes in the gubernatorial race. The results now showed Tower's margin at 14,902 votes instead of the 12,088 lead reported by the Texas Election Bureau two days earlier, while Clements's margin shrank from 18,612 to 18,437.[15] Oaks concluded, "There is no great variance at all," and added that results from only two counties remained unavailable: Dallas, because of computer problems, and Bell, because the office had closed in honor of Veterans Day.[16]

The Krueger campaign, however, took strong exception to the conclusions of Oaks. The campaign requested another canvass, claiming that its post-election check of the results showed there were major discrepancies in the outcome. In some counties, for example, they claimed that those who voted a straight Democratic ballot were kept separate and not reported for Krueger.[17] Oaks replied, "We believe that our informal canvass shows that they are now counted in."[18] Krueger's staff considered requesting a formal recount of the state but decided that the expense and uncertainty of the result simply did not warrant it.[19] Disappointed, Krueger now conceded the results.

Hill reluctantly called for a recount. He did not expect the results to shift to his favor, however. Dramatic shifts in vote totals from recounts remain rare in American political contests, especially with margins in the thousands as faced by the Democrats. Hill said that he felt that he owed it to his supporters to see if any changes would occur. "My supporters felt that in a race that close—they just felt that we should ask for a recount. They had worked so hard. I felt real friendly toward the people who worked for me. It's pretty hard [to win] on a recount," he commented.[20]

The Republicans rapidly organized to defend their leads. Calls for elections attorneys spread nationwide, and the campaigns raised funds to beat back the challenges. In recounts, not only do campaigns face legal bills but the campaigns must also foot the bill for recounting the ballots. In a November 13 letter, Tower noted to Republicans nationwide that not only his campaign faced a recount, but two other recounts now proceeded in Virginia and West Virginia.[21] Tower stated in his appeal, "We face a critical recount challenge. Krueger and Hill have asked for a recount in 42 counties in which more than 70 percent of the total votes were cast. . . . Big Labor has made it a special goal to overturn this election. Key operatives have been sent to Texas to find additional votes."[22] Another Tower letter estimated the recount costs between $75,000 and $250,000.[23]

Accusations of ballot fraud had occurred in a number of Texas elections in years past. In fact, *D Magazine* reported a number of cases of ballot fraud that had erupted in Dallas in recent years. Some eleven precincts in the Fair Park neighborhood of Dallas, just south of downtown had found themselves embroiled in controversy a few years before over these accusations.[24] The courts, however, had dismissed the cases.[25]

The recount yielded interesting results, with modest changes in the election totals. None of the totals, however, produced any lead changes. Mike Dodge, a Dallas attorney working for the Republicans, said that volunteers rechecked vote totals in 76 counties and found that Krueger had gained roughly 3,700 votes. Dodge had concluded that Dallas County had run "a pretty clean election."[26] Krueger had gained 29 votes in Dallas County. If Dallas could not produce any more significant changes, it would almost prove that the recount would not yield success for the Democrats. The 39 counties that used punch card ballots, even more notorious in the wake of the 2000 presidential election twenty-two years later, would become the targets of recounts. These counties included some of the most heavily populated counties in the state, including Chambers, Galveston, Midland, San Patricio, Victoria, Tarrant, El Paso, Jefferson, Tom Green, Lubbock, Montgomery, Travis, Bexar, Harris, Dallas, Smith, Harrison, Hidalgo, Cameron, Pecos, Anderson, Collin, Wichita, Nacogdoches, Grayson, and Nueces. Hill had won nearly half of these counties. The concern among Republicans in the meantime had heightened. A Bexar County official reported that the Clements campaign had paid for armed guards to protect election recounts.[27]

Hill commented with resignation, "I don't think in all probability there'll be any change in the outcome of either election."[28] Both campaigns maintained that they wanted to make sure that all votes were counted in those counties. The Hill campaign had bitterly criticized the Republican County Judge in Harris County for refusing a recount request and said they would go to court to force the recount.[29]

All four campaigns carefully watched the recount, armed with armies of attorneys and die-hard supporters. One Tower official dutifully reported the results of the recount in Bexar County to the Tower campaign office, noting results that became typical of the recount. "There were very small vote shifts," wrote the Tower operative, "They are as follows: U. S. Senator: Tower +3 votes, Krueger +119, for a Krueger net gain of +116 votes; Governor: Clements +4, Hill –189, for a Clements net gain of +193 votes. All errors were of a mechanical or reporting nature."[30] In Bexar County, the handful of discrepancies from the 170,000 votes cast resulted not from malfeasance but minor glitches in the tabulation machines. No evidence of any fraud has ever emerged. Answered Hill on whether he believed that any vote fraud occurred: "No particular evidence. I don't have any smoking gun."[31]

The recount changed the numbers slightly, but the overall result remained: Tower had won reelection and Bill Clements had scored an upset victory. Oaks presented the unofficial results, that with 42 percent turnout, Clements had defeated Hill by 16,860 votes.[32] The results would become official when approved by the state legislature on January 9. Oaks also certified the Tower victory of 12,227 votes over Krueger, or 0.6 percent. After the long process, the secretary declared, "So far as I know, this is the last canvass in 1978."[33]

In 252 of the state's 254 counties, the Democrats lost votes from the primary to the general election.[34] Only in two counties, Mason and Zavala, did the Democrats gain votes. Hill, however, lost both counties (see appendix D). The party lost 610,939 votes between the two elections, or 34.4 percent of its primary voters. Republican inroads in the rural counties had become clear. A county-level comparison of Hill's support in 1978 compared to Dolph Briscoe's support in 1972 indicates that Hill experienced critical losses in the countryside, primarily in the small-town, rural areas of West Texas.[35]

Post-election comments by Democratic Congressman Kent Hance of West Texas reflect this analysis. Hance said that bitterness over Hill's primary defeat of Briscoe, a West Texas native, caused more conservative rural Democrats in that part of the state to vote for Clements, but he perceived this as a passing thing.[36] Democratic Congressman Charlie Wilson of East Texas disagreed. "The cities have been where the Republican votes are. Now, the rural areas are growing, changing. Instead of being all poor farmers, factory workers and all that, you get tons of white-collar insurance salesmen, real-estate people, all that kind of stuff."[37] Wilson concluded that those who do not think the conservative Democrats are going Republican had fooled themselves.[38] Hance himself would switch to the Republican Party in the 1980s.

An analysis of the results from the primary to the election demonstrates some interesting facts. In each of four counties, Dallas, Tarrant, Travis, and Bexar, the loss of primary voters exceeded the margin of victory. In McLennan County, more than 15,000 primary voters did not vote for the Democratic candidate in the fall.[39] Hill, however, had gained voters: 21,534 in Bexar County from the primary to the general election, 44,494 votes in Dallas County, 20,119 in Tarrant, and 4,199 in Travis. He had gained more than 3,000 in McLennan County, now carrying the county by a comfortable margin as opposed to his loss in the primary. Hill lost thirty-five counties that he had won in the primary, mainly in the conservative, rural counties of the Panhandle and West Texas and the Dallas–Fort Worth metroplex. However, he won dozens more counties, mainly rural, across South and Central Texas that he had lost in the primaries. John Hill gained votes in 142 counties from the primary to the general election, with no change in one county, rural Collingsworth in the Panhandle. This gave him a total gain of 234,574 votes from the primary to the general election, or 25.2 percent increase of his primary total. However, he lost votes in 111 counties. The loss of votes in these counties equaled 34,978, more than twice the victory margin. Almost 3.8 percent of Hill's primary voters failed to vote for him in November. A collapse of Democratic cohesion from the primary to the election and problems in mobilizing voters ultimately crippled Hill's efforts. Although the Hill campaign remained aware of the acrimony in Democratic ranks and the risks of low turnout among Democrats, they clearly underestimated its impact in the critical months following the primary in which they planned the general election strategy. Once the problems became increasingly apparent in the weeks before the election, the Hill campaign could not easily alter its course.

The two minor party candidates, Mario C. Compean of the La Raza Unida Party and Sara J. Johnston of the Socialist Workers Party, proved little more than a distraction to the larger battle between Clements and Hill. Compean won a scant 14,213 votes, or 0.59 percent of the vote, while Johnston won only 4,624 votes, or 0.19 percent.[40] By themselves, neither total exceeded the narrow 17,000-vote victory margin, but their combined 18,837 votes did. Hill pointed to the LRU and the Socialist Workers Party as having an impact on the narrow margin.[41] Senate LRU candidate Luis A. Diaz de Leon and his 17,869 votes had a much clearer impact on the margin of the senate race of roughly 12,000 votes. It is unlikely, however, that a significant portion of these voters would have turned to either Hill or Clements in the general election in their absence (or Krueger or Tower, respectively), but these votes had an impact in such a close contest. Compean had loudly voiced his disgust at the Democratic Party that his voters would not likely have voted for Hill. In fact, the margins of victory for Clements in Harris and Dallas counties each exceeded the Republican's statewide victory margin. In Ector and Midland counties, the Clements margin of victory exceeded his statewide total—in two small, conservative counties that the Democrats had won in 1974.

Hill won 157 of the state's 254 counties to 96 counties won by Clements, with the LRU's last stronghold of Zavala County voting for Compean. He won the deep South Texas county with 51.1 percent of the vote, besting the second-place Hill by 740 votes. La Raza Unida, once a threatening force in South Texas politics in the early 1970s, now stood on the brink of extinction. More important for the Republicans lay in the fact that they gained votes in every Texas county from the 1974 to the 1978 election.

In the other major contests, for senate and lieutenant governor, these races produced markedly different results (see appendix F). Tower won only 84 counties to 168 won by Krueger, with Zavala County voting for the LRU candidate Luis de Leon, and one tie between Tower and Krueger. Tower won in six counties that Clements lost, while Tower tied or lost in seventeen counties that Clements won. "We were outspent three-to-one," admitted Krueger.[42] In the lieutenant governor's race, the popular Democratic incumbent William P. Hobby won an easy victory over underfunded Republican Gaylord Marshall. Hobby won the race by 674,000 votes, capturing 250 counties.

In Dallas and Tarrant counties, Clements beat Hill by three-to-one margins in the upper-class white precincts, but Hill won the African American precincts in these counties with roughly 95 percent of the vote.[43] Hill narrowly edged Clements in the blue-collar neighborhoods of these counties, with turnout between the traditionally Democratic blue-collar white and African American neighborhoods almost half that of the upper-class white neighborhoods.

Hill won Bexar County, though by a slender margin 8,000 votes or 51.5 percent of the vote (see appendix C).[44] The Clements campaign had pinpointed Dallas as a problem area and it received more television spots and an extra campaign stop by the Republican in the final days. The strategy reaped handsome rewards for Clements as he captured Dallas County alone by 46,000 votes, or 58 percent of the electorate, and won adjacent Tarrant County by 7,000 votes. The northern suburban counties of Denton, Rockwall, and Collin, which Hill had won in the primary, voted for Clements; but the southern suburban counties of Johnson and Ellis, which Hill had lost in the spring, now turned to the Democrat. As predicted by Republican officials, Cooke County, north of the metroplex, went for Clements by a margin of 558 votes.

The power of the suburban Republican vote had begun to appear by the late 1970s. The outlying counties from the large city still remained overwhelmingly Democratic at the local level but saw an increasing Republican vote at the state and national levels. Denton, Rockwall, and Collin counties, for example, still had no local Republican elected officials in 1978 but voted for Clements nevertheless. By the 1990s, these counties had shifted from primarily rural Democratic counties to heavily urbanized Republican strongholds and had become symbolic of the rising Republican strength in the state. By 2004, of these three counties, only Denton County could boast an elected Democratic official.[45]

As election day approached in 1978, Republicans had feared that a late loss of support in the Houston area had put their hopes in jeopardy. Clements had called Harris County the key to the election late in the campaign, and the result proved this was no exaggeration. The relative closeness of the result demonstrates the depths of their concerns. Clements carried the county by 23,000 votes, or 52.9 percent of the total vote. Although a large number of votes in comparison to the final vote tallies, the close percentages made Republicans uncomfortable. In other areas, the distribution of votes and change in the voting pattern indicated a major shift in favor of the Republicans. The Midland-Odessa area, oil towns that served as the epicenter of West Texas Republicanism, produced some of the more interesting results. The Republicans had taken little interest in the 1974 contest, allowing Dolph Briscoe to carry both of these counties. But four years later, 10,085 Republicans in Ector County and 9,032 Republicans in adjacent Midland County surged to the polls, while the Democrats had no vote change in vote totals in Ector and lost 320 votes in Midland. In addition, the rubber chicken incident had apparently done no damage to Clements in Amarillo. He won Potter County by 303 votes and gained for the party 2,180 votes from their margin four years earlier (see appendix E).

El Paso and Austin voted for Hill by wide margins as he won both Travis and El Paso counties by at least 8,000 votes each. Charges by the Republicans of a political purge of the two Galveston County Democratic precinct chairmen who favored Clements had created a considerable stir, but Hill won the county by 4,200 votes. Voter interest had surged in the county, as more than 10,600 more voters turned out for the 1978 election than in 1974, with more than two-thirds of the increase favoring Clements. Despite the charges of misdeeds against both campaigns, Hill captured Webb County with 62 percent of the vote, though the Republicans gained 2,489 votes from 1974 to 1978. The widest percentage margins lay in Glasscock County, where 77.7 percent of voters cast ballots for Clements, and in Starr County, where Hill won with 87.8 percent.

Voter registration and turnout may also have served as a factor. A lower proportion of the voting-age electorate was registered to vote in the 1978 general election, 60.63 percent, than the 64.61 percent registered in 1974 and the 60.86 percent registered in 1976.[46] A large of number of Texans newly registered between the primary and the general election, as only 54.09 percent of voting-age Texans had registered by the May 1978 primaries. Typically, the higher the registration rate, the higher the proportion of Democrats. Early voting reports also showed very high turnout in many Republican precincts. The higher turnout for a presidential election and the high registration rate may have helped the Democrats to win the state in 1976, though by a comparatively close margin of 130,000 votes. In fact, of the counties carried by Clements, only seven had a turnout lower than 40 percent, while nearly half of the Hill counties fell below the 40 percent turnout.[47] In fact, throughout the first half of the twentieth century, turnout of eligible voters in presidential elections in the South remained very low. Voter interest had certainly increased due at least in part because many Texas voters now believed that a Republican could win. Republicans who had never bothered voting in the general election because they believed their candidates would lose now went to the polls in the belief that they could win and their votes were not wasted.

An analysis by the Southwestern Voter Registration Project showed that the turnout in predominantly Mexican American precincts was higher in 1978 than it had been in 1974, but only 27 percent of registered voters in these precincts went to the polls.[48] This was far short of the nearly 42 percent of total voters. Of the twenty-eight counties where at least half of the residents had Hispanic surnames, primarily along the Rio Grande, the Democrats gained votes from the primary to the general election in only Zavala County. In eighteen of these counties, the Democrats lost more than half of their votes from the primary to the general election, and Hill lost votes from the primary to the general election in fifteen counties. Hill had lost fifteen of these counties in the primary and won nineteen in the general election. In the twenty-eight counties with more than 25 percent African American population, primarily in East Texas, Hill gained votes from the primary in only eight counties. In twelve of the counties with large African American populations, the Democrats lost more than half of their voters from the primary. Hill won twenty-three of the counties with sizable African American populations in the primary and won twenty-six of these counties in the general election. Clearly, low turnout in minority communities added to Hill's problems.

The drop in total Democratic votes cast between the primary and the election remains among the more striking of the statistics from the 1978 election. Interestingly, Democratic primary turnout in the past remained highest in overwhelmingly Democratic states because there few Republicans stayed home on primary election day. As the general election results grew closer in many of those states, primary turnout declined.[49] In addition, primary voters usually involve themselves more in politics and make themselves more knowledgeable about candidates and issues and usually tend to be more likely to vote in primaries if they belong to the majority party or to the party that most often has competitive primaries.[50]

In states or localities that lean strongly toward one party or another, the party primary often serves as the regular election since alternative party candidates have little chance of victory. In this case, voters cross party lines to vote in the primaries to have a voice in the political process. The virtual absence of party competition in the South during the period of African American disfranchisement, from the 1890s to the 1960s, remained associated with extremely low levels of turnout, even among white voters. And both turnout and competition in the South have increased since African Americans have joined the electorate.[51]

Differences in the level of turnout for any given type of election vary with the amount of interest in that particular race.[52] Presidential elections and hotly contested races for senator or governor can spur higher turnout. The massive amount of resources spent in the 1978 election on advertising only increased as the election became closer, drawing still more interest in the campaign. In tight contests, individuals who ordinarily remain somewhat passive or indifferent to political issues can realize the importance of their vote.

While this rings true in most cases, exceptions have occurred. The 1968, 1976, and 1980 elections suggest that the expectation of a close race does not invariably lead to heightened turnout nor, as the 1984 campaign attested, does the expectation of a landslide necessarily depress turnout.[53] In some instances, the excitement generated by a particular political figure can mobilize a fair portion of the electorate. Clements had managed both by energizing his own base of supporters and by closing the massive gap in the polls.

Immediately after the Clements victory results had become clear, analysts began trying to explain why the election had concluded in the manner it had and what the results meant. Post-election survey results determined that the most important issue for Clements was the cost of government, which included the burden of a growing bureaucracy, followed by education issues and then energy issues.[54] Clements himself explained the results as a matter of personality rather than any particular issue. "It was an issue of personality, my personality and my approach to leading Texas," he explained.[55] "They [voters] just decided it was time to change. They were looking for a fresh face in the political scene. John Hill had been around a long time in many offices." John Tower realized how close he had come to losing and credited the Clements campaign with helping him to victory.

The Republicans' tight organizations had helped carry the party's two leading candidates over the finish line. As Tower noted in his 1991 memoir, "Our political game plans dovetailed nicely. Clements had concentrated time and resources on the rural areas, and my solid base in the urban areas assisted him. . . . The downside was that we [the Tower campaign] had run a terrible campaign, making, along the way, just about every mistake imaginable."[56]

Pollster Lance Tarrance carefully explained the polling data, particularly daily tracking polls that the Republicans had used to identify key issues among the electorate and how the party managed to pinpoint their weakest areas. As he explained, both campaigns nearly lost. He noted that his charts showed Tower lost his Senate seat two times in October before recovering in the final days of the campaign.[57] "The Krueger campaign, from October 29 to November 5, witnessed a slow but steady decline in support for seven straight days which enabled the Tower campaign to reorganize and surge forth in those last days."[58] As Tower campaign manager Nola F. Heale explained, "If the election had been held on November 1, we might have lost."[59] Meanwhile, a sharp break in the undecided vote in favor of Clements late in the contest helped him surge to victory. Explained Tarrance, "The Hill and Clements contest closed about November 2 with a sharp decline in the undecided vote. What is interesting about the governor's race is that both Hill and Clements were winning equal amounts of the last-minute undecided voters."[60]

He theorized further that the Hill campaign probably underestimated the Clements campaign and erred in waiting for Clements to make a colossal mistake. He also stated that Hill had made a critical mistake to assume the mantle of the governorship after the primary. Stated Tarrance, "Hill had Dolph Briscoe beaten early in the spring and he did it on energy, actively. Clements's government background convinced many voters he's not a politician; but he knows his way around."[61] Tarrance added that no one issue sealed the election for Clements, and suggested that the Republican's success centered around his media campaign, his ability to get out his vote Tuesday, the name recognition he gained in the May primary, and the fact he didn't run out of gas and kept fighting to the very last.[62]

Hill had difficulty gaining any traction among voters in the wake of the onslaught by Clements and the Republicans. He had also been hurt by perceptions that he was a liberal, while most Texans saw themselves as moderate-conservative.[63] When asked about the polls that had showed him ahead, Hill himself seemed somewhat mystified and explained that his campaign and other polling firms had polled based on the traditional voters in Texas elections. Explained Hill, "It was a distorted electorate we couldn't poll because polls are based on traditional voting patterns. Some areas were having the usual and groups of voters were voting heavily because of certain issues. You just can't poll that."[64] He blamed his defeat on a number of different factors, including the millions spent by Clements, his last-minute circulation of allegations by Rev. Lester Roloff calling Hill anti-Christian, and a large group of non-traditional voters who cast their ballots for Clements.[65]

The political climate had also shifted away from the Democrats, compounding Hill's problems. Reflecting on the election years later, Hill explained, "Timing is everything. At this time Reagan was in the wings, Carter was not popular in Texas—I'm not blaming Carter for my defeat, I'm just trying to give you an idea of the times—California was just out of Proposition 13. The conservative tide was rising. When they [Republicans] smelled victory, they went for it."[66]

Political analysts usually point to the 1978 gubernatorial election as the election that turned Texas into a two-party state. In the first years after the election, it remained unclear whether this had truly happened in Texas, and the subsequent successes by Republicans have cast further doubt on this analysis. A large-scale transfer of party affection in a single election can be quite short-term, or the temporary "flash-in-the-pan," a different sort of phenomenon from that which occurs in elections marked by broad and lasting shifts in party strength.[67] Voter revolts against a party or a candidate had occurred in the South in elections past, and voters returned to their traditional voting habits with the next election. This may have occurred with the 1974 election as revulsion from the Watergate scandal—coupled with weak Republican opposition—inflated Democratic strength in the state. Analysis of the 1962, 1970, and 1972 elections indicated very close margins in the gubernatorial elections, which demonstrated an emerging pattern as the Republicans gained strength in Texas.[68]

The Democrats had managed to keep the conservatives within their ranks for many years despite inroads by the Republicans, which slowly eroded Democratic strength. Ideologically, many Texans had aligned with the Republicans but stayed with the Democratic Party for various reasons. Until 1978, frustrated Republican leaders had remained unable to convince these voters to switch sides. Many other Republicans had simply not bothered to vote, believing that Democratic strength had remained so overpowering that their vote could not make a significant difference.

The 1978 Texas elections did not produce an ideological realignment in the state, only the beginnings of a partisan realignment. Bill Clements succeeded in convincing his supporters that their votes would not be wasted on him. He energized existing Republicans by convincing them that he had a realistic chance of victory and convinced conservative Democrats that he best represented their interests. As a result, Clements managed to increase the Republican turnout by 669,560 votes, or by 130.2 percent over 1974, compared to Democratic gains of 150,113 votes, or 14.8 percent. New Republican voters, many of them lifelong Democrats, broke the Democratic Party's century-old lock on statewide offices.

Bill Clements had awakened the latent Republican strength in the state and roused it to become an even more potent force in Texas politics. The Texas

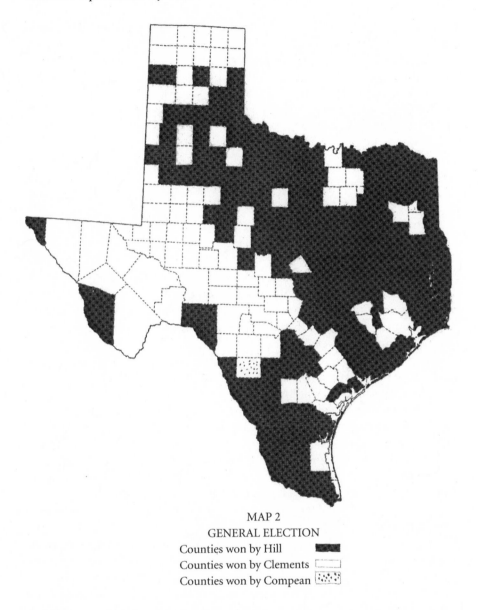

MAP 2
GENERAL ELECTION
Counties won by Hill
Counties won by Clements
Counties won by Compean

Republican Party would not fall into a slumber again for the foreseeable future, taking the role of dominance that the Democrats once claimed. Republicans became the most powerful political party in Texas by the end of the 1990s, eclipsing the relative parity of a two-party system. The Democrats, however, began to watch their strength wither after 1978 and slide from dominance in the 1970s to the brink of political irrelevance by the beginning of the twenty-first century.

CHAPTER 7

THE ONCE AND FUTURE GOVERNOR

"THIS WAS A CAMPAIGN never to be repeated," said David Dean.[1] Praise and blame circulated around the state almost immediately to answer the question of why the election ended with a Republican victory. The drive and resources of the Bill Clements campaign had taken the state by storm, stunning observers with his victory.

Some Democrats questioned whether Dolph Briscoe and his family had undermined John Hill's campaign, either by the governor's inaction or the open condemnation of Hill by members of his family. The outgoing governor defended himself at a speech in Austin. "I campaigned to help those who asked. Hill did not ask."[2] He dismissed charges that Janey Briscoe's support of Clements cost Hill the election. "There were many other factors," claimed Briscoe and turned his attention to the immediate problem of convincing voters to support the Democratic Party again, "The problem is to bring back to the Democratic Party those who left it in the recent election. We are going to have to get the independent voters back by presenting them a party and a platform they can support."[3]

Liberal commentator and lobbyist Jim Hightower blasted what he saw as the complacency of the Hill campaign. "It is a misconception to think that the GOP's win was strictly the result of slick advertising. . . . In the end, Hill's campaign was not a botched-up campaign at all; it was a carefully calculated loss. Hill's deliberate, don't-rock-the-boat, we'll-win-if-we-just-hold-on general election campaign is the same formula that has won for Democratic nominees before."[4]

Hill campaign manager John Rogers admitted that the campaign had miscalculated in the general election. "We did a lot of things right in the primary and we did a lot of things wrong in the general election."[5] Hill in particular blamed the late wave of advertising by the Republicans with his loss. "I think it was the result of that TV," he noted, "It was completely unexpected."[6] The television ads portrayed Hill in the worst manner possible. Hill lamented that

Clements had managed to cast the race in terms of Hill's character and what the Republican derided as radical liberal politics. "The race never developed into as much about issues. It was always personal attacks—what kind of a person I was—the perception of me as a city-slicker, big-spending liberal. But it worked."[7] When the opponent becomes able to determine the issues of the debate, it places the other candidate in a dangerous position of having to wage a campaign based on that candidate's weaknesses, real or perceived, which the opposition can exploit without mercy. Clements seized that opportunity.

With the bottomless well of finances available, Clements did not falter in the late stages of the campaign and had the resources available for a late surge of advertising and get-out-the-vote activities. To employ the expression used at that time, Clements did not run out of gas, which allowed him to continue to charge forward to victory. The victory proved the theories Clements espoused about the Texas electorate throughout the election, although his totals remained shy of the 53-percent victory total he had predicted.

John Hill had waged a traditional campaign in the general election, but Bill Clements spent the 1978 election season rewriting the rules for Texas campaigns. But Hill's strategy for winning the election nearly worked, faltering by some 16,900 votes. Despite Clements's intensity, mobilization, careful attention to detail, and millions of dollars spent, the Republican's campaign nearly failed. A failure would likely have set back Republican efforts in the state by years, and a Republican governor may not have emerged until the late 1980s or 1990s. All of the ingredients needed for a Republican breakthrough in 1978 occurred. The end of the Democratic lock on the governorship could almost as easily have happened with Dolph Briscoe as the nominee. Briscoe had nearly lost the 1972 election, which would have made Hank Grover the state's first Republican governor since Reconstruction.

Comparatively, in Arkansas, a series of unpopular policy and tax decisions cost then-Gov. Bill Clinton his bid for re-election in 1980 against the relatively unknown conservative Frank White. White became the first modern conservative Republican elected in Arkansas, but lost in a rematch to Clinton in 1982.[8] These victories in Texas and Arkansas proved that the Republicans had become a significant political power capable of toppling long-standing Democratic dynasties across the South.

As for Texas, Republican State Sen. Ike Harris of Dallas proposed that a combination of factors all contributed to Hill's loss:

> It goes back to what I've always said. For a Republican to get elected governor in this state, there are a whole lot of ifs that have to fall into place, and they just all fell into place. . . . Money had a lot to do with it; his [Clements's] ability to get himself known, the name identification which is a basic. The turnout was strong—2.3 million. . . . Our folks got to the polls. The traditional straight-Democratic voting precincts results indicate a poor turnout.[9]

Only 27 percent of Hispanics, for example, turned up to vote, compared to some 40 percent of the total electorate. Hill had clearly failed to mobilize his backers in the general election while Clements succeeded. Continued Harris, "I think Hill came off very poorly in the campaign—a surprise to me—particularly in the debates. . . . Not that Clements was outstanding. I'm not suggesting that. It's just that Hill came off poorly. . . . He acted like he was governor in advance of the election, and I think that put him in the role of incumbency, which you don't necessarily want to be in these days."[10] Pollster Lance Tarrance agreed with these latter sentiments. "He [Hill] was caught off-guard all year. That famous trip to Washington, D.C., after the primary to tell national leaders how Texas would be run shocked a lot of people," commented the pollster, "He started his campaign off as governor. . . . Hill, with all due respect, underestimated the money and the tenacity of the Republican effort."[11]

The disaffection of the Briscoe Democrats, the unpopularity of Jimmy Carter in Texas, the superiority of funds possessed by Clements, the special tax relief session of the state legislature, the failure to mobilize Democratic voters, the damage from fights with La Raza Unida, and many other factors contributed to Hill's defeat. Hill, however, could not quite repair all of the fractures and divisions within the party. Clements exploited this division and presented himself as a palatable alternative for conservative Democrats used to conservative candidates.

The damage from all of these issues weighing against Hill became too much for his campaign to bear. Each of these issues slowly added up against the Democrat. His trip to Washington to meet with President Carter in the weeks after the primary only inflamed the bitter loss that the Briscoe loyalists still felt. Coupled with his years of feuding with the Briscoe family and allies, he had damaged his standing with this faction of the party. Hill waged a modest campaign in accordance with the traditional Texas election practices of the time, and based his entire campaign strategy on traditional ideas about Texas politics. But he found himself unprepared for the force and effectiveness of the Clements campaign. By effectively tying the unpopular Democratic president with the Democratic attorney general of the state, Clements placed Hill on the defensive and reinforced many of the doubts that independent and conservative voters had about Hill. The La Raza Unida Party had aired doubts about Democratic motives regarding the Hispanic community on many occasions throughout the 1970s, but Hill could not quite overcome them as the LRU candidate repeatedly denounced Hill in his travels across Texas.

Hill, seeing polls showing him with a respectable lead throughout the race, did not expect such an unconventional plan of attack from the Republicans. Clements, however, had discovered a wealth of new voters eager to support the Republican's campaign, which fell under the radar of the Hill campaign. Using traditional polling methods, the Hill campaign could not accurately gauge the support of these voters who had either not voted in Texas previously or had voted only sporadically. Clements, using modern polling techniques, identified their voters and concentrated all of their efforts on getting these supporters to vote. The innovation and resources of the Clements campaign allowed the Republicans to outmaneuver Hill, whose campaign seemed lethargic in comparison.

After an exceptionally close election and an agonizing recount, Texans realized that they now had a Republican governor. A few short years before, they would have considered the idea impossible. As the reality of the results set in, reactions across the Lone Star State ranged from shock to bitter disappointment to overwhelming joy. Republicans celebrated. But the bitter recriminations from the Democrats would linger. Mostly, the people of Texas wondered what to expect.

Newspapers reflected a mix of surprise and skepticism. The *Dallas Morning News* observed, "Clements won the office in one of the most spectacular and expensive campaigns in the state's history. He was an underdog in both the Republican Primary and the general election. But with the intense drive and energy that marked his career as a successful businessman, Clements surprised oddsmakers."[12]

His victory had been the result of dogged determination, careful targeting of voters, and a wealth of resources to find these voters, but many others wondered if the same intensity and abrasiveness that Clements showed in the campaign would mix well with an overwhelmingly Democratic legislature used to a Democratic governor and a strictly Democratic agenda. The *Austin American-Statesman* commented, "His programs for 'total change in Austin' may not come to full fruition, and some of his campaign ideas are impassable but he's got some good notions which fit with his desire that he is going to be a governor for 'all Texans.'"[13]

His success or failure as governor would depend on how well he worked with legislators, observers repeated. Other editorial writers noted, "History will view Clements's administration, not on the basis of whether he was a Republican, but on how well he handled the problems that he will face. And we think most Texans will use the same guidelines today."[14] This would help determine whether the Clements victory served simply as an aberration or a true shift in Texas politics toward a two-party state. In the near-term, it would also determine whether Clements could survive a reelection campaign in 1982.

Dolph Briscoe's departure did little to repair the fracture between the conservatives and the moderates among Texas Democrats. In an address to the state legislature, Briscoe took a final swipe at Hill, hinting at the charges he had leveled at the attorney general during the primary. "Society may be asking too much of its public schools by way of social engineering. It is a good time to examine this situation, and I am glad my successor comes into office free of any obligations to increase spending without taking a hard look at the educational results."[15] The outgoing governor lavished praise on his successor. "To my successor, Governor William P. Clements, Jr. go my best wishes and hopes for the success of his administration. . . . Political parties are important, but more important is the welfare of the people of Texas."[16] As he returned to Uvalde, Briscoe predicted cooperation between Clements and the Democratic legislature.

House Speaker Billy Clayton accepted the rise of the modern Republicans with a sense of resignation. "Texas has always been a majority-conservative state, anyway, from a philosophical standpoint. . . . Certainly we are a two-philosophy state. You still have a coalition of Republicans and conservative democrats that works together quite well in the legislative process."[17] Clayton had never appreciated the political leanings of John Hill. He had worked to embarrass Hill with the summer special session on tax relief and seemed to prefer the conservatism of Clements. "As I view the circumstances and the campaign platform on which he ran, I can't see that there is going to be a great deal of change," said Clayton.[18]

Texas Republicans and other fans of Bill Clements gathered in Austin on the night before the inauguration to savor the victory once more. The Republican Party's "Victory Reception" drew a mix of presidential aspirants for 1980, particularly George Bush and John Connally, as well as a handful of Democratic officeholders, while raising $500,000 for the state Republican Party.[19] Billed as "The Best Party in 105 Years," more than 3,500 people swarmed into Austin's Municipal Auditorium to celebrate the inauguration of Clements. The victory, however sweet for Republicans, still left some dumbfounded. Paul Eggers, the Republican gubernatorial candidate in 1968 and 1970 commented, "I didn't think we would win until the late 1980s or the 1990s."[20]

Whether a near-miss would have created a frustrated and down-hearted Republican Party unable to capture the governor's mansion for another decade remains uncertain. Since they had won, Republicans reflected on what the future might bring their organization. Connally boasted, "The Republican Party could well be the principal party in the state by the end of the Clements administration. I don't view this election as a fluke . . . I think there is a major shift going on in the state. Clements was able to penetrate the rural conservative who has been inclined to vote Democratic."[21] His prediction, however, would take a decade longer to come true. Bush, with a more cautious outlook, expressed his hopes that the two parties would achieve a degree of equality between the two parties rather than Republican domination of Texas. "This is a start toward two-party government. It assures fair play and neutrality at the top of state government and it brings hope to other Republican candidates."[22]

In his inaugural address, Clements declared a new day for Texas.[23] He outlined the direction for state government that he foresaw, operating in the same manner that had made him a success in the energy industry. "I want to conduct government in a businesslike manner, with elected officials and government leaders responsible to the taxpayers just as a board of directors and company officials are responsible to the stockholders."[24] He continued, "[Texas] is a frontier in the sense of unparalleled economic opportunity. It is a place where people can realize their dreams and aspirations and a place where free enterprise can flourish without laboring under the yoke of a burdensome government."[25] He took a few moments in his address to commend the service of Gov. Dolph Briscoe, Lt. Gov. Bill Hobby, and Speaker Billy Clayton. He also recognized the task of working with a Democratic legislature and called for cooperation between the two parties. "All of us, all Texans, must lock arms and work together. We must shape a new alliance of greatness, an alliance that will perpetuate enhance the blessings our Almighty God has bestowed upon our state."[26]

A deep recession had gripped the nation by 1982, and the style of Clements had worn thin with many voters. These factors and an aggressive campaign helped the Democrats recover in 1982 as the party swept all statewide offices, thrusting Atty. Gen. Mark White into the governor's chair. But the 1982 election demonstrated that the Republican victory of 1978 was no fluke. Democratic turnout had recovered as the party gained more than 530,000 votes over 1978, but the Republicans gained more than 282,000 votes.[27] Clements lost votes in only 48 counties between the 1978 and 1982 elections, and gained votes in 205 counties; while the Democrats lost votes in 13 counties and gained votes in 242 counties.

Amid the statistics, one important fact stands out: The conservative Democrats who had voted for Clements in the previous election stayed with the Republican in the following election. Once Clements convinced these Democrats to vote Republican, most stayed Republican. Conservative Democrats had given the Republicans new strength and would continue to send Republicans to office across the state in increasing numbers. Clearly, the two-party Texas had come to life. In turn, this strength helped Clements defeat White in a bitter contest for a second term in 1986.

For the next fifteen years, an appearance of relative parity prevailed in Texas politics. Although Democrats controlled the state legislature, the parties split two of the four gubernatorial elections between 1978 and 1990, and both parties claimed one U.S. senator.[28] By the mid-1990s, however, that parity began to unravel, as the Republicans overtook the Democrats for control of the state's politics, winning every statewide election in a streak beginning in 1996, capturing the state Senate by 1997, and taking the state House of Representatives by 2002. In the wake of a bitter congressional redistricting fight in 2003, the Democrats lost their last source of domination in the state, the congressional delegation, with the fall of four incumbent congressmen in the 2004 general election.[29] Although the Democrats and Republicans both won the state four times in presidential elections between 1948 and 1976, the most important fact for Texas Republicans remained that the party had won every presidential election in the state since 1980. "Certainly, the political scene has not been the same since my election," wrote Clements in 2004. "I suspect that I was merely a part of the change and not necessarily the cause."[30]

The Clements election would foreshadow the rise of the conservative Republicans into national prominence with the election of Ronald Reagan as president in 1980. The conservatives would control the Republican Party for the next generation and would come to dominate most of the political dialogue in the South. The once-solidly Democratic South had become almost solidly Republican at the presidential level. Longtime North Carolina Sen. Jesse Helms, after winning election in the 1970s and serving through the 1990s, became practically synonymous with conservative Republicanism. Arkansas would see another conservative Republican become governor, former president of the Arkansas Baptist Convention Mike Huckabee, in 1996.[31] In Louisiana, conservative Gov. Buddy Roemer switched to the Republican Party in 1987. Conservative Democratic State Sen. Mike Foster switched to the Republican Party to run for Louisiana governor in 1995, and portraying himself as "a Christian and a gun owner," convincingly won two terms.[32] Georgia would be the last southern Democratic state to fall to the rule of conservative Republicans, with the election of a Republican governor and U.S. senator in 2002 for the first time since Reconstruction.[33]

David Dean served as secretary of state under Clements from 1981 to 1983. Neither Dolph Briscoe nor Preston Smith ever sought election again after 1978. Smith died in Lubbock after a lengthy illness in October 2003.[34]

John Hill later became Chief Justice of the Texas Supreme Court. As Chief Justice, Hill was charged with administering the oath of office to the governor in 1987, Bill Clements. Hill chuckled years later as he recalled a friend's comments, "'That has got to be one of the most ironic things—John Hill swearing in Bill Clements as governor.'"[35] Hill expressed no regrets over his career or his campaign in 1978. "I'm a lucky guy. I've got a great wife, who I feel did not get enough credit. She got me a whole lot of votes. I've got 3 fine children and 10 grandchildren. . . . I'm proud of the race I ran. I feel like Lou Gehrig: I'm the luckiest man alive."[36] He added, "I'm very grateful to the people. . . . I'm the only man in the history of Texas to serve as secretary of state, attorney general and Chief Justice of the Supreme Court. I think I've made a difference."[37] Hill stated that in the years since both he and Clements have become friends and have worked together on a number of civic causes.

In a 1999 interview, Hill commented on the pronounced change in state politics over the ensuing two decades. "Well, what has happened is that a lot of people who considered themselves conservative Democrats have shifted into the Republican Party. . . . Either conservative or moderate conservative distinguished from liberal. The Democratic Party base is now of an overwhelmingly liberal bent. There are still 100 or more counties in Texas that are probably unchanged in terms of the old moderate conservative Democratic roots."[38] He added that Texas Democrats faced an uphill fight by 2002. "They're in bad shape right now. . . . They've lost a lot of conservatives to the Republicans. They've been too oriented toward the liberal side."[39]

Lance Tarrance largely agreed with Hill's assessment of problems facing the once supreme Democratic organization. He commented, "In the last twenty, twenty-five years, Texas has moved from a very incipient two-party state to where it's going to be a fairly Republican state."[40] Looking to the future of politics in the state, Tarrance commented, "It's all Republican."[41]

David Dean, however, took an alternate view. He postulated that in the same way that the breakdown of Democratic cohesion allowed the Republicans to gain strength, a similar breakdown may allow the Democrats to regain a measure of their political strength. "The 'Eleventh Commandment' will wear thin after a while," said Dean, referring to Ronald Reagan's injunction for Republicans to never criticize one another. "Our country thrives on diversity. It's the reason for a strong two-party system in the United States. It's a big state. Big enough for two parties. Not all that long ago, there were no [Republican] statewide elected office holders."[42] Dean commented on the election, "[It] was a watershed year. It was the growing up of Texas from one era to another, one political party to another."[43]

Bob Krueger answered about the Democratic future with his usual optimism: "We're going to come back."[44]

With the 2006 election for governor, Dean's prediction seemed to start to emerge. Republican Comptroller Carole Keeton Strayhorn, angry with incumbent Republican Gov. Rick Perry, ran a spirited campaign as an independent rather than challenge him in the primary.[45] But Democratic candidate Chris Bell remained unable to capitalize on this division throughout much of the election season.

Since the 1950s, the Texas Republican Party has continued to grow at the expense of the Democratic Party. By 1978, the Republicans found themselves in a position to capitalize on this new strength. The 1978 election saw the twilight of the age of unquestioned Democratic superiority in the state. The Republican Party had demonstrated that it could win statewide elections and began to attract more Democrats looking for both a conservative organization and a party that could win statewide elections, and it began to attract more Democrats looking for both a conservative organization and a party that could win. A new era of Texas politics had begun, but the ultimate shape that Texas politics would take remained unclear in the immediate months after the Hill-Clements contest.

In some respects, Texas politics at the statewide level has changed little. By the early twenty-first century, Texas had become a state where one party, a conservative party, controls the state government. The difference has become which party label that conservative party has chosen to wear. Because of the 1978 election, a transformation began from conservative Democratic domination to conservative Republican domination of the state. The Democratic monopoly had ended, ushering in a dawn of Republican dominance that eclipsed the Democrats.

The Democrats, however, retain a measure of strength at the local levels. Some regions of the state remain overwhelmingly Democratic, and most major cities have Democratic mayors. The traditional conservatism of Texas may well stay intact for the foreseeable future, unless a major demographic shift occurs or some major event forces conservatives to reconsider their ideas. Election results reflect not only a strong affection for or revulsion against a particular candidate, but also reflect population shifts and changes of ideology. The Democrats, or any organization that draws its appeal and support from lower- and middle-income Texans, will likely face difficulties financing campaigns against wealthier Republicans, but states such as New York and California have shown that these are not insurmountable obstacles. In the future, Texas Democrats have to overcome the name-brand loyalty of many Republicans and project the image of both political viability and personal relevance to issues that individual Texans hold dear.

Political fortunes shift endlessly. The Texas Democrats began to enter a nighttime of despair in 1978, but the Republicans would soon see their brightest days. Texas could reverse itself yet again at some point in the future in favor of the Democrats. The voters, however, will ultimately determine the future course of politics in the Lone Star State. What issues the coming generations of voters will find important is uncertain. Men may not know what the future pages of history will read, but they are not powerless in creating the future.

PRESIDENTIAL ELECTION TOTALS IN TEXAS, 1968–1988[1]

Year	Candidate	Party[2]	Votes	Percentage	Change in Votes[3]
1968	Hubert H. Humphrey	Democratic	1,266,804	41.55%	−397,011
	Richard M. Nixon	Republican	1,227,844	39.88%	+269,278
	George C. Wallace	American Ind.	548,269	18.97%	—
TOTAL			**3,078,917**	**100.00%**	**+452,106**
1972	George McGovern	Democratic	1,154,289	33.28%	−112,515
	Richard M. Nixon	Republican	2,298,896	66.29%	+1,071,052
	Linda Jenness	Socialist Lbr.	8,664	0.25%	—
	John G. Schmitz	American Ind.	6,039	0.17%	−542,230
TOTAL			**3,467,888**	**100.00%**	**+388,971**
1976	Jimmy Carter	Democratic	2,082,319	51.14%	+928,030
	Gerald R. Ford	Republican	1,953,300	47.97%	−345,596
	Thomas Anderson	American	11,442	0.28%	—
	Peter Camejo	Socialist Wrk.	1,723	0.04%	—
	Eugene McCarthy	Independent	20,118	0.49%	—
TOTAL			**4,071,884**	**100.00%**	**+603,996**
1980	Jimmy Carter	Democratic	1,881,147	41.42%	−201,172
	Ronald Reagan	Republican	2,510,705	55.28%	+ 557,405
	Ed Clark	Libertarian	37,643	0.83%	—
	John Anderson	Independent	111,613	2.46%	—
	Write-ins		529	0.01%	—
TOTAL			**4,541,637**	**100.00%**	**+ 469,753**
1984	Walter Mondale	Democratic	1,949,276	36.11%	+68,129
	Ronald Reagan	Republican	3,433,428	63.61%	+922,723

Year	Candidate	Party[2]	Votes	Percentage	Change in Votes[3]
1984	Lyndon LaRouche	Independent	14,613	0.27%	—
(cont.)	Gus Hall	Write-In	126	0.00%	—
	Sonia Johnson	Write-In	87	0.00%	—
	Dennis Serrette	Write-In	41	0.00%	—
TOTAL			**5,397,571**	**100.00%**	**+855,934**
1988	George Bush	Republican	3,036,829	55.95%	−396,599
	Michael Dukakis	Democratic	2,352,748	43.35%	+403,472
	Ron Paul	Libertarian	30,355	0.56%	—
	Lenora Fulani	New Alliance	7,208	0.13%	—
	Bobby Locke	Write-In	98	0.00%	—
	Willa Kenoyer	Write-In	62	0.00%	—
	James Warren	Write-In	110	0.00%	—
TOTAL			**5,427,410**	**100.00%**	**+29,839**

DEMOCRATIC PRIMARY RESULTS BY COUNTY[1]

County	Dolph Briscoe	John Hill	Preston Smith	Briscoe +/− 1974[2]	County +/− 1974	County +/− 1982
Anderson	3443	3332	405	−871	+1969	−1918
Andrews	1132	727	172	−709	−501	+183
Angelina	2808	5825	564	−3290	−4467	+3167
Aransas	1024	1156	79	−115	+587	−646
Archer	736	874	84	−714	−130	−438
Armstrong	323	400	63	−101	+229	−316
Atascosa	2645	3052	152	−241	+1895	−1257
Austin	1447	1592	180	−736	+301	−1984
Bailey	295	618	123	−555	+72	+10
Bandera	1272	1016	105	−344	+301	−949
Bastrop	1993	2803	278	−839	+1129	+27
Baylor	751	680	85	−399	+110	−746
Bee	2118	1674	111	−668	−50	−2291
Bell	7913	8590	944	−87	+5486	−8403
Bexar	42259	66175	2455	−14353	+1359	−38366
Blanco	313	361	39	−212	+85	−419
Borden	182	164	33	−177	−46	−21
Bosque	1529	1405	185	−596	+434	+179
Bowie	6687	7215	855	−1504	+3376	−425
Brazoria	9302	9509	659	−288	+4053	−8241
Brazos	4897	8298	409	−466	+5479	−3061
Brewster	891	700	120	−199	+102	−324
Briscoe	183	570	73	−382	+153	−168
Brooks	1227	1777	100	−266	+11	+56
Brown	2901	2902	362	+299	+1860	−1286
Burleson	863	1782	176	−789	+388	−850
Burnet	1749	3084	304	−697	+1936	−1506

County	Dolph Briscoe	John Hill	Preston Smith	Briscoe +/- 1974[2]	County +/- 1974	County +/- 1982
Caldwell	1669	1925	216	−1085	+173	−915
Calhoun	1639	2362	175	−495	+1047	−976
Callahan	1601	1457	161	−35	+1283	−1730
Cameron	8590	13027	1141	−1966	+5594	+2407
Camp	1097	1184	101	−257	+538	+114
Carson	780	996	221	−214	+655	−605
Cass	2172	2800	455	−1748	+357	+1005
Castro	426	1356	247	−938	+256	−230
Chambers	1617	1808	231	−381	+817	−165
Cherokee	2457	3767	328	−1803	+727	−927
Childress	881	671	151	−541	+27	−953
Clay	1121	1072	106	−496	+163	+603
Cochran	377	764	191	−379	+377	−200
Coke	610	363	72	−169	+112	+119
Coleman	1182	895	126	−1427	−889	−1025
Collin	4228	5506	429	−1485	+2449	−4471
Collingsworth	524	783	128	−344	+385	−271
Colorado	1131	1194	110	−1408	−955	−425
Comal	2171	2180	198	−599	+946	−2732
Comanche	1259	1544	165	−1027	+170	+233
Concho	751	400	41	+68	+403	−219
Cooke	2419	2689	343	−1549	+224	−2348
Coryell	2066	1914	314	−752	+794	−543
Cottle	294	605	234	−332	+363	−492
Crane	666	561	116	−283	+127	−320
Crockett	495	233	20	−112	−19	−142
Crosby	639	1110	236	−527	+579	−707
Culberson	289	311	31	−240	−26	−103
Dallam	432	540	129	−11	+501	−173
Dallas	54108	64123	7541	−15601	+13195	−69361
Dawson	1183	1003	285	−948	−368	+443
Deaf Smith	1269	2389	432	−878	+1341	−1709
Delta	473	945	102	−879	−131	−240
Denton	4544	7195	510	−3003	+69	−6504
De Witt	1205	1113	87	−1286	−825	−114
Dickens	332	759	106	−536	+140	−5
Dimmit	1401	1886	98	−390	+799	−348
Donley	428	849	151	−150	+517	−408
Duval	2776	2162	117	−623	+1022	+30
Eastland	1887	1782	164	−1570	−508	−692
Ector	3896	3457	670	−1213	+1145	−1564
Edwards	412	140	26	−77	+38	−179
Ellis	3870	3698	448	−2157	+378	−1930

County	Dolph Briscoe	John Hill	Preston Smith	Briscoe +/− 1974[2]	County +/− 1974	County +/− 1982
El Paso	14848	26946	1355	+552	+18132	−12582
Erath	2252	2206	260	−1705	−131	−836
Falls	2409	1884	214	−73	+1224	−1629
Fannin	2179	2474	238	−2256	−1438	+353
Fayette	1555	2206	153	−1608	−762	+158
Fisher	828	1036	111	−725	+93	−35
Floyd	962	1198	189	−826	+207	−1336
Foard	455	407	72	−183	+176	−357
Fort Bend	5279	6141	570	−761	+3138	−7845
Franklin	551	839	84	−332	+339	−564
Freestone	1445	1568	138	−878	+330	−968
Frio	1883	2025	70	−273	+1461	−1068
Gaines	1175	1332	390	−702	+502	−1420
Galveston	11118	13303	790	−3770	−499	−8747
Garza	439	703	100	−260	+226	−397
Gillespie	596	565	56	−262	+201	−763
Glasscock	240	82	31	−15	+52	−16
Goliad	850	474	36	−75	+80	−527
Gonzales	1633	1429	104	−1133	−411	−580
Gray	1821	1883	413	−565	+915	−1906
Grayson	6106	7035	470	−1768	+3131	−8434
Gregg	5124	6564	483	−4096	+938	−2834
Grimes	1355	1346	138	−766	+40	−190
Guadalupe	3359	3413	311	+612	+3224	−2410
Hale	2499	3108	608	−700	+2196	−3631
Hall	328	694	143	−740	−152	+104
Hamilton	890	856	111	−1296	−118	−192
Hansford	461	595	168	−451	+44	−458
Hardeman	761	866	162	−483	+230	−480
Hardin	3067	3858	340	−451	+808	+644
Harris	76546	89890	9774	−18798	+10940	−94675
Harrison	4127	5027	397	−1626	+1659	−670
Hartley	459	463	117	−102	+334	−330
Haskell	1260	1480	173	−1123	+105	−1300
Hays	1922	4561	250	−1778	+755	−2247
Hemphill	419	456	94	−226	+56	−402
Henderson	2609	3920	321	−2586	−96	+91
Hidalgo	12748	13758	704	−1563	+3740	−2369
Hill	2951	2136	331	−635	+1259	−734
Hockley	1470	2751	343	−2461	−462	−1272
Hood	1125	1120	102	−527	+338	+1830
Hopkins	2460	2704	482	−852	+1618	−1896
Houston	1748	2732	259	−949	+1117	−513

County	Dolph Briscoe	John Hill	Preston Smith	Briscoe +/– 1974[2]	County +/– 1974	County +/– 1982
Howard	3326	2621	443	–281	+1513	–2447
Hudspeth	347	301	16	–91	+114	–91
Hunt	3627	4601	482	–2268	+1030	–2375
Hutchinson	2083	1943	455	–734	+588	–1454
Irion	253	147	17	–54	–10	–180
Jack	871	525	65	–400	–133	–244
Jackson	1333	1185	108	+169	+1156	–369
Jasper	2202	3136	264	–1020	+855	+820
Jeff Davis	285	235	35	+38	+246	–336
Jefferson	13801	17093	923	–4979	+2322	+7673
Jim Hogg	870	1284	69	–82	+265	–35
Jim Wells	4348	4064	380	–897	+135	–415
Johnson	4080	4006	272	–893	+2139	+1704
Jones	2239	1947	271	–342	+1404	–1808
Karnes	1964	1199	92	–814	–424	–1135
Kaufman	2460	3399	403	–1221	+1683	–828
Kendall	551	546	11	+15	+451	–792
Kenedy	106	54	6	–27	0	+25
Kent	242	351	78	–203	+146	–169
Kerr	1528	1349	137	–848	+47	–1656
Kimble	602	265	33	–252	–98	–258
King	36	84	12	–64	+8	+44
Kinney	474	389	36	–144	+66	–180
Kleberg	2013	2592	172	–344	+286	+32
Knox	546	626	129	–475	+100	–194
Lamar	3470	4770	664	–1991	+2083	–3370
Lamb	1164	2208	282	–1711	+63	–562
Lampasas	1421	1289	119	–214	+851	–669
La Salle	704	515	34	–395	–124	+219
Lavaca	1585	1626	131	–960	–60	–463
Lee	576	1074	126	–1098	–571	+270
Leon	1324	1428	138	–712	+400	–989
Liberty	3028	4116	351	–2006	+9	–1156
Limestone	1748	1982	373	+66	+2096	–149
Lipscomb	381	621	145	+42	+654	–194
Live Oak	1391	999	89	–573	–20	–784
Llano	1024	1584	129	–731	+424	–402
Loving	22	25	3	–17	0	+6
Lubbock	8393	14015	4514	–6777	+4496	–9694
Lynn	700	1183	322	–356	+986	–278
McCulloch	1217	910	216	–389	+465	–425
McLennan	16944	14341	1499	+3122	+14079	–9251
McMullen	171	96	11	–195	–157	–119

County	Dolph Briscoe	John Hill	Preston Smith	Briscoe +/– 1974[2]	County +/– 1974	County +/– 1982
Madison	978	1249	158	−834	+88	−452
Marion	947	922	94	−375	+143	−280
Martin	723	370	99	+257	+639	−301
Mason	254	212	27	−718	−679	−40
Matagorda	2289	2255	249	−1009	+131	−1406
Maverick	1118	2528	45	−859	+139	+536
Medina	2998	1704	132	−187	+1012	−1360
Menard	355	252	26	−134	+33	+41
Midland	2688	2091	411	−1192	−43	−3129
Milam	1910	2863	242	−149	+2094	−32
Mills	791	692	112	−360	+224	−572
Mitchell	986	839	88	−565	+2	+282
Montague	1682	1299	208	−879	+28	+91
Montgomery	5796	8134	841	−917	+4922	−6025
Moore	1376	2038	428	−104	+1792	−1134
Morris	1184	1644	182	−1296	−288	+245
Motley	302	397	71	−200	+141	−239
Nacogdoches	2328	3732	266	−1707	+487	+123
Navarro	3534	4764	356	−632	+3585	−2183
Newton	709	1285	98	−899	+190	+750
Nolan	1786	1879	159	−1177	+325	−739
Nueces	14951	21905	1517	−7431	−298	−4579
Ochiltree	736	622	184	−632	−255	−432
Oldham	316	425	91	−167	+193	−391
Orange	4894	7313	380	−3058	+817	+1668
Palo Pinto	2548	2113	277	+171	+1839	−1612
Panola	2685	2303	206	−1010	+341	−1344
Parker	3250	3835	334	−1692	+934	−2662
Parmer	467	1007	317	−1023	−70	−529
Pecos	2149	1477	391	−109	+929	−1151
Polk	1734	3624	283	−1408	+1072	−551
Potter	4117	5815	1020	−1798	+1687	−2901
Presidio	633	553	67	−237	+68	−348
Rains	511	765	90	−583	−39	−105
Randall	2815	4133	688	−1957	+578	−1852
Reagan	558	490	64	−375	−152	−262
Real	746	349	34	+387	+739	−316
Red River	1683	1952	360	−1288	+111	−300
Reeves	1678	1093	362	−2	+905	−392
Refugio	1229	1064	92	−277	+246	−96
Roberts	122	140	20	−139	−53	−77
Robertson	1398	1978	266	−1327	−227	−238
Rockwall	1323	1600	209	−412	+946	−1188

County	Dolph Briscoe	John Hill	Preston Smith	Briscoe +/- 1974[2]	County +/- 1974	County +/- 1982
Runnels	1334	707	92	−384	+118	+112
Rusk	2992	4493	451	−3596	−531	−1470
Sabine	980	1756	138	−822	+236	+92
San Augustine	704	1355	113	−708	+230	+454
San Jacinto	1209	1757	148	−633	+365	−116
San Patricio	5108	4516	535	−16	+2462	−2959
San Saba	617	565	63	−354	+121	+4
Schleicher	596	196	29	−53	+60	−197
Scurry	2324	1632	328	−950	+476	−2147
Shackelford	590	589	62	+39	+551	−494
Shelby	2155	2732	300	−1224	+596	−817
Sherman	322	472	89	−174	+220	−144
Smith	7575	9202	793	−3618	+2424	−7892
Somervell	666	597	106	−88	+306	−352
Starr	1695	2773	74	−1288	+438	−694
Stephens	1330	983	111	−219	+565	−280
Sterling	245	109	20	−63	+164	−51
Stonewall	506	492	66	−230	+166	−461
Sutton	519	274	34	+99	+323	−171
Swisher	561	1661	254	−646	+763	−49
Tarrant	34354	43543	2854	−7486	+15498	−38657
Taylor	9914	7570	652	+547	+6464	−9121
Terrell	277	163	16	−271	−281	+43
Terry	881	1707	232	−1208	+236	−1061
Throckmorton	385	402	59	−379	−96	−250
Titus	1724	2428	469	−1268	+756	+112
Tom Green	5506	4175	405	−1044	+720	−3295
Travis	20315	44183	3474	−14860	+173	−15313
Trinity	1041	1547	88	−1216	−409	+1412
Tyler	1150	1929	242	−1152	−16	+481
Upshur	2132	2973	224	−2598	−960	−362
Upton	572	387	76	−367	−232	−293
Uvalde	4505	759	58	+1050	+1548	−1618
Val Verde	2261	1456	163	−525	+176	+415
Van Zandt	2678	3772	337	−1330	+1670	−1085
Victoria	4596	4905	369	+279	+3984	−2230
Walker	2114	4105	370	−1785	+837	−1791
Waller	1795	1424	314	+2	+972	−954
Ward	1313	1241	251	−493	+510	+361
Washington	1233	2470	285	−1588	+274	−1025
Webb	5445	10245	429	+923	+9386	−6339
Wharton	2562	3182	303	−2035	−701	−1698
Wheeler	711	1152	276	−724	+298	−1048

County	Dolph Briscoe	John Hill	Preston Smith	Briscoe +/- 1974[2]	County +/- 1974	County +/- 1982
Wichita	7071	6897	699	−4016	−611	−8163
Wilbarger	1888	2149	271	−217	+1812	−1937
Willacy	1133	1434	100	−944	−144	+783
Williamson	3624	5258	708	−960	+3488	−1952
Wilson	2366	2318	214	−292	+1143	−971
Winkler	965	954	155	−496	+114	−1036
Wise	1589	1841	140	−1857	−690	−335
Wood	2054	2850	203	−660	+1613	−445
Yoakum	788	1066	260	−680	+167	−165
Young	1523	1661	127	−885	+310	−1534
Zapata	900	801	29	+29	+264	−50
Zavala	627	268	24	−394	−212	+1123
TOTAL	**753,309**	**932,245**	**92,202**	**−272,323**	**+256,552**	**−520,378**
	(42.4%)	(52.4%)	(5.2%)	(−26.6%)	(+14.4%)	(−29.3%)

1978 GUBERNATORIAL ELECTION TOTALS AND PERCENTAGES[1]

County	John Hill	Bill Clements	Mario C. Compean[2]	Sara J. Johnston[3]	Hill Vote %[4]	Clements Vote %
Anderson	3777	3180	1	7	54.2	45.8
Andrews	753	1588	3	0	32.1	67.9
Angelina	5384	3499	0	0	60.6	39.4
Aransas	1072	1516	12	7	41.1	58.2
Archer	939	672	0	0	58.3	41.7
Armstrong	353	354	0	0	49.9	50.1
Atascosa	2210	2030	12	6	51.9	47.7
Austin	1665	1845	3	1	47.4	52.6
Bailey	715	819	18	0	46.1	52.7
Bandera	1028	1580	1	5	39.3	60.7
Bastrop	2651	1820	14	6	59.0	41.0
Baylor	814	494	0	0	62.2	37.8
Bee	1423	2076	78	8	39.7	57.9
Bell	10378	8779	141	41	53.7	45.4
Bexar	87709	79832	2148	530	51.5	46.9
Blanco	708	766	0	2	48.0	52.0
Borden	149	162	0	0	47.9	52.1
Bosque	1948	1698	5	3	53.3	46.7
Bowie	5889	5718	27	13	50.6	49.4
Brazoria	13190	12299	81	33	51.5	48.5
Brazos	7623	7298	110	51	50.5	48.4
Brewster	595	881	8	2	40.0	59.3
Briscoe	548	226	1	0	70.8	29.2
Brooks	1220	435	22	3	72.6	25.9
Brown	3548	2935	3	3	54.7	45.3
Burleson	1712	703	6	0	70.7	29.3
Burnet	2669	2207	5	2	54.7	45.3

County	John Hill	Bill Clements	Mario C. Compean[2]	Sara J. Johnston[3]	Hill Vote %[4]	Clements Vote %
Caldwell	2315	1727	24	9	56.8	42.4
Calhoun	2006	1641	16	4	54.7	44.8
Callahan	1476	1288	1	3	53.3	46.7
Cameron	13224	10601	273	108	54.6	43.8
Camp	998	695	1	0	59.0	41.0
Carson	975	872	2	1	52.9	47.1
Cass	3563	2521	1	4	58.5	41.5
Castro	1651	866	51	2	64.2	33.7
Chambers	1636	1060	2	9	60.4	39.2
Cherokee	3679	2351	1	1	60.1	39.9
Childress	885	722	1	0	55.1	44.9
Clay	1458	940	0	1	60.8	39.2
Cochran	725	521	5	0	58.0	41.6
Coke	692	536	0	0	56.4	43.6
Coleman	1217	1079	1	0	52.9	47.1
Collin	8232	13779	34	33	37.3	62.4
Collingsworth	783	474	0	2	62.2	37.6
Colorado	1699	1494	4	2	53.1	46.9
Comal	3017	5035	22	3	37.4	62.6
Comanche	1784	935	2	3	65.5	34.5
Concho	498	446	1	1	52.6	47.4
Cooke	2442	3000	2	7	45.0	55.0
Coryell	2493	2475	8	2	50.1	49.9
Cottle	579	263	1	0	68.7	31.3
Crane	322	685	2	2	32.2	67.8
Crockett	349	541	11	1	40.0	60.0
Crosby	1473	668	28	5	67.8	32.2
Culberson	333	392	8	0	45.4	54.6
Dallam	517	651	1	1	44.4	55.6
Dallas	108617	154901	1518	744	40.9	58.3
Dawson	1770	2155	55	1	44.5	54.1
Deaf Smith	1680	1787	58	1	47.6	50.7
Delta	809	292	0	1	73.4	26.6
Denton	9870	11630	68	50	45.7	53.8
De Witt	1471	1889	11	1	43.6	56.0
Dickens	794	266	5	0	74.6	25.4
Dimmit	1327	925	33	9	57.8	42.2
Donley	725	502	3	0	58.9	41.1
Duval	2188	692	44	1	74.8	23.7
Eastland	2230	1834	5	3	54.8	45.2
Ector	5174	13491	226	31	27.3	71.3
Edwards	189	351	1	1	35.0	65.0
Ellis	4758	4256	7	6	52.7	47.3

County	John Hill	Bill Clements	Mario C. Compean[2]	Sara J. Johnston[3]	Hill Vote %[4]	Clements Vote %
El Paso	31809	23490	0	0	57.5	42.5
Erath	2413	2273	5	1	51.4	48.6
Falls	2634	1543	7	7	62.8	37.2
Fannin	4207	2171	3	4	65.9	34.1
Fayette	2150	1726	2	4	55.4	44.6
Fisher	1178	560	4	1	67.9	32.1
Floyd	1255	997	11	1	55.4	44.0
Foard	669	178	1	0	78.9	21.1
Fort Bend	7750	11298	98	30	40.4	58.9
Franklin	719	379	0	0	65.5	34.5
Freestone	1493	1229	1	2	54.8	45.2
Frio	1520	1436	210	7	47.9	45.3
Gaines	1238	1356	15	0	47.5	52.0
Galveston	17396	13120	162	100	56.5	42.6
Garza	547	439	4	1	55.2	44.8
Gillespie	944	2595	1	3	26.6	73.4
Glasscock	94	326	1	0	22.3	77.7
Goliad	564	579	2	0	49.3	50.6
Gonzales	1634	1292	5	1	55.7	44.3
Gray	2658	3792	1	2	41.2	58.8
Grayson	7534	6835	30	13	52.3	47.4
Gregg	7230	9763	29	13	42.4	57.3
Grimes	2076	1388	3	4	60.0	40.0
Guadalupe	3550	5081	31	6	41.0	58.6
Hale	3207	3356	98	11	48.1	50.3
Hall	817	513	0	2	61.3	38.7
Hamilton	1051	1025	1	1	50.7	49.3
Hansford	582	897	0	0	39.4	60.6
Hardeman	1198	668	2	0	64.2	35.8
Hardin	5331	3127	3	2	63.0	37.0
Harris	167814	190728	1025	849	46.6	52.9
Harrison	4611	4008	28	17	53.2	46.3
Hartley	573	645	2	0	47.1	52.9
Haskell	1554	854	3	0	64.6	35.4
Hays	3819	2657	46	12	58.4	40.7
Hemphill	435	511	0	1	46.0	54.0
Henderson	4304	3819	7	3	53.0	47.0
Hidalgo	17697	13557	448	128	55.6	42.6
Hill	2453	2199	5	2	52.7	47.3
Hockley	2680	1821	22	3	59.2	40.2
Hood	1716	1580	2	1	52.1	47.9
Hopkins	2684	1704	2	0	61.2	38.8
Houston	2419	1280	3	0	65.4	34.6

County	John Hill	Bill Clements	Mario C. Compean[2]	Sara J. Johnston[3]	Hill Vote %[4]	Clements Vote %
Howard	2676	3575	68	8	42.3	56.5
Hudspeth	221	247	4	3	48.0	52.0
Hunt	4404	3613	2	6	54.9	45.1
Hutchinson	2884	3670	3	7	44.1	55.9
Irion	152	219	1	0	41.1	58.9
Jack	869	677	0	0	56.2	43.8
Jackson	1549	1400	4	1	52.6	47.4
Jasper	2969	1692	1	2	63.7	36.3
Jeff Davis	189	278	1	0	40.6	59.4
Jefferson	24693	16034	54	90	60.4	39.2
Jim Hogg	1359	311	15	0	80.7	18.5
Jim Wells	3102	2339	58	5	56.4	42.5
Johnson	5684	4658	6	8	54.9	45.0
Jones	2367	1784	6	0	56.9	43.1
Karnes	1413	1394	9	2	50.1	49.5
Kaufman	3342	2456	2	2	57.7	42.3
Kendall	994	2284	0	3	30.3	69.7
Kenedy	62	63	2	0	48.8	49.6
Kent	330	194	0	0	63.0	37.0
Kerr	2391	5283	7	2	31.2	68.8
Kimble	461	702	4	1	39.9	60.1
King	67	79	0	0	45.9	54.1
Kinney	235	332	0	1	41.6	58.4
Kleberg	2512	2176	140	8	51.9	45.0
Knox	918	390	0	0	70.2	29.8
Lamar	4735	2909	5	11	61.8	38.0
Lamb	2261	1851	36	5	54.4	44.6
Lampasas	1178	1337	1	1	46.8	53.2
La Salle	1004	805	237	5	49.0	39.2
Lavaca	2096	1483	3	2	58.4	41.6
Lee	1030	781	1	0	56.8	43.2
Leon	1189	812	3	0	59.3	40.7
Liberty	3720	2476	0	2	60.0	40.0
Limestone	2541	1690	0	0	60.1	39.9
Lipscomb	378	553	0	0	40.6	59.4
Live Oak	725	1111	3	0	39.6	60.4
Llano	1577	1632	3	0	49.2	50.8
Loving	19	38	0	0	33.3	66.7
Lubbock	16963	21094	528	76	43.9	54.6
Lynn	1203	807	11	0	59.5	39.9
McCulloch	936	1198	0	0	43.9	56.1
McLennan	17405	16642	100	15	50.9	48.7
McMullen	102	224	2	1	31.0	69.0

County	John Hill	Bill Clements	Mario C. Compean[2]	Sara J. Johnston[3]	Hill Vote %[4]	Clements Vote %
Madison	930	600	1	1	60.7	39.3
Marion	1091	727	1	1	60.1	39.9
Martin	366	666	1	2	35.7	64.3
Mason	527	803	1	0	39.7	60.3
Matagorda	2478	2356	8	3	51.1	48.9
Maverick	1627	606	36	0	71.7	26.7
Medina	1872	2852	26	2	39.4	60.0
Menard	375	398	0	0	48.5	51.5
Midland	4632	13808	80	30	25.0	74.4
Milam	2935	1674	5	1	63.7	36.3
Mills	639	584	0	1	52.3	47.7
Mitchell	947	866	2	1	52.1	47.9
Montague	1901	1568	1	2	54.8	45.2
Montgomery	7159	8998	23	14	44.2	55.6
Moore	1325	1599	3	1	45.3	54.7
Morris	1622	1101	0	2	59.6	40.4
Motley	295	381	0	0	43.6	56.4
Nacogdoches	3728	3026	6	15	55.3	44.7
Navarro	3992	2681	6	1	59.8	40.2
Newton	1454	503	2	2	74.3	25.7
Nolan	1859	1790	2	3	51.0	49.0
Nueces	25702	21472	634	131	53.6	44.8
Ochiltree	478	1328	0	0	26.5	73.5
Oldham	361	319	0	0	53.1	46.9
Orange	7492	4572	4	10	62.0	38.0
Palo Pinto	2487	2011	3	3	55.2	44.8
Panola	2044	1743	1	2	54.0	46.0
Parker	4328	3517	2	5	55.2	44.8
Parmer	1164	1212	7	0	49.1	50.9
Pecos	1172	1705	20	6	40.4	58.7
Polk	2305	1418	1	1	61.9	38.1
Potter	7188	7491	73	36	48.6	50.7
Presidio	521	447	8	4	53.2	45.6
Rains	675	309	0	0	58.6	31.4
Randall	6235	9854	22	10	38.7	61.1
Reagan	299	514	0	0	36.8	63.2
Real	347	569	12	1	37.4	61.2
Red River	1652	1086	2	1	60.4	39.6
Reeves	1627	1660	261	12	45.7	46.6
Refugio	1725	1202	17	2	58.6	40.8
Roberts	134	253	0	0	34.6	65.4
Robertson	2042	788	1	4	72.2	27.8
Rockwall	1128	1676	4	1	40.2	59.7

County	John Hill	Bill Clements	Mario C. Compean[2]	Sara J. Johnston[3]	Hill Vote %[4]	Clements Vote %
Runnels	1142	1671	6	3	40.5	59.2
Rusk	3217	3346	13	10	48.8	50.8
Sabine	1104	469	1	2	70.0	30.0
San Augustine	1136	584	1	2	65.9	34.1
San Jacinto	1093	699	2	1	61.1	38.9
San Patricio	4232	4250	88	23	49.2	49.5
San Saba	927	606	3	2	60.6	39.4
Schleicher	290	489	0	0	37.2	62.8
Scurry	1410	2183	22	4	39.0	60.3
Shackelford	532	505	0	0	51.3	48.7
Shelby	2229	1514	1	1	59.6	40.4
Sherman	437	524	1	1	45.6	54.4
Smith	10232	14133	23	16	41.9	57.9
Somervell	700	365	1	0	65.8	34.2
Starr	3591	466	32	3	87.8	11.4
Stephens	944	1012	2	1	48.3	51.7
Sterling	121	230	0	0	34.5	65.5
Stonewall	448	237	0	0	65.4	34.6
Sutton	366	612	6	0	37.8	62.2
Swisher	2123	620	8	2	77.1	22.5
Tarrant	63662	70709	327	290	47.2	52.4
Taylor	9526	12576	46	38	42.9	56.7
Terrell	151	265	6	0	35.8	62.8
Terry	1612	1502	17	1	51.5	48.0
Throckmorton	400	230	1	0	63.4	36.5
Titus	2108	1505	1	0	58.4	41.6
Tom Green	6674	7773	46	22	46.0	53.6
Travis	48382	38856	811	456	54.7	43.9
Trinity	1340	676	4	1	66.3	33.7
Tyler	1653	1107	3	1	59.8	40.2
Upshur	2509	1923	2	0	56.6	43.4
Upton	357	653	1	1	35.5	64.5
Uvalde	1306	3158	47	0	29.0	70.0
Val Verde	2607	2732	15	4	48.7	51.0
Van Zandt	3550	2504	5	3	58.6	41.3
Victoria	5211	6291	94	24	44.8	54.1
Walker	3059	2504	1	3	55.5	44.5
Waller	1595	1509	1	4	51.3	48.7
Ward	847	1532	9	1	35.5	64.1
Washington	1825	2073	1	3	46.9	53.1
Webb	5433	3019	255	38	62.1	34.5
Wharton	3619	3086	9	8	53.8	45.9
Wheeler	906	769	0	2	54.1	45.9

County	John Hill	Bill Clements	Mario C. Compean[2]	Sara J. Johnston[3]	Hill Vote %[4]	Clements Vote %
Wichita	11312	10348	33	27	52.1	47.6
Wilbarger	1688	1259	0	0	57.3	42.7
Willacy	1473	1100	18	6	56.7	42.4
Williamson	6089	5943	22	15	50.5	49.2
Wilson	1790	1555	12	2	53.3	46.3
Winkler	997	1413	8	1	41.6	58.4
Wise	2545	1888	3	2	57.5	42.5
Wood	2427	2080	1	5	53.8	46.2
Yoakum	759	889	7	1	45.8	53.7
Young	1999	1713	1	1	53.9	46.1
Zapata	765	416	5	2	64.4	35.0
Zavala	1204	741	2036	5	30.2	18.6
TOTAL	**1,166,919** (49.24%)	**1,183,828** (49.96%)	**14,213** (0.59%)	**4,624** (0.19%)	**49.24%**	**49.96%**

DEMOCRATIC TURNOUT, 1978 GUBERNATORIAL ELECTION[1]

County	John Hill	Bill Clements	Mario C. Compean	Sara J. Johnston	Primary Difference[2]	Hill Difference[3]
Anderson	3777	3180	1	7	−3403	+334
Andrews	753	1588	3	0	−1278	+26
Angelina	5384	3499	0	0	−3813	−441
Aransas	1072	1516	12	7	−1187	−84
Archer	939	672	0	0	−755	+65
Armstrong	353	354	0	0	−433	−47
Atascosa	2210	2030	12	6	−3639	−842
Austin	1665	1845	3	1	−1554	+73
Bailey	715	819	18	0	−321	+97
Bandera	1028	1580	1	5	−1365	+12
Bastrop	2651	1820	14	6	−2423	−152
Baylor	814	494	0	0	−702	+134
Bee	1423	2076	78	8	−2480	−251
Bell	10378	8779	141	41	−7069	+1788
Bexar	87709	79832	2148	530	−23180	+21534
Blanco	708	766	0	2	−5	+347
Borden	149	162	0	0	−230	−15
Bosque	1948	1698	5	3	−1171	+543
Bowie	5889	5718	27	13	−8868	−1326
Brazoria	13190	12299	81	33	−6280	+3681
Brazos	7623	7298	110	51	−5981	−675
Brewster	595	881	8	2	−1116	−105
Briscoe	548	226	1	0	−278	−22
Brooks	1220	435	22	3	−1884	−557
Brown	3548	2935	3	3	−2617	+646
Burleson	1712	703	6	0	−1109	−70
Burnet	2669	2207	5	2	−2468	−415

County	John Hill	Bill Clements	Mario C. Compean	Sara J. Johnston	Primary Difference[2]	Hill Difference[3]
Caldwell	2315	1727	24	9	−1495	+390
Calhoun	2006	1641	16	4	−2170	−356
Callahan	1476	1288	1	3	−1743	+19
Cameron	13224	10601	273	108	−9534	+197
Camp	998	695	1	0	−1384	−168
Carson	975	872	2	1	−1022	−21
Cass	3563	2521	1	4	−1864	+763
Castro	1651	866	51	2	−378	+295
Chambers	1636	1060	2	9	−2020	172
Cherokee	3679	2351	1	1	−2873	88
Childress	885	722	1	0	−818	+214
Clay	1458	940	0	1	−841	+386
Cochran	725	521	5	0	−607	−39
Coke	692	536	0	0	−353	+329
Coleman	1217	1079	1	0	−986	+322
Collin	8232	13779	34	33	−1931	+2726
Collingsworth	783	474	0	2	−652	0
Colorado	1699	1494	4	2	−736	+505
Comal	3017	5035	22	3	−1532	+837
Comanche	1784	935	2	3	−1184	+240
Concho	498	446	1	1	−694	+98
Cooke	2442	3000	2	7	−3009	−247
Coryell	2493	2475	8	2	−1801	+579
Cottle	579	263	1	0	−554	26
Crane	322	685	2	2	−1021	−239
Crockett	349	541	11	1	−399	+116
Crosby	1473	668	28	5	−512	+363
Culberson	333	392	8	0	−298	+22
Dallam	517	651	1	1	−584	−23
Dallas	108617	154901	1518	744	−17155	+44494
Dawson	1770	2155	55	1	−701	+767
Deaf Smith	1680	1787	58	1	−2410	−709
Delta	809	292	0	1	−711	−136
Denton	9870	11630	68	50	−2370	+2675
De Witt	1471	1889	11	1	−934	+358
Dickens	794	266	5	0	−403	+35
Dimmit	1327	925	33	9	−2058	−599
Donley	725	502	3	0	−703	−124
Duval	2188	692	44	1	−2867	+26
Eastland	2230	1834	5	3	−1603	+448
Ector	5174	13491	226	31	−2849	+1717
Edwards	189	351	1	1	−389	+49
Ellis	4758	4256	7	6	−3258	+1060

County	John Hill	Bill Clements	Mario C. Compean	Sara J. Johnston	Primary Difference[2]	Hill Difference[3]
El Paso	31809	23490	0	0	−11340	+4863
Erath	2413	2273	5	1	−2305	+207
Falls	2634	1543	7	7	−1873	+750
Fannin	4207	2171	3	4	−684	+1733
Fayette	2150	1726	2	4	−1764	−56
Fisher	1178	560	4	1	−797	+142
Floyd	1255	997	11	1	−1094	+57
Foard	669	178	1	0	−265	+262
Fort Bend	7750	11298	98	30	−4240	+1609
Franklin	719	379	0	0	−755	−120
Freestone	1493	1229	1	2	−1658	−75
Frio	1520	1436	210	7	−2458	−505
Gaines	1238	1356	15	0	−1659	−94
Galveston	17396	13120	162	100	−7815	−4093
Garza	547	439	4	1	−695	−156
Gillespie	944	2595	1	3	−273	+379
Glasscock	94	326	1	0	−259	+12
Goliad	564	579	2	0	−796	+90
Gonzales	1634	1292	5	1	−1532	+205
Gray	2658	3792	1	2	−1459	+775
Grayson	7534	6835	30	13	−6077	+499
Gregg	7230	9763	29	13	−4941	+666
Grimes	2076	1388	3	4	−763	+730
Guadalupe	3550	5081	31	6	−3533	−137
Hale	3207	3356	98	11	−3008	+99
Hall	817	513	0	2	−348	+123
Hamilton	1051	1025	1	1	−806	−195
Hansford	582	897	0	0	−682	−13
Hardeman	1198	668	2	0	−591	+332
Hardin	5331	3127	3	2	−1934	+1473
Harris	167814	190728	1025	849	−8306	+77924
Harrison	4611	4008	28	17	−4940	−416
Hartley	573	645	2	0	−466	+110
Haskell	1554	854	3	0	−1359	+74
Hays	3819	2657	46	12	−2914	−742
Hemphill	435	511	0	1	−534	−21
Henderson	4304	3819	7	3	−2546	+384
Hidalgo	17697	13557	448	128	−9513	+3939
Hill	2453	2199	5	2	−2965	+317
Hockley	2680	1821	22	3	−1884	−71
Hood	1716	1580	2	1	−631	+596
Hopkins	2684	1704	2	0	−2962	−20
Houston	2419	1280	3	0	−2320	−313

County	John Hill	Bill Clements	Mario C. Compean	Sara J. Johnston	Primary Difference[2]	Hill Difference[3]
Howard	2676	3575	68	8	−3714	+55
Hudspeth	221	247	4	3	−443	−80
Hunt	4404	3613	2	6	−4306	−197
Hutchinson	2884	3670	3	7	−1597	+941
Irion	152	219	1	0	−265	+5
Jack	869	677	0	0	−592	+344
Jackson	1549	1400	4	1	−1077	+364
Jasper	2969	1692	1	2	−2633	−167
Jeff Davis	189	278	1	0	−366	−46
Jefferson	24693	16034	54	90	−7124	+7600
Jim Hogg	1359	311	15	0	−864	+75
Jim Wells	3102	2339	58	5	−5690	−962
Johnson	5684	4658	6	8	−2674	+1678
Jones	2367	1784	6	0	−2090	+420
Karnes	1413	1394	9	2	−1842	+214
Kaufman	3342	2456	2	2	−2920	−57
Kendall	994	2284	0	3	−114	+448
Kenedy	62	63	2	0	−104	+8
Kent	330	194	0	0	−341	−21
Kerr	2391	5283	7	2	−623	+1042
Kimble	461	702	4	1	−439	+196
King	67	79	0	0	−65	−17
Kinney	235	332	0	1	−664	−154
Kleberg	2512	2176	140	8	−2265	−80
Knox	918	390	0	0	−383	+292
Lamar	4735	2909	5	11	−4169	−35
Lamb	2261	1851	36	5	−1393	+53
Lampasas	1178	1337	1	1	−1651	−111
La Salle	1004	805	237	5	−249	+489
Lavaca	2096	1483	3	2	−1246	+470
Lee	1030	781	1	0	−746	−44
Leon	1189	812	3	0	−1701	−239
Liberty	3720	2476	0	2	−3775	−396
Limestone	2541	1690	0	0	−1562	+559
Lipscomb	378	553	0	0	−776	−250
Live Oak	725	1111	3	0	−1754	−274
Llano	1577	1632	3	0	−1160	−7
Loving	19	38	0	0	−31	−6
Lubbock	16963	21094	528	76	−9959	+2948
Lynn	1203	807	11	0	−1002	+20
McCulloch	936	1198	0	0	−1407	+26
McLennan	17405	16642	100	15	−15379	+3064
McMullen	102	224	2	1	−176	+6

County	John Hill	Bill Clements	Mario C. Compean	Sara J. Johnston	Primary Difference[2]	Hill Difference[3]
Madison	930	600	1	1	−1455	−319
Marion	1091	727	1	1	−872	+169
Martin	366	666	1	2	−826	−4
Mason	527	803	1	0	+34	+315
Matagorda	2478	2356	8	3	−2315	+223
Maverick	1627	606	36	0	−2064	−901
Medina	1872	2852	26	2	−2962	+168
Menard	375	398	0	0	−258	+123
Midland	4632	13808	80	30	−558	+2541
Milam	2935	1674	5	1	−2080	+72
Mills	639	584	0	1	−956	−53
Mitchell	947	866	2	1	−966	+108
Montague	1901	1568	1	2	−1288	+602
Montgomery	7159	8998	23	14	−7612	−975
Moore	1325	1599	3	1	−2517	−713
Morris	1622	1101	0	2	−1388	−22
Motley	295	381	0	0	−475	−102
Nacogdoches	3728	3026	6	15	−2598	−4
Navarro	3992	2681	6	1	−4662	−772
Newton	1454	503	2	2	−638	−169
Nolan	1859	1790	2	3	−1965	−20
Nueces	25702	21472	634	131	−12671	+3797
Ochiltree	478	1328	0	0	−1064	−144
Oldham	361	319	0	0	−471	−64
Orange	7492	4572	4	10	−5095	+179
Palo Pinto	2487	2011	3	3	−2451	+374
Panola	2044	1743	1	2	−3150	−259
Parker	4328	3517	2	5	−3091	+493
Parmer	1164	1212	7	0	−627	+57
Pecos	1172	1705	20	6	−2845	−305
Polk	2305	1418	1	1	−3336	−1319
Potter	7188	7491	73	36	−3764	+1373
Presidio	521	447	8	4	−732	−32
Rains	675	309	0	0	−691	−90
Randall	6235	9854	22	10	−1401	+2102
Reagan	299	514	0	0	−813	−191
Real	347	569	12	1	−782	−2
Red River	1652	1086	2	1	−2343	−300
Reeves	1627	1660	261	12	−2368	+534
Refugio	1725	1202	17	2	−1408	+632
Roberts	134	253	0	0	−148	−6
Robertson	2042	788	1	4	−1600	+64
Rockwall	1128	1676	4	1	−2004	−472

County	John Hill	Bill Clements	Mario C. Compean	Sara J. Johnston	Primary Difference[2]	Hill Difference[3]
Runnels	1142	1671	6	3	−911	+435
Rusk	3217	3346	13	10	−4719	−1276
Sabine	1104	469	1	2	−1770	−652
San Augustine	1136	584	1	2	−1036	−219
San Jacinto	1093	699	2	1	−2021	−664
San Patricio	4232	4250	88	23	−5927	−284
San Saba	927	606	3	2	−318	+362
Schleicher	290	489	0	0	−531	+94
Scurry	1410	2183	22	4	−2874	−222
Shackelford	532	505	0	0	−709	−57
Shelby	2229	1514	1	1	−2958	−503
Sherman	437	524	1	1	−446	−35
Smith	10232	14133	23	16	−7338	+1030
Somervell	700	365	1	0	−669	+103
Starr	3591	466	32	3	−951	+818
Stephens	944	1012	2	1	−1480	−39
Sterling	121	230	0	0	−253	+12
Stonewall	448	237	0	0	−616	−44
Sutton	366	612	6	0	−461	+92
Swisher	2123	620	8	2	−353	+462
Tarrant	63662	70709	327	290	−17089	+20119
Taylor	9526	12576	46	38	−2610	+1956
Terrell	151	265	6	0	−305	−12
Terry	1612	1502	17	1	−1208	−95
Throckmorton	400	230	1	0	−446	−2
Titus	2108	1505	1	0	−2513	−320
Tom Green	6674	7773	46	22	−3412	+2499
Travis	48382	38856	811	456	−19590	+4199
Trinity	1340	676	4	1	−1336	−207
Tyler	1653	1107	3	1	−1668	−276
Upshur	2509	1923	2	0	−2820	−464
Upton	357	653	1	1	−678	−30
Uvalde	1306	3158	47	0	−4016	+547
Val Verde	2607	2732	15	4	−1273	+1151
Van Zandt	3550	2504	5	3	−3237	−222
Victoria	5211	6291	94	24	−4659	+306
Walker	3059	2504	1	3	−3530	−1046
Waller	1595	1509	1	4	−1938	−171
Ward	847	1532	9	1	−1958	−394
Washington	1825	2073	1	3	−2163	−645
Webb	5433	3019	255	38	−10686	−4812
Wharton	3619	3086	9	8	−2428	+437
Wheeler	906	769	0	2	−1233	−246

County	John Hill	Bill Clements	Mario C. Compean	Sara J. Johnston	Primary Difference[2]	Hill Difference[3]
Wichita	11312	10348	33	27	−3355	+4415
Wilbarger	1688	1259	0	0	−2620	−461
Willacy	1473	1100	18	6	−1194	+39
Williamson	6089	5943	22	15	−3501	+831
Wilson	1790	1555	12	2	−3108	−528
Winkler	997	1413	8	1	−1077	+43
Wise	2545	1888	3	2	−1025	+704
Wood	2427	2080	1	5	−2680	−423
Yoakum	759	889	7	1	−1355	+307
Young	1999	1713	1	1	−1312	+338
Zapata	765	416	5	2	−965	−36
Zavala	1204	741	2036	5	+285	+936
TOTAL	**1,166,919**	**1,183,828**	**14,213**	**4,624**	**−610,939**	**+234,574**
	(49.24%)	(49.96%)	(0.59%)	(0.19%)	(−34.4%)	(+25.2%)

GUBERNATORIAL VOTING TRENDS, 1974–1982[1]

County	John Hill	Bill Clements	Democrats +/- 1974[2]	Republicans +/- 1974	Democrats +/-1982	Republicans +/- 1982
Anderson	3777	3180	+659	+2436	+1271	+525
Andrews	753	1588	−204	+1129	+390	−32
Angelina	5384	3499	−28	+1793	+4028	+1787
Aransas	1072	1516	+171	+1037	+754	+416
Archer	939	672	−280	+514	+482	+331
Armstrong	353	354	−114	+140	+70	+100
Atascosa	2210	2030	+382	+1408	+1048	+523
Austin	1665	1845	+253	+1239	+657	+304
Bailey	715	819	−2	+333	+296	+197
Bandera	1028	1580	+73	+1175	−66	+109
Bastrop	2651	1820	+538	+1092	+1815	+516
Baylor	814	494	−221	+344	+228	+131
Bee	1423	2076	−1185	+1310	+1661	+162
Bell	10378	8779	+4533	+6719	+1059	+1998
Bexar	87709	79832	+22500	+42687	+12181	+16609
Blanco	708	766	+3	+494	+184	+188
Borden	149	162	−135	+84	+13	+13
Bosque	1948	1698	+163	+1271	+471	+134
Bowie	5889	5718	−1352	+4078	+3758	+1483
Brazoria	13190	12299	+3276	+7389	+6514	+2755
Brazos	7623	7298	+2811	+5348	+2018	+2090
Brewster	595	881	−15	+335	+555	+42
Briscoe	548	226	−135	+67	+100	+78
Brooks	1220	435	+6	+326	+1279	0
Brown	3548	2935	+660	+2184	+1657	+80
Burleson	1712	703	+399	+540	+755	+233
Burnet	2669	2207	+569	+1131	+572	+1759

County	John Hill	Bill Clements	Democrats +/– 1974[2]	Republicans +/– 1974	Democrats +/–1982	Republicans +/– 1982
Caldwell	2315	1727	+406	+1111	+1210	+160
Calhoun	2006	1641	+342	+1182	+1313	+365
Callahan	1476	1288	+142	+970	+319	+107
Cameron	13224	10601	+3828	+5890	+6871	+3195
Camp	998	695	–3	+503	+762	+299
Carson	975	872	–205	+280	+349	+240
Cass	3563	2521	+625	+1828	+1773	+130
Castro	1651	866	+541	+430	–127	+139
Chambers	1636	1060	–147	+620	+1382	+427
Cherokee	3679	2351	+574	+1422	+1356	+494
Childress	885	722	–379	+292	+222	+39
Clay	1458	940	–214	+688	+840	+239
Cochran	725	521	+178	+259	+79	+139
Coke	692	536	–111	+429	+225	+194
Coleman	1217	1079	–333	+803	+527	+205
Collin	8232	13779	–1251	+8942	+6099	+11072
Collingsworth	783	474	–152	+188	+105	–3
Colorado	1699	1494	–277	+860	+736	+391
Comal	3017	5035	–490	+2939	+756	+1393
Comanche	1784	935	+1	+669	+914	+950
Concho	498	446	–174	+350	+216	–84
Cooke	2442	3000	+149	+2177	+1259	+885
Coryell	2493	2475	+551	+1883	+325	+769
Cottle	579	263	–179	+179	+174	–32
Crane	322	685	–479	+521	+521	+51
Crockett	349	541	–161	+440	+99	–91
Crosby	1473	668	+549	+309	–171	–14
Culberson	333	392	–68	+284	+238	–48
Dallam	517	651	–155	+262	+156	+39
Dallas	108617	154901	+7970	+77628	+46720	+32755
Dawson	1770	2155	+293	+1319	+285	–363
Deaf Smith	1680	1787	+359	+928	+397	+595
Delta	809	292	–340	+120	+399	+23
Denton	9870	11630	+2576	+7689	+5243	+6513
De Witt	1471	1889	+70	+1192	+567	+398
Dickens	794	266	+38	+104	+65	–6
Dimmit	1327	925	–420	+714	+855	–180
Donley	725	502	+16	+199	+26	+30
Duval	2188	692	–826	+618	+1246	+162
Eastland	2230	1834	–420	+1231	+1065	+330
Ector	5174	13491	0	+10085	+4783	+20
Edwards	189	351	–122	+278	+46	–17
Ellis	4758	4256	+168	+3301	+3229	+1048

County	John Hill	Bill Clements	Democrats +/- 1974[2]	Republicans +/- 1974	Democrats +/-1982	Republicans +/- 1982
El Paso	31809	23490	+7592	+9449	+5916	+8402
Erath	2413	2273	−411	+1421	+1562	+351
Falls	2634	1543	+792	+1258	+316	+199
Fannin	4207	2171	+1100	+1734	+1311	−364
Fayette	2150	1726	+245	+1039	+880	+728
Fisher	1178	560	+84	+449	+299	−135
Floyd	1255	997	+87	+390	+113	+12
Foard	669	178	+118	+127	−75	+28
Fort Bend	7750	11298	+2548	+8216	+4657	+4103
Franklin	719	379	−91	+283	+515	+232
Freestone	1493	1229	−1	+972	+1149	+190
Frio	1520	1436	−660	+1193	+636	−219
Gaines	1238	1356	+252	+852	−149	−303
Galveston	17396	13120	+3532	+7122	+11345	+1846
Garza	547	439	+48	+190	+29	+35
Gillespie	944	2595	−588	+1205	+444	+526
Glasscock	94	326	−210	+276	+82	−62
Goliad	564	579	+50	+424	+372	+261
Gonzales	1634	1292	+36	+949	+399	+302
Gray	2658	3792	−419	+1082	+582	+631
Grayson	7534	6835	−35	+4462	+5293	−1477
Gregg	7230	9763	+228	+5575	+6123	+602
Grimes	2076	1388	+796	+1081	+93	−177
Guadalupe	3550	5081	+895	+3081	+1640	+1824
Hale	3207	3356	+500	+1283	+390	+592
Hall	817	513	−384	+153	+296	+36
Hamilton	1051	1025	−183	+757	+449	−24
Hansford	582	897	−223	+296	+13	+225
Hardeman	1198	668	+50	+437	−112	−147
Hardin	5331	3127	+3107	+2500	+1891	−203
Harris	167814	190728	+37192	+94491	+72465	+40317
Harrison	4611	4008	+386	+2437	+2070	+2573
Hartley	573	645	−76	+394	+70	+58
Haskell	1554	854	−210	+713	+102	+184
Hays	3819	2657	+698	+1125	+1684	+1205
Hemphill	435	511	−34	+162	+194	+185
Henderson	4304	3819	+600	+2694	+3245	+678
Hidalgo	17697	13557	+8930	+8964	+13595	+4214
Hill	2453	2199	−377	+1705	+1624	+212
Hockley	2680	1821	+346	+932	−220	+267
Hood	1716	1580	+217	+1283	+720	+1007
Hopkins	2684	1704	+104	+1225	+1533	+355
Houston	2419	1280	+671	+897	+1305	+275

County	John Hill	Bill Clements	Democrats +/– 1974[2]	Republicans +/– 1974	Democrats +/–1982	Republicans +/– 1982
Howard	2676	3575	–2153	+2107	+2019	+49
Hudspeth	221	247	–475	+115	+99	+9
Hunt	4404	3613	+652	+2489	+3208	+1386
Hutchinson	2884	3670	–334	+1087	+311	+614
Irion	152	219	–76	+143	+113	+49
Jack	869	677	+12	+503	+332	+197
Jackson	1549	1400	+52	+980	+751	+358
Jasper	2969	1692	+983	+1175	+2059	+430
Jeff Davis	189	278	–42	+194	+73	+3
Jefferson	24693	16034	+1619	+6761	+15337	+2673
Jim Hogg	1359	311	+149	+24	+167	–60
Jim Wells	3102	2339	–31	+1643	+3218	+303
Johnson	5684	4658	+783	+3385	+4578	+1846
Jones	2367	1784	–596	+1314	–745	+991
Karnes	1413	1394	+21	+1056	+558	+118
Kaufman	3342	2456	+536	+1788	+2904	+1003
Kendall	994	2284	–13	+1343	+13	+455
Kenedy	62	63	–75	+52	+91	–21
Kent	330	194	–17	+125	+108	–22
Kerr	2391	5283	–465	+3312	+633	+875
Kimble	461	702	–367	+533	+78	–103
King	67	79	–50	+58	+48	+4
Kinney	235	332	–230	+288	+355	+82
Kleberg	2512	2176	–328	+1417	+1634	+70
Knox	918	390	–106	+276	+71	+51
Lamar	4735	2909	–586	+1553	+2259	+83
Lamb	2261	1851	+473	+997	–237	–64
Lampasas	1178	1337	+72	+1030	+970	–25
La Salle	1004	805	–203	+691	+632	–87
Lavaca	2096	1483	+267	+1096	+769	+489
Lee	1030	781	+145	+443	+762	+244
Leon	1189	812	+7	+647	+637	+111
Liberty	3720	2476	+638	+1623	+3213	+1002
Limestone	2541	1690	+657	+1388	+727	–47
Lipscomb	378	553	–123	+101	+113	+112
Live Oak	725	1111	–244	+833	+460	+108
Llano	1577	1632	+245	+831	+770	+388
Loving	19	38	–15	+27	+1	–1
Lubbock	16963	21094	+6750	+7481	+3952	+4128
Lynn	1203	807	+232	+431	–56	+93
McCulloch	936	1198	–197	+1023	+834	+232
McLennan	17405	16642	+2178	+11736	+5307	+1959
McMullen	102	224	–103	+173	+33	–36

County	John Hill	Bill Clements	Democrats +/– 1974[2]	Republicans +/– 1974	Democrats +/–1982	Republicans +/– 1982
Madison	930	600	+25	+474	+484	–130
Marion	1091	727	–78	+476	+665	+331
Martin	366	666	–302	+541	+219	–147
Mason	527	803	–54	+527	+29	–153
Matagorda	2478	2356	+138	+1665	+1380	+432
Maverick	1627	606	+701	+454	+1193	+72
Medina	1872	2852	–760	+2232	+1037	+53
Menard	375	398	–134	+275	+104	+53
Midland	4632	13808	–320	+9032	+1379	+1954
Milam	2935	1674	+869	+1229	+1201	+40
Mills	639	584	–66	+457	+285	–35
Mitchell	947	866	–439	+615	+438	+52
Montague	1901	1568	–149	+1214	+1123	+196
Montgomery	7159	8998	+93	+5785	+7064	+5887
Moore	1325	1599	–323	+510	+344	+418
Morris	1622	1101	+70	+818	+1261	+179
Motley	295	381	–126	+218	+67	–63
Nacogdoches	3728	3026	–452	+1638	+1241	+1331
Navarro	3992	2681	+750	+1952	+1528	+220
Newton	1454	503	+349	+313	+1630	+13
Nolan	1859	1790	–212	+1232	+688	–113
Nueces	25702	21472	+5357	+13618	+12753	+3885
Ochiltree	478	1328	–432	+118	+439	+509
Oldham	361	319	–65	+96	+5	+6
Orange	7492	4572	–937	+2891	+7791	+965
Palo Pinto	2487	2011	–39	+1489	+1612	+470
Panola	2044	1743	–123	+1192	+1020	+448
Parker	4328	3517	+15	+2381	+2648	+1516
Parmer	1164	1212	–53	+429	–167	+220
Pecos	1172	1705	+9	+1320	+391	–142
Polk	2305	1418	+500	+988	+1867	+386
Potter	7188	7491	+55	+2180	+1856	+1821
Presidio	521	447	–325	+311	+383	–19
Rains	675	309	+38	+220	+676	+251
Randall	6235	9854	+523	+3112	+1664	+4609
Reagan	299	514	–125	+414	+211	–9
Real	347	569	–29	+520	+370	+70
Red River	1652	1086	–965	+607	+1275	+55
Reeves	1627	1660	+678	+1350	+876	+105
Refugio	1725	1202	+770	+968	–269	–228
Roberts	134	253	–138	+86	+46	+10
Robertson	2042	788	+94	+593	+848	+135
Rockwall	1128	1676	–45	+1192	+973	+1295

County	John Hill	Bill Clements	Democrats +/- 1974[2]	Republicans +/- 1974	Democrats +/-1982	Republicans +/- 1982
Runnels	1142	1671	−757	+1233	+442	+265
Rusk	3217	3346	−42	+1790	+1346	+1585
Sabine	1104	469	−306	+271	+550	+326
San Augustine	1136	584	+401	+437	+325	+139
San Jacinto	1093	699	+334	+484	+1388	+171
San Patricio	4232	4250	+1164	+3173	+2817	+454
San Saba	927	606	+470	+507	+237	−67
Schleicher	290	489	−202	+374	+141	−100
Scurry	1410	2183	−740	+1509	+364	−37
Shackelford	532	505	+43	+365	+72	+37
Shelby	2229	1514	+151	+1119	+752	+298
Sherman	437	524	−63	+208	−12	+74
Smith	10232	14133	+3411	+7039	+4646	+3203
Somervell	700	365	+182	+288	+227	+54
Starr	3591	466	+390	+372	+1159	+376
Stephens	944	1012	−84	+726	+452	+352
Sterling	121	230	−81	+177	+112	+10
Stonewall	448	237	−87	+173	+269	+94
Sutton	366	612	−45	+486	+146	+17
Swisher	2123	620	+478	+122	+8	+181
Tarrant	63662	70709	+3653	+41978	+44309	+32792
Taylor	9526	12576	+244	+8403	+2695	+2532
Terrell	151	265	−221	+179	+171	−1
Terry	1612	1502	+78	+696	+265	+75
Throckmorton	400	230	−113	+163	+49	+25
Titus	2108	1505	−208	+999	+1826	+661
Tom Green	6674	7773	+262	+4592	+3092	+2299
Travis	48382	38856	+14170	+11627	+26767	+11554
Trinity	1340	676	−267	+464	+982	+122
Tyler	1653	1107	−331	+641	+1327	+161
Upshur	2509	1923	+17	+1203	+1892	+715
Upton	357	653	−386	+429	+201	−163
Uvalde	1306	3158	−1882	+2876	+1470	−443
Val Verde	2607	2732	−76	+2303	+832	−399
Van Zandt	3550	2504	−3	+1688	+2230	+641
Victoria	5211	6291	+1750	+4836	+1171	+3039
Walker	3059	2504	+13	+1570	+1748	+425
Waller	1595	1509	+342	+1161	+1131	+491
Ward	847	1532	−93	+1123	+764	+14
Washington	1825	2073	+625	+1297	+1613	+1148
Webb	5433	3019	+1259	+2489	+4090	+894
Wharton	3619	3086	+778	+2277	+2331	+790
Wheeler	906	769	−265	+175	+266	+204

County	John Hill	Bill Clements	Democrats +/− 1974[2]	Republicans +/− 1974	Democrats +/−1982	Republicans +/− 1982
Wichita	11312	10348	−2168	+6428	+4012	+1259
Wilbarger	1688	1259	−960	+728	+1132	+372
Willacy	1473	1100	+406	+780	+1012	+204
Williamson	6089	5943	+1920	+4341	+4127	+2676
Wilson	1790	1555	+202	+1152	+901	+537
Winkler	997	1413	+285	+1145	+170	−403
Wise	2545	1888	+188	+1403	+1678	+538
Wood	2427	2080	+134	+1124	+1490	+806
Yoakum	759	889	−145	+375	+117	+149
Young	1999	1713	+134	+1269	+713	+769
Zapata	765	416	−90	+336	+498	+195
Zavala	1204	741	−419	+627	+888	−244
TOTAL	1,166,919	1,183,828	+150,113	+669,560	+530,951	+282,109
	(49.24%)	(49.96%)	(+14.8%)	(+130.2%)	(+45.5%)	(+23.8%)

1978 GENERAL ELECTION RESULTS BY COUNTY[1]

County	GOVERNOR		U.S. SENATE		LT. GOVERNOR	
	John Hill	Bill Clements	John Tower	Robert Krueger	William P. Hobby	Gaylord Marshall
Anderson	3777	3180	2610	4168	476	1686
Andrews	753	1588	1190	936	1421	859
Angelina	5384	3499	3466	4946	6438	2248
Aransas	1072	1516	1316	1087	1561	942
Archer	939	672	609	985	1228	292
Armstrong	353	354	359	341	464	193
Atascosa	2210	2030	2067	2023	2787	1098
Austin	1665	1845	1787	1673	2320	970
Bailey	715	819	886	624	901	519
Bandera	1028	1580	1558	1053	1510	929
Bastrop	2651	1820	1901	2555	3270	911
Baylor	814	494	523	762	942	286
Bee	1423	2076	1815	1370	2253	1129
Bell	10378	8779	9179	9398	12098	5423
Bexar	87709	79832	79889	84569	98694	54534
Blanco	708	766	775	698	897	451
Borden	149	162	158	145	208	77
Bosque	1948	1698	1635	1932	2436	1000
Bowie	5889	5718	5671	5816	8142	2778
Brazoria	13190	12299	10964	11645	17257	7355
Brazos	7623	7298	7479	7267	10272	3961
Brewster	595	881	713	743	869	492
Briscoe	548	226	295	452	590	119
Brooks	1220	435	408	1230	1365	222
Brown	3548	2935	2777	3657	4415	1788

County	GOVERNOR		U.S. SENATE		LT. GOVERNOR	
	John Hill	Bill Clements	John Tower	Robert Krueger	William P. Hobby	Gaylord Marshall
Burleson	1712	703	674	1696	1923	354
Burnet	2669	2207	2228	2563	3221	1300
Caldwell	2315	1727	1711	2191	2732	974
Calhoun	2006	1641	1446	2072	2633	762
Callahan	1476	1288	1212	1504	1963	623
Cameron	13224	10601	11093	11813	12613	7954
Camp	998	695	641	1018	1190	345
Carson	975	872	850	964	1218	549
Cass	3563	2521	2534	3394	4242	1310
Castro	1651	866	1093	1343	1835	535
Chambers	1636	1060	1080	1351	2080	627
Cherokee	3679	2351	2340	3549	4380	1296
Childress	885	722	675	881	1125	388
Clay	1458	940	841	1509	1788	443
Cochran	725	521	596	597	868	288
Coke	692	536	443	777	884	242
Coleman	1217	1079	1173	1157	1529	862
Collin	8232	13779	12101	8299	11235	9957
Collingsworth	783	474	520	707	867	286
Colorado	1699	1494	1553	1581	1986	854
Comal	3017	5035	4502	3552	4064	3671
Comanche	1784	935	954	1711	2010	557
Concho	498	446	342	594	650	205
Cooke	2442	3000	2875	2493	3283	1818
Coryell	2493	2475	2609	2311	3406	1483
Cottle	579	263	323	508	661	131
Crane	322	685	503	503	584	381
Crockett	349	541	440	449	538	248
Crosby	1473	668	837	1256	1670	323
Culberson	333	392	368	315	456	200
Dallam	517	651	614	524	69	417
Dallas	108617	154901	142290	117076	135329	106272
Dawson	1770	2155	1909	1772	2542	987
Deaf Smith	1680	1787	1926	1459	2117	1236
Delta	809	292	330	751	877	138
Denton	9870	11630	10826	10375	12363	7801
De Witt	1471	1889	1801	1531	1999	1149
Dickens	794	266	314	728	839	127
Dimmit	1327	925	840	1316	1616	395
Donley	725	502	579	603	785	309
Duval	2188	692	535	2324	2496	243

County	GOVERNOR		U.S. SENATE		LT. GOVERNOR	
	John Hill	Bill Clements	John Tower	Robert Krueger	William P. Hobby	Gaylord Marshall
Eastland	2230	1834	1789	2198	2717	1193
Ector	5174	13491	11007	7446	973	8665
Edwards	189	351	303	236	310	177
Ellis	4758	4256	4009	4902	5944	2450
El Paso	31809	23490	25324	28233	35938	16635
Erath	2413	2273	2240	2395	3131	1291
Falls	2634	1543	1448	2474	3190	616
Fannin	4207	2171	1863	4233	4748	976
Fayette	2150	1726	1753	2072	2787	910
Fisher	1178	560	629	1051	1375	215
Floyd	1255	997	984	1244	1502	612
Foard	669	178	216	581	663	81
Fort Bend	7750	11298	11229	7508	11333	7120
Franklin	719	379	378	690	840	187
Freestone	1493	1229	1144	1522	1885	656
Frio	1520	1436	1286	1561	1875	690
Gaines	1238	1356	1244	1266	1756	631
Galveston	17396	13120	12469	17560	19847	8370
Garza	547	439	471	478	667	227
Gillespie	944	2595	2444	1076	1319	2115
Glasscock	94	326	249	166	241	148
Goliad	564	579	565	548	744	317
Gonzales	1634	1292	1321	1540	2035	633
Gray	2658	3792	3703	2657	3498	2573
Grayson	7534	6835	6144	7278	9561	4251
Gregg	7230	9763	9920	6557	8580	6175
Grimes	2076	1388	1184	1983	2303	631
Guadalupe	3550	5081	5050	3565	5074	4688
Hale	3207	3356	3430	3023	4216	2100
Hall	817	513	471	739	988	280
Hamilton	1051	1025	985	1074	1322	633
Hansford	582	897	989	487	834	522
Hardeman	1198	668	691	1112	1404	296
Hardin	5331	3127	3065	5146	6364	1357
Harris	167814	190728	192381	155075	196720	136111
Harrison	4611	4008	4369	3913	5528	2063
Hartley	573	645	627	584	773	388
Haskell	1554	854	937	1404	1895	399
Hays	3819	2657	2600	3460	4609	1674
Hemphill	435	511	545	379	600	285
Henderson	4304	3819	3408	4558	5331	2171

County	GOVERNOR		U.S. SENATE		LT. GOVERNOR	
	John Hill	Bill Clements	John Tower	Robert Krueger	William P. Hobby	Gaylord Marshall
Hidalgo	17697	13557	13730	16321	17275	9768
Hill	2453	2199	1965	2551	3218	1035
Hockley	2680	1821	1931	2503	3235	1065
Hood	1716	1580	1516	1714	2152	1001
Hopkins	2684	1704	1618	2557	3236	740
Houston	2419	1280	1119	2893	2812	669
Howard	2676	3575	3226	2997	4455	1783
Hudspeth	221	247	231	218	306	106
Hunt	4404	3613	3583	4139	5262	2270
Hutchinson	2884	3670	3571	2946	3940	2270
Irion	152	219	172	195	220	120
Jack	869	677	664	859	1093	364
Jackson	1549	1400	1231	1664	2077	678
Jasper	2969	1692	1833	2723	3522	895
Jeff Davis	189	278	226	225	256	153
Jefferson	24693	16034	16582	23599	29561	9996
Jim Hogg	1359	311	628	995	1356	145
Jim Wells	3102	2339	2117	3269	3761	1243
Johnson	5684	4658	4572	5682	6941	2948
Jones	2367	1784	1656	2352	2960	744
Karnes	1413	1394	1408	1353	1934	716
Kaufman	3342	2456	2332	3392	4096	1372
Kendall	994	2284	2074	1165	1441	1658
Kenedy	62	63	58	70	101	17
Kent	330	194	180	307	378	74
Kerr	2391	5283	4690	2937	3576	3650
Kimble	461	702	604	574	716	345
King	67	79	90	51	97	31
Kinney	235	332	311	232	336	157
Kleberg	2512	2176	2117	2531	3201	1264
Knox	918	390	467	826	1090	163
Lamar	4735	2909	2587	5054	5635	1581
Lamb	2261	1851	2006	1953	2795	983
Lampasas	1178	1337	1277	1178	1564	781
La Salle	1004	805	658	1153	1039	283
Lavaca	2096	1483	1461	2101	2645	783
Lee	1030	781	802	976	1270	438
Leon	1189	812	736	1186	1378	418
Liberty	3720	2476	2734	3453	4512	1327
Limestone	2541	1690	1659	2397	3033	865
Lipscomb	378	553	590	309	492	332

| County | GOVERNOR | | U.S. SENATE | | LT. GOVERNOR | |
	John Hill	Bill Clements	John Tower	Robert Krueger	William P. Hobby	Gaylord Marshall
Live Oak	725	1111	1008	797	1101	606
Llano	1577	1632	1489	1679	2015	1067
Loving	19	38	36	20	30	21
Lubbock	16963	21094	20473	15068	23548	13490
Lynn	1203	807	824	1122	1513	352
McCulloch	936	1198	905	1182	1365	619
McLennan	17405	16642	16526	17241	22710	10074
McMullen	102	224	204	126	206	97
Madison	930	600	608	877	1109	301
Marion	1091	727	753	1033	1238	429
Martin	366	666	560	443	650	285
Mason	527	803	695	629	688	537
Matagorda	2478	2356	2243	2529	3285	1320
Maverick	1627	606	603	1582	1719	380
Medina	1872	2852	2717	1947	2908	1520
Menard	375	398	290	479	539	181
Midland	4632	13808	12672	5448	7356	9692
Milam	2935	1674	1579	2892	3449	879
Mills	639	584	518	682	828	316
Mitchell	947	866	645	1142	1243	485
Montague	4901	1568	1406	1978	2400	792
Montgomery	7159	8998	8116	6349	9749	6003
Moore	1325	1599	1465	1430	1349	1473
Morris	1622	1101	1174	1491	1968	555
Motley	295	381	379	281	401	212
Nacogdoches	3728	3026	2901	3449	4695	1822
Navarro	3992	2681	2639	3939	4762	1550
Newton	1454	503	497	1401	1580	267
Nolan	1859	1790	1867	1654	2530	901
Nueces	25702	21472	22076	24306	31358	12573
Ochiltree	478	1328	1316	462	909	762
Oldham	361	319	337	339	483	161
Orange	7492	4572	4503	7465	8694	2836
Palo Pinto	2487	2011	1982	2512	3126	1189
Panola	2044	1743	1631	2055	2711	808
Parker	4328	3517	3622	4158	5290	2263
Parmer	1164	1212	1376	954	1428	789
Pecos	1172	1705	1158	1495	1933	875
Polk	2305	1418	1419	2156	2651	764
Potter	7188	7491	7343	7133	9170	5024
Presidio	521	447	388	505	656	218

County	GOVERNOR		U.S. SENATE		LT. GOVERNOR	
	John Hill	Bill Clements	John Tower	Robert Krueger	William P. Hobby	Gaylord Marshall
Rains	675	309	375	594	722	176
Randall	6235	9854	9794	5882	8936	6830
Reagan	299	514	863	436	529	251
Real	347	569	414	482	543	251
Red River	1652	1086	1008	1634	1971	472
Reeves	1627	1660	1211	1701	2264	729
Refugio	1725	1202	1127	1741	2188	509
Roberts	134	253	231	153	213	151
Robertson	2042	788	767	1980	2296	394
Rockwall	1128	1676	1541	1219	1472	1161
Runnels	1142	1671	1345	1464	1777	836
Rusk	3217	3346	3422	2679	3388	1854
Sabine	1104	469	544	1002	1176	301
San Augustine	1136	584	601	1082	1303	299
San Jacinto	1093	699	701	1011	1251	371
San Patricio	4232	4250	4057	4138	5327	2212
San Saba	927	606	586	918	1111	270
Schleicher	290	489	380	397	490	247
Scurry	1410	2183	1907	1440	2240	1255
Shackelford	532	505	486	517	694	243
Shelby	2229	1514	1479	2177	2774	754
Sherman	437	524	499	451	596	305
Smith	10232	14133	13481	10161	12860	9840
Somervell	700	365	365	700	795	190
Starr	3591	466	856	3192	3585	272
Stephens	944	1012	1012	913	1300	529
Sterling	121	230	163	191	223	106
Stonewall	448	237	230	436	529	101
Sutton	366	612	470	455	608	286
Swisher	2123	620	790	1892	2269	358
Tarrant	63662	70709	69124	62725	73185	50406
Taylor	9526	12576	11906	9801	14729	6586
Terrell	151	265	231	182	244	144
Terry	1612	1502	1486	1550	2180	790
Throckmorton	400	230	216	397	480	110
Titus	2108	1505	1511	1997	2642	751
Tom Green	6674	7773	6280	7191	9265	480
Travis	48382	38856	40610	45754	62979	20558
Trinity	1340	676	639	1240	1451	343
Tyler	1653	1107	1049	1633	1971	603
Upshur	2509	1923	1983	2387	2983	1095

County	GOVERNOR		U.S. SENATE		LT. GOVERNOR	
	John Hill	Bill Clements	John Tower	Robert Krueger	William P. Hobby	Gaylord Marshall
Upton	357	653	522	479	589	374
Uvalde	1306	3158	2646	1699	2733	1365
Val Verde	2607	2732	2059	2569	3101	1370
Van Zandt	3550	2504	2508	3618	4309	1465
Victoria	5211	6291	6084	5062	7097	3530
Walker	3059	2504	2569	2751	3902	1190
Waller	1595	1509	1387	1649	2153	760
Ward	847	1532	1202	1147	1469	800
Washington	1825	2073	2024	1821	2557	1175
Webb	5433	3019	2703	5498	6879	1310
Wharton	3619	3086	3103	3447	4576	1762
Wheeler	906	769	809	837	1077	489
Wichita	11312	10348	10280	10226	14528	6677
Wilbarger	1688	1259	1375	1608	2139	667
Willacy	1473	1100	1163	1287	1609	685
Williamson	6089	5943	609	5828	7931	3500
Wilson	1790	1555	1533	1746	2214	911
Winkler	997	1413	1129	1199	1568	707
Wise	2545	1888	1888	2452	3004	1143
Wood	2427	2080	2013	2397	3040	1207
Yoakum	759	889	867	721	1003	550
Young	1999	1713	1720	1967	2463	1233
Zapata	765	416	414	747	840	337
Zavala[2]	1204	741	676	1303	1383	319
TOTAL	**1,166,919**	**1,183,828**	**1,151,376**	**1,139,149**	**1,434,613**	**760,642**
	(49.24%)	(49.96%)	(49.9%)	(49.3%)	(65.35%)	(34.65%)

TEXAS VOTER REGISTRATION AND TURNOUT TOTALS, 1970–1990[1]

Election	% Voter Turnout	Total Voter Turnout	Voters Registered	% Voters Registered	Voting-Age Population
1970 Democratic Primary	24.37%	1,011,300	4,149,250	57.75%	7,185,274
1970 Republican Primary	2.63%	109,021	4,149,250	57.75%	7,185,274
1970 General	53.89%	2,235,847	4,149,250	57.75%	7,185,274
1972 Democratic Primary	56.63%	2,192,903	3,872,462	50.09%	7,731,571
1972 Republican Primary	2.94%	114,007	3,872,462	50.09%	7,731,571
1972 General	86.94%	3,471,281	3,872,462	50.09%	7,731,571
1974 Democratic Primary	28.44%	1,521,306	5,348,343	64.61%	8,278,089
1974 Republican Primary	1.29%	69,101	5,348,343	64.61%	8,278,089
1974 General	30.94%	1,654,984	5,348,343	64.61%	8,278,089
1976 Democratic Primary	28.47%	1,529,168	5,370,593	60.86%	8,824,677
1976 Republican Primary	6.63%	356,307	5,370,593	60.86%	8,824,677
1976 General	64.83%	4,071,884	6,281,149	71.18%	8,824,677
1977 Amendment	9.54%	565,516	5,924,891	65.13%	9,097,491
1978 Democratic Primary	35.76%	1,812,896	5,069,267	54.09%	9,371,178
1978 Republican Primary	3.12%	158,403	5,069,267	54.09%	9,371,178
1978 General	41.71%	2,369,764	5,681,875	60.63%	9,371,178
1979 Amendment	7.79%	444,377	5,700,828	59.11%	9,643,927
1980 Democratic Primary	25.67%	1,377,767	5,367,973	53.83%	9,971,392
1980 Republican Primary	9.81%	526,769	5,367,973	53.83%	9,971,392
1980 General	68.40%	4,451,637	6,639,661	66.59%	9,971,392
1981 Amendment	12.55%	832,266	6,629,092	64.31%	10,308,552
1982 Democratic Primary	21.64%	1,318,663	6,093,632	56.95%	10,699,706
1982 Republican Primary	4.36%	265,794	6,093,632	56.95%	10,699,706
1982 General	49.74%	3,191,091	6,414,988	59.95%	10,699,706
1983 Amendment	11.75%	65,045	6,511,134	58.84%	11,065,220
1984 Democratic Primary	21.34%	1,463,449	6,859,334	60.42%	11,352,126
1984 Republican Primary	4.91%	336,814	6,859,334	60.42%	11,352,126

Election	% Voter Turnout	Total Voter Turnout	Voters Registered	% Voters Registered	Voting-Age Population
1984 General	68.32%	5,397,571	7,900,167	69.59%	11,352,126
1985 Amendment	12.05%	956,909	7,942,831	68.40%	11,613,066
1986 Democratic Primary	13.79%	1,096,552	7,951,368	67.11%	11,847,825
1986 Republican Primary	6.85%	544,719	7,951,368	67.11%	11,847,825
1986 General	47.23%	3,441,460	7,287,173	61.51%	11,847,825
1987 Amendment	30.56%	2,243,239	7,340,638	60.88%	12,056,634
1988 Democratic Primary	22.78%	1,767,045	7,757,502	63.38%	12,239,280
1988 Republican Primary	13.08%	1,014,956	7,757,502	63.38%	12,239,280
1988 General	66.17%	5,427,410	8,201,856	67.01%	12,239,280
1989 Amendment	14.12%	1,157,121	8,192,240	66.09%	12,395,782
1990 Democratic Primary	17.95%	1,487,260	8,285,307	66.14%	12,526,224
1990 Republican Primary	10.32%	855,231	8,285,307	66.14%	12,526,224
1990 General	50.55%	3,892,746	8,285,307	66.14%	12,526,224

GUBERNATORIAL ELECTION RESULTS, 1968–1990[1]

Year	Candidate	Party	Votes	Percentage	Change in Votes
1968	Preston Smith	Democratic	1,662,019	56.99%	+624,502
	Paul Eggers	Republican	1,254,333	43.01%	+886,308
TOTAL			**2,916,352**	**100.00%**	**+1,510,810**
1970	Preston Smith	Democratic	1,232,506	53.44%	−429,513
	Paul Eggers	Republican	1,073,831	46.56%	−180,502
TOTAL			**2,306,337**	**100.00%**	**−610,015**
1972	Dolph Briscoe	Democratic	1,633,493	47.96%	+399,987
	Henry C. Grover	Republican	1,533,986	45.04%	+460,155
	Ramsey Muniz	La Raza Unida	214,118	6.29%	—
	Deborah Leonard	Socialist	24,103	0.71%	—
TOTAL			**3,405,700**	**100.00%**	**+1,099,363**
1974	Dolph Briscoe	Democratic	1,016,334	61.42%	−617,159
	Jim Granberry	Republican	514,725	31.11%	−1,019,261
	Ramsey Muniz	La Raza Unida	93,295	5.64%	−120,823
	S. W. McDonnell	American	22,208	1.34%	—
	Sherry Smith	Socialist	8,171	0.49%	−15,932
TOTAL			**1,654,733**	**100.00%**	**−1,750,967**
1978	Bill Clements	Republican	1,183,828	49.96%	+669,103
	John Hill	Democratic	1,166,919	49.24%	+150,585
	Mario Compean	La Raza Unida	14,213	0.59%	−79,082
	Sara J. Johnston	Socialist Worker	4,624	0.19%	−3,547
TOTAL			**2,369,584**	**100.00%**	**+714,851**

Year	Candidate	Party	Votes	Percentage	Change in Votes
1982	Mark White	Democratic	1,697,870	53.21%	+530,951
	Bill Clements	Republican	1,465,937	45.94%	+282,109
	David Hutzelman	Independent	19,143	0.61%	—
	Bob Poteet	Constitution	8,065	0.25%	—
TOTAL			**3,188,015**	**100.00%**	**+818,431**
1986	Bill Clements	Republican	1,813,779	52.71%	+347,842
	Mark White	Democratic	1,584,515	46.05%	−113,355
	Theresa Doyle	Libertarian	42,496	1.24%	—
TOTAL			**3,440,790**	**100.00%**	**+252,775**
1990	Ann W. Richards	Democratic	1,925,670	49.47%	+341,155
	Clayton Williams	Republican	1,826,431	46.92%	+12,652
	Jeff Daiell	Libertarian	129,128	3.32%	+86,632
	Write-Ins		11,517	0.29%	—
TOTAL			**3,892,746**	**100.00%**	**+451,956**

NOTES

CHAPTER 1

1. *Austin American-Statesman,* November 9, 1978; *Dallas Morning News,* November 9, 1978.

2. U.S. Department of Labor, Bureau of Labor Statistics, Employment and Earnings, States and Areas, 1939–78 (Washington, D.C.: U.S. Government Printing Office): 620–623.

3. For more information on Reconstruction in Texas, see Randolph B. Campbell, *Grass-Roots Reconstruction in Texas, 1865–1880* (Baton Rouge, La.: Louisiana State University Press, 1997); and James M. Smallwood, *Time of Hope, Time of Despair: Black Texans During Reconstruction* (Port Washington, NY: Kennikut Press, 1981).

4. For more on Reconstruction, see James M. Smallwood, Barry A. Crouch, and Larry Peacock, *Murder and Mayhem: The War of Reconstruction in Texas* (College Station, Tex.: Texas A&M University Press, 2003). For a brief synopsis on the history of southern politics after Reconstruction, see George Brown Tindall, *The Persistent Tradition in New South Politics* (Baton Rouge, La.: Louisiana State University Press, 1975).

5. Campbell, *Grass-Roots Reconstruction in Texas,* 24; James Marten, *Texas Divided: Loyalty and Dissent in the Lone Star State, 1856–1874* (Lexington, Ky.: University Press of Kentucky, 1990), 145.

6. James Lamare, J. L. Polinard, and Robert D. Winkle, "Texas: Lone Star (Wars) State," in *The New Politics of the Old South,* ed. Charles S. Bullock and Bradley R. Rice (New York: Rowman and Littlefield, 1983), 246.

7. "Texas Secretary of State," www.sos.state.tx.us.

8. George Brown Tindall, *The Emergence of the New South, 1913–1945* (Baton Rouge: Louisiana State University Press, 1967), 251.

9. George Norris Green, *The Establishment in Texas Politics* (Westport, Conn.: Greenwood Press, 1979), 12.

10. V. O. Key Jr., *Southern Politics in State and Nation* (New York: Alfred A. Knopf, 1949), 259.

11. Numan V. Bartley and Hugh D. Graham, *Southern Politics and the Second Reconstruction* (Baltimore: Johns Hopkins, 1975), 24.

12. Ricky F. Dobbs, "Towards a Two-Party South: Allan Shivers and Texas Politics, 1934–1957" (Ph. D. diss., Texas A&M University, 1996), 36–37.

13. Green, *The Establishment in Texas Politics*, 16.

14. Ibid., 17.

15. Chandler Davidson, *Race and Class in Texas Politics* (Princeton, N.J.: Princeton, 1990): 159.

16. Ibid.

17. Dobbs, "Towards a Two-Party South," 40–41.

18. David C. Perry and Alfred J. Watkins, "People, Profit, and the Rise of the Sunbelt Cities," in *The Rise of the Sunbelt Cities*, ed. David C. Perry and Alfred J. Watkins (Beverly Hills, Cal.: Sage Publications, 1978): 288.

19. David R. Goldfield, *Cotton Fields and Skyscrapers: Southern City and Region, 1607–1980* (Baton Rouge, La.: Louisiana State University Press), 150.

20. Ibid., 142.

21. Perry and Watkins, "People, Profit, and the Rise of the Sunbelt Cities," 280.

22. Lamare et al., "Texas: Lone Star (Wars) State," 246.

23. Green, *The Establishment in Texas Politics*, 3.

24. Charles L. Prysby and John W. Books, *Political Behavior and the Local Context* (New York: Praegar, 1991): 102.

25. Marten, *Texas Divided*, 145–151; and Key, *Southern Politics in State and Nation*, 275.

26. David R. Goldfield, *Black, White, and Southern: Race Relations and Southern Culture, 1940 to the Present* (Baton Rouge, La.: Louisiana State University Press, 1990), 195.

27. Key, *Southern Politics in State and Nation*, 255.

28. Bernard L. Weinstein and Robert E. Firestine, *Regional Growth and Decline in the United States: The Rise of the Sunbelt and the Decline of the Northeast* (New York: Praeger Publishers, 1978): 19.

29. Gordon E. Baker studies the relationship between urban and rural political power that had developed by the mid-twentieth century in Gordon E. Baker, *Rural versus Urban Political Power* (New York: Random House, 1955).

30. Dobbs, "Towards a Two-Party South," 146.

31. Ibid., 191.

32. Davidson, *Race and Class in Texas Politics*, 160.

33. Dobbs, "Towards a Two-Party South," 203.

34. Numan V. Bartley and Hugh D. Graham, *Southern Politics and the Second Reconstruction* (Baltimore: Johns Hopkins Press, 1975): 185.

35. Ibid., 83.

36. Nicol C. Rae, *The Decline and Fall of the Liberal Republicans: From 1952 to the Present* (New York: Oxford University Press, 1989), 49.

37. Earl Black, *Southern Governors and Civil Rights: Racial Segregation as a Campaign Issue in the Second Reconstruction* (Cambridge, Mass.: Harvard University Press, 1976), 45.

38. Davidson, *Race and Class in Texas Politics*, 164.

39. Numan V. Bartley, *The New South 1945–1980* (Baton Rouge, La.: Louisiana State University Press, 1995), 196.

40. Black, *Southern Governors and Civil Rights*, 128.

41. Davidson, *Race and Class in Texas Politics*, 178.

42. Green, *The Establishment in Texas Politics*, 198.

43. *Dallas Times Herald*, November 1, 1960.

44. John Tower Papers, Special Collections, Southwestern University, Georgetown, Tex.

45. Alexander P. Lamis, *The Two-Party South* (New York: Oxford University Press, 1988), 195.

46. Ibid., 195–196.

47. Bartley, *The New South*, 387; R. K. Gaddie and Scott E. Buchanan, "Oklahoma: GOP Realignment in the Buckle of the Bible Belt," *The New Politics of the Old South: An Introduction to Southern Politics*, ed. Charles S. Bullock III and Mark J. Rozell (New York: Rowman & Littlefield Publishers, 1998): 207.

48. Green, *The Establishment in Texas Politics*, 9.

49. Goldfield, *Black, White, and Southern*, 195.

50. Lamis, *The Two-Party South*, 196.

51. Goldfield, *Black, White, and Southern*, 195.

52. Wayne Parent and Peter A. Petrakis, "Populism Left and Right: Politics of the Rural South," In *The Rural South Since World War II*, ed. R. Douglas Hurt (Baton Rouge, La.: Louisiana State University Press, 1998): 151.

53. Howard P. Chudacoff and Judith E. Smith, *The Evolution of American Urban Society*, 4th ed. (Englewood Cliffs, N.J.: Prentice Hall, 1994), 262–263.

54. Goldfield, *Black, White, and Southern*, 203.

55. Ibid., Goldfield, *Cotton Fields and Skyscrapers*, 165.

56. Lamis, *The Two-Party South*, 196.

57. Davidson, *Race and Class in Texas Politics*, 201.

58. Parent and Petrakis, "Populism Left and Right," 150.

59. Bartley and Graham, *Southern Politics and the Second Reconstruction*, 127.

60. Malcolm E. Jewell, *Parties and Primaries: Nominating State Governors* (New York: Praeger): 215.

61. Parent and Petrakis, "Populism Left and Right," 151.

62. Lamis, *The Two-Party South*, 209.

63. Bartley and Graham, *Southern Politics and the Second Reconstruction*, 134–35.

64. Black, *Southern Governors and Civil Rights*, 126–27.

65. Jerry Conn, *Preston Smith: The Making of a Texas Governor* (Austin: Jenkins Publishing Co., 1972), 74.

66. Wanda Evans, *Preston Smith: The People's Governor* (Lubbock, Tex.: Millenia Books, 1999): 64–67.

67. Green, *The Establishment in Texas Politics*, 196.

68. U.S. Department of Commerce, Bureau of the Census, Statistical Abstract of the United States, 1979 (Washington, D.C.: U.S. Government Printing Office), 449, 465.

69. Jackson, *Crabgrass Frontier*, 154.

70. Key, *Southern Politics in State and Nation*, 673.

71. David R. Goldfield, *Region, Race, and Cities: Interpreting the Urban South* (Baton Rouge, La.: Louisiana State University Press, 1997), 290.

72. Goldfield, *Cotton Fields and Skyscrapers*, 192–93.

73. Bob Bullock, *The Texas Economy—1970 and 1980* (Austin: Comptroller of Public Accounts, 1981), 1.

74. Goldfield, *Cotton Fields and Skyscrapers,* 152.

75. Beth Anne Shelton et al. *Houston: Growth and Decline in a Sunbelt Boomtown* (Philadelphia: Temple University Press, 1989), 22.

76. Ibid., 19.

77. Ibid., 11.

78. Goldfield, *Black, White, and Southern,* 246.

79. Bullard, *Invisible Houston,* 135–36.

80. Kenneth T. Jackson, *Crabgrass Frontier: The Suburbanization of the U.S.* (New York: Oxford University Press, 1985), 154.

81. Patricia Evridge Hill, *Dallas: The Making of a Modern City* (Austin: University of Texas Press, 1996), 164.

82. Clifton McCleskey et al., *The Government and Politics of Texas* (Boston: Little, Brown): 11.

83. Davidson, *Race and Class in Texas Politics,* 65.

84. Ibid., 69.

85. Bullock, *The Texas Economy—1970 and 1980,* 3–4.

86. Ibid., 168; and Black, *Southern Governors and Civil Rights,* 131.

87. Ann Fears Crawford and Crystal S. Ragsdale, *Women in Texas: Their Lives, Their Experiences, Their Accomplishments* (Burnet, Tex.: Eakin Press, 1982): 290.

88. McCleskey et al. *The Government and Politics of Texas,* 94–95.

89. "Texas Secretary of State," www.sos.state.tx.us.

90. Crawford and Ragsdale, *Women in Texas,* 292.

91. "Texas Secretary of State," www.sos.state.tx.us; Mike Kingston et al., ed. *The Texas Almanac's Political History of Texas* (Austin: Eakin Press, 1992), 308–315.

92. "Texas Presidential Elections," Texas Secretary of State, www.sos.state.tx.us.

93. Prysby and Books, *Political Behavior and the Local Context,* 102.

94. Alwyn Barr, *Black Texans: A History of African-American in Texas, 1528–1995,* 2nd ed. (Norman, Okla.: University of Oklahoma Press, 1996), 210.

95. Shelton et al. *Houston,* 4, 84.

96. Davidson, *Biracial Politics: Conflict and Coalition in the Metropolitan South* (Baton Rouge, La.: Louisiana State University Press, 1972): 113; Shelton et al., *Houston,* 96; and Geoffrey Fox, *Hispanic Nation: Culture, Politics, and the Constructing of Identity* (Secaucus, N.J.: Birch Lane Press, 1996), 155.

97. Shelton et al., *Houston,* 96; and Fox, *Hispanic Nation,* 155. For more on the history of Hispanic civil rights groups in Texas, see Carl Allsup, *The American G. I. Forum: Origins and Evolution* (Austin: University of Texas Press, 1982).

98. Davidson, *Biracial Politics,* 87.

99. Bullock, *The Texas Economy—1970 and 1980,* 2.

100. Bob Bullock, *1980 Census of Population: Gross Migration for Counties: 1975 to 1980* (Washington, D.C.: Government Printing Office, 1984), 222.

101. Jackson, *Crabgrass Frontier,* 155; and Arnold Fleischmann, "Sunbelt Boosterism: The Politics of Postwar Growth and Annexation in San Antonio," in *The Rise of the Sunbelt Cities,* ed. David C. Perry and Alfred J. Watkins (Beverly Hills, Cal.: Sage Publications, 1978), 168.

102. Ibid., 6; and Russell Howard, "Energy for the Growing South," in *The Economics of*

Southern Growth, ed. E. Blaine Liner and Lawrence K. Lynch (Durham, N.C.: The Southern Growth Policies Board, 1977), 90.

103. Bernard L. Weinstein and Robert E. Firestine, *Regional Growth and Decline in the United States: The Rise of the Sunbelt and the Decline of the Northeast* (New York: Praeger Publishers, 1978): 19.

104. William H. Miernyk, "The Changing Structure of the Southern Economy," in *The Economics of Southern Growth,* ed. E. Blaine Liner and Lawrence K. Lynch (Durham, N.C.: The Southern Growth Policies Board, 1977), 41.

105. U.S. Department of Labor, Bureau of Labor Statistics, Employment and Earnings, States and Areas, 1939–78 (Washington, D.C.: U.S. Government Printing Office, 1979), 620.

106. Ibid., 620.

107. Ibid., 508.

108. Ibid.

Chapter 2

1. *Dallas Morning News,* March 5, 1978, clipping in Dolph Briscoe Papers, Center for American History, University of Texas, Austin.

2. For more on the structure of Texas government and the state political system, see Richard H. Kraemer, Charldean Newell, and David F. Prindle, *Texas Politics,* 6th ed. (St. Paul, Minn.: West Publishing, 1996).

3. Malcolm E. Jewell, *Parties and Primaries: Nominating State Governors* (New York: Praeger, 1984), 214.

4. Ibid., 239.

5. Dolph Briscoe, *Report to the 66th Legislature of Texas from Dolph Briscoe, Governor of Texas 1973–1979* (Austin: State of Texas, 1979), 1.

6. Ibid., 2.

7. Dolph Briscoe, *Destiny by Choice: The Inaugural Addresses of the Governors of Texas,* ed. Marvin DeBoer (Fayetteville, Ark.: University of Arkansas Press, 1992): 438.

8. Briscoe, *Destiny By Choice,* 439.

9. Briscoe, *Report,* 7, 68.

10. Briscoe, *Destiny by Choice,* 432.

11. Briscoe, *Report,* 47.

12. Walt Parker, "Interview with Walt Parker, July 17, 1973," interview by Ron Marcello (Denton: North Texas State University, 1973), 34.

13. James F. Lea, *Contemporary Southern Politics* (Baton Rouge: Louisiana State University Press, 1988), 273.

14. Bill Clayton, "Interview with Speaker Bill Clayton, June 29, 1977," interview by Ron Marcello (Denton: North Texas State University, 1977): 30.

15. Robert Krueger, Interview with the author, New Braunfels, Texas, March 25, 2004.

16. Gibson D. Lewis, "Interview with Rep. 'Gib' Lewis, August 29, 1979," interview by Ron Marcello (Denton: North Texas State University, 1980): 47–50.

17. Lea, *Contemporary Southern Politics,* 239–40.

18. Briscoe, *Report,* 6.

19. "Bum Steer Awards '78," *Texas Monthly* (January 1978: 74–81), 78.

20. David Dean, Interview with the author, November 26, 2002.

21. Krueger, Interview with the author, March 25, 2004.

22. Chandler Davidson, *Race and Class in Texas Politics* (Princeton, N.J.: Princeton University, 1990), 80.

23. Numan V. Bartley and Hugh D. Graham, *Southern Politics and the Second Reconstruction* (Baltimore: Johns Hopkins Press, 1975), 171.

24. George Norris Green, *The Establishment in Texas Politics, The Primitive Years, 1938–1957* (Westport, Conn.: Greenwood Press, 1979), 7.

25. Oscar Mauzy, "Interview with Sen. Oscar Mauzy, July 17, 1975," interview by Ron Marcello (Denton: North Texas State University, 1975), 39.

26. Alexander P. Lamis, *The Two-Party South* (New York: Oxford University Press, 1988), 200.

27. David Montejano, *Anglos and Mexican in the Making of Texas* (Austin: University of Texas Press, 1987), 289.

28. Lamis, *The Two-Party South,* 200.

29. Montejano, *Anglos and Mexican in the Making of Texas,* 278.

30. Lamis, *The Two-Party South,* 201.

31. Montejano, *Anglos and Mexican in the Making of Texas,* 289–290.

32. David Dean, Interview with the author, Dallas, Texas, November 26, 2002.

33. *Dallas Morning News,* November 3, 1977, clipping in Dolph Briscoe Papers.

34. *Dallas Morning News,* November 8, 1977, clipping in Dolph Briscoe Papers.

35. Ibid.

36. See John L. Hill Jr., *A Practical Primer for Texas Consumers* (Austin: Attorney General's Office, State of Texas, 1975).

37. *Dallas Morning News,* November 2, 1977, clipping in Dolph Briscoe Papers.

38. John L. Hill Jr. *Oral History Interview with the Honorable John L. Hill Jr.,* Sheree Scarborough, ed. (Austin: Texas Bar Foundation, 1999), 27.

39. John L. Hill Jr., Interview with the author, Houston, Texas, September 26, 2002.

40. Ibid.

41. Ibid.

42. Dean, Interview with the author, November 26, 2002.

43. Martin V. Melosi, "Dallas-Fort Worth: Marketing the Metroplex," in *Sunbelt Cities: Politics and Growth Since World War II,* ed. Richard M. Bernard and Bradley R. Rice (Austin, Tex.: University of Texas Press, 1983: 162–95), 175.

44. Lea, *Contemporary Southern Politics,* 89.

45. Earl Black, *Southern Governors and Civil Rights: Racial Segregation as a Campaign Issue in the Second Reconstruction* (Cambridge, Mass.: Harvard University Press, 1976), 350.

46. David R. Goldfield, *Black, White, and Southern: Race Relations and Southern Culture, 1940 to the Present* (Baton Rouge: Louisiana State University Press, 1990), 178.

47. Lea, *Contemporary Southern Politics,* 83.

48. Ibid., 92–93.

49. Ibid., 94.

50. Clifton McCleskey et al. *The Government and Politics of Texas* (Boston: Little, Brown, 1978), 121.

51. Laurence Moreland et al. explore the many facets of African American political participation in *Blacks in Southern Politics* (New York: Praeger, 1987).

52. McCleskey et al. *The Government and Politics of Texas,* 119.

53. James W. Lamare, J. L. Polinard, and Robert D. Wrinkle, "Texas: Lone Star (Wars) State," in *The New Politics of the Old South: An Introduction to Southern Politics,* ed. Charles S. Bullock III and Mark J. Rozell (New York: Rowman & Littlefield Publishers, 1998), 245–60, 253.

54. David R. Johnson, "San Antonio: The Vicissitudes of Boosterism," in *Sunbelt Cities: Politics and Growth Since World War II,* ed. Richard M. Bernard and Bradley R. Rice (Austin: University of Texas Press, 198): 232–54, 248.

55. Louis DeSipio, *Counting on the Latino Vote: Latinos as a New Electorate* (Charlottesville, Va.: University of Virginia Press, 1996), 112.

56. Lamare, "Texas: Lone Star (Wars) State," 253.

57. Black, *Southern Governors and Civil Rights,* 126–27.

58. Bartley, Graham, *Southern Politics and the Second Reconstruction,* 83.

59. Lamis, *The Two-Party South,* 197–98.

60. Ibid.

61. Earl Black and Merle Black, *The Vital South: How Presidents Are Elected* (Cambridge, Mass.: Harvard University Press, 1992), 332.

62. Poll, March 1977, John Tower Papers, Special Collections, Southwestern University, Georgetown, Tex.

63. Ibid.

64. *Dallas Morning News,* March 5, 1978, clipping in Dolph Briscoe Papers.

65. Jerry Conn, *Preston Smith: The Making of a Texas Governor* (Austin: Jenkins Publishing Co., 1972), 40.

66. Ibid., 60.

67. Ibid., 76–77.

68. Ibid., 125–26.

69. Preston Smith, *Destiny By Choice,* 427.

70. Ibid., 431.

71. Ibid.

72. See Preston Smith, *Programs for People* (Austin: State of Texas, 1973).

73. Ibid., 13.

74. Green, *The Establishment in Texas Politics,* 205.

75. Lewis, "Oral Interview," 45, 47.

76. Tom Creighton, "Interview with Sen. Tom Creighton, July 15, 1975," interview by Ron Marcello (Denton: North Texas State University, 1976), 2.

77. Parker, "Oral Interview," 4, 31.

78. Oscar Mauzy, "Interview with Sen. Oscar Mauzy, October 23, 1978," interview by Ron Marcello (Denton: North Texas State University, 1979): 45.

79. *Dallas Morning News,* November 3, 1977, clipping in Dolph Briscoe Papers.

80. Jon Ford, "Dolph, John, and Preston," *Texas Monthly* (November 1977): 110.

81. Hill, Interview with the author, September 26, 2002.

82. Ford, "Dolph, John, and Preston," *Texas Monthly* (November 1977): 110.

83. Ibid.

84. David Dean, Interview with the author, November 26, 2002.

85. John Bloom, "Two for the Road," *Texas Monthly* (April 1978): 74.

86. Ibid.

87. Ibid.

88. Ibid., 75.

89. Texas State Library, Prints and Photographs Collection, Dolph Briscoe, www.tsl.state
.tx.us/governors/modern/briscoe-p03.html.

90. Cora Oltersdorf, *The Alcalde* 88 (September/October 2000), http://utopia.utexas
.edu/articles/alcalde/briscoe.html?sec=texas%E2%8A%82=law.

91. Texas State Library, www.tsl.state.tx.us/governors/modern/briscoe-p03.html.

92. Fred Agnich, "Interview with Rep. Fred Agnich, September 9, 1977," interview by Ron
Marcello (Denton: North Texas State University, 1976): 22.

93. Louis, Boyles, and Grove poll, March 1978, John Tower Papers.

94. *Houston Chronicle,* March 2, 1978, clipping in Dolph Briscoe Papers.

95. John Bloom, "He Who Would Be Governor," *Texas Monthly* (April 1978): 76.

96. V. O. Key Jr., *Southern Politics in State and Nation* (New York: Alfred A. Knopf, 1949):
658.

97. James C. Cobb, *Industrialization and Southern Society, 1877–1984* (Lexington, Ky.:
University of Kentucky Press, 1984): 136–37.

98. *Austin American-Statesman,* March 5, 1978; and *San Antonio Express-News,* March 5,
1978, clipping in Dolph Briscoe Papers.

99. *Texas Observer,* March 31, 1978.

100. Kruger, Interview with the author, March 25, 2004.

101. *Texas Monthly* (May 1978): 88.

102. Ibid.

103. *Beaumont Enterprise,* March 10, 1978, clipping in Dolph Briscoe Papers.

104. Ibid., March 9, 1978, clipping in Dolph Briscoe Papers.

105. *Dallas Morning News,* March 5, 1978, clipping in Dolph Briscoe Papers.

106. Ibid.

107. Key, *Southern Politics in State and Nation,* 261.

108. Charles D. Hadley and Lewis Bowman demonstrate the evolution of grassroots
party activists in the South by the mid-1990s in *Party Activists in Southern Politics: Mirrors
and Makers of Change,* ed. Charles D. Hadley and Lewis Bowman (Knoxville, Tenn.: University of Tennessee Press, 1998).

109. McCleskey et al. *The Government and Politics of Texas,* 85.

110. Earl Black and Merle Black explain discuss this electoral shift and how it affected the
presidential vote in the South in *The Vital South: How Presidents Are Elected* (Cambridge,
Mass.: Harvard University Press, 1992): 242.

111. Earl Black and Merle Black, *Politics and Society in the South* (Cambridge, Mass.:
Harvard University Press, 1987), 256.

112. Lamis, *The Two-Party South,* 196.

113. Bartley and Graham, *Southern Politics and the Second Reconstruction,* 133.

114. Black and Black, *Politics and Society in the South,* 278.

115. Clayton, "Interview with Speaker Bill Clayton, April 2, 1982," interview by Ron Marcello (Denton: North Texas State University, 1982), 1–2.

116. Lewis, "Oral Interview," 22.

117. Richard K. Scher, *Politics in the New South: Republicanism, Race, and Leadership in the Twentieth Century* (Armonk, N.Y.: M.E. Sharpe, 1997): 273.

118. *San Antonio Express,* May 3, 1978.

119. *Dallas Times Herald,* April 23, 1978.

120. Ibid.

121. Ibid.

122. Ibid.

123. *Austin American-Statesman,* May 2, 1978.

124. *Houston Post,* May 3, 1978.

125. *Dallas Morning News,* March 2, 1978, clipping in Dolph Briscoe Papers.

126. Ibid.

127. *Dallas Morning News,* March 5, 1978, clipping in Dolph Briscoe Papers.

128. *Dallas Morning News,* March 3, 1978, clipping in Dolph Briscoe Papers.

129. Ibid.

130. *Dallas Morning News,* March 5, 1978, clipping in Dolph Briscoe Papers.

131. Ibid.

132. *Dallas Morning News,* March 8, 1978, clipping in Dolph Briscoe Papers.

133. Ibid.

134. *Dallas Morning News,* April 17, 1978, clipping in Dolph Briscoe Papers.

135. *Houston Chronicle,* March 2, 1978; *Fort Worth Star-Telegram,* March 2, 1978, clipping in Dolph Briscoe Papers.

136. *Dallas Morning News,* June 15, 1978, clipping in Dolph Briscoe Papers.

137. Ibid.

138. *Dallas Morning News,* March 8, 1978, clipping in Dolph Briscoe Papers; *Houston Post,* March 8, 1978, clipping in Dolph Briscoe Papers; *Houston Chronicle,* March 8, 1978; *Fort Worth Star-Telegram,* March 8, 1978; *Austin American-Statesman,* March 8, 1978.

139. David Dean, Interview with the Author, November 26, 2002.

140. *Dallas Morning News,* March 21, 1978, clipping in Dolph Briscoe Papers.

141. Ibid., March 23, 1978, clipping in Dolph Briscoe Papers.

142. Ibid., April 1, 1978, clipping in Dolph Briscoe Papers.

143. Ibid.

144. *Dallas Times Herald,* April 23, 1978.

145. *Dallas Morning News,* April 16, 1978, clipping in Dolph Briscoe Papers.

146. Ibid.

147. *Dallas Morning News,* June 19, 1978.

148. *Dallas Morning News,* April 19, 1978, clipping in Dolph Briscoe Papers.

149. *Dallas Times Herald,* April 23, 1978.

150. Bernard L. Weinstein and Robert E. Firestine, *Regional Growth and Decline in the United States: The Rise of the Sunbelt and the Decline of the Northeast* (New York: Praeger Publishers, 1978), 31.

151. *Austin American-Statesman,* May 2, 1978.

152. *Dallas Morning News,* April 24, 1978, clipping in Dolph Briscoe Papers.

153. *San Antonio Express-News,* April 2, 1978, clipping in Dolph Briscoe Papers.

154. *Austin American-Statesman,* May 2, 1978.

155. *Dallas Morning News,* April 19, 1978, clipping in Dolph Briscoe Papers.

156. John Bloom, "He Who Would Be Governor," *Texas Monthly* (April 1978): 78.

157. *Dallas Times Herald,* April 23, 1978.

158. Ibid.

159. *Houston Post,* May 3, 1978.

160. Ibid., May 6, 1978.

161. Mauzy, "Interview with Sen. Oscar Mauzy, July 17, 1975," interview by Ron Marcello (Denton: North Texas State University, 1975): 17–18.

162. *Dallas Morning News,* March 24, 1978, clipping in Dolph Briscoe Papers.

163. Ibid., March 29, 1978, clipping in Dolph Briscoe Papers.

164. *Austin American-Statesman,* June 18, 1978.

165. *Dallas Morning News,* April 27, 1978, clipping in Dolph Briscoe Papers.

166. Ibid., April 10, 1978, clipping in Dolph Briscoe Papers.

167. Ibid., April 1, 1978, clipping in Dolph Briscoe Papers.

168. Ibid., May 2, 1978, clipping in Dolph Briscoe Papers.

169. Paul Burka, "Election Tip Sheet," *Texas Monthly* (April 1978: 116–121): 117.

170. *Dallas Morning News,* April 19, 1978, clipping in Dolph Briscoe Papers.

171. *Houston Post,* April 15, 1978, clipping in Dolph Briscoe Papers; *Dallas Morning News,* April 19, 1978, clipping in Dolph Briscoe Papers.

172. *Dallas Morning News,* April 22, 1978, clipping in Dolph Briscoe Papers.

173. *Dallas Times Herald,* April 23, 1978.

174. *Dallas Morning News,* March 13, 1978, clipping in Dolph Briscoe Papers.

175. *Dallas Times Herald,* April 23, 1978.

176. *Abilene Reporter-News,* March 19, 1978, clipping in Dolph Briscoe Papers.

177. *San Antonio Express-News,* April 30, 1978, clipping in Dolph Briscoe Papers.

178. *Houston Chronicle,* March 12, 1978, clipping in Dolph Briscoe Papers.

179. *Dallas Morning News,* April 23, 1978, clipping in Dolph Briscoe Papers.

180. *Dallas Times Herald,* April 22, 1978.

181. Ibid., May 5, 1978.

182. *Houston Post,* May 2, 1978.

183. Ibid., May 5, 1978.

184. *Houston Post,* May 2, 1978; and *Dallas Morning News,* May 4, 1978.

185. Ibid.

186. David Dean, Interview with the author, November 26, 2002.

187. *Dallas Times Herald,* May 1, 1978; *Dallas Times Herald,* May 6, 1978; *Fort Worth Star-Telegram,* May 5, 1978; *Dallas Morning News,* May 3, 1978, clipping in Dolph Briscoe Papers.

188. *Dallas Times Herald,* May 2, 1978.

189. *Houston Post,* May 2, 1978.

190. *Dallas Times Herald,* May 2, 1978.

191. *Houston Post,* May 2, 1978.

192. *Fort Worth Star-Telegram,* May 3, 1978.

193. Ibid.

194. *San Antonio Express,* May 4, 1978.

195. *Fort Worth Star-Telegram,* May 5, 1978.

196. *Houston Post,* May 6, 1978.

197. *San Antonio Express,* May 3, 1978.

198. *Houston Post,* May 5, 1978.

199. Ibid.

200. Ibid., May 6, 1978.

201. Ibid.

202. Ibid.

203. *Fort Worth Star-Telegram,* May 3, 1978; and *Houston Post,* May 6, 1978.

204. *Houston Post,* May 6, 1978.

205. *Austin American-Statesman,* May 8, 1978.

206. Ibid.

207. Ibid.

208. "Texas Secretary of State," www.sos.state.tx.us; Mike Kingston, et al., ed. *The Texas Almanac's Political History of Texas* (Austin: Eakin Press, 1992): 264–267.

209. *Dallas Morning News,* May 8, 1978.

210. *Dallas Morning News,* May 18, 1978, clipping in Dolph Briscoe Papers.

211. *Dallas Times Herald,* May 8, 1978.

Chapter 3

1. *Texas Observer,* October 18, 1977.

2. Lance Tarrance, Interview with the author, Houston, Texas, October 8, 2002.

3. Ibid.

4. O. Douglas Weeks, "Texas: Land of Conservative Expansiveness," in *The Changing Politics of the South,* ed. William C. Havard (Baton Rouge, La.: Louisiana State University Press, 1972), 205.

5. Ibid., 202.

6. Glenn A. Robinson, "The Electorate in Texas," in *Texas at the Crossroads: People, Politics, and Policy,* ed. Anthony Champagne and Edward J. Harpham (College Station, Tex.: Texas A&M Press, 1987: 68–107), 71.

7. Weeks, "Texas: Land of Conservative Expansiveness," *Changing Politics of the South,* 209.

8. "Texas Secretary of State," www.sos.state.tx.us.

9. Weeks, "Texas: Land of Conservative Expansiveness," *Changing Politics of the South,* 209.

10. V. O. Key, *Southern Politics in State and Nation* (New York: Alfred A. Knopf, 1949), 278.

11. Clifton McCleskey et al., *The Government and Politics of Texas* (Boston: Little, Brown, 1978): 92.

12. Alexander Heard, *A Two-Party South?* (Chapel Hill, N.C.: University of North Carolina Press, 1952): 133–134.

13. Weeks, "Texas: Land of Conservative Expansiveness," *Changing Politics of the South,* 218.

14. Ibid., 223.

15. Alma Box, "Interview with Alma Box, August 19, 1993," interview by Kristi Strickland (Denton: University of North Texas, 1993): 8; Betty Andujar, "Interview with Sen. Betty

Andujar, September 6, 1979," interview by Ronald E. Marcello (Denton: North Texas State University, 1979): 3; Barbara Campbell, "Interview with Barbara Campbell, May 6, 1993," interview by Kristi Strickland (Denton: University of North Texas, 1993): 21.

16. Roger M. Olien, *From Token to Triumph, The Texas Republicans Since 1920* (Dallas: SMU Press, 1982), 243.

17. John Tower Papers, Special Collections, Southwestern University, Georgetown, Texas.

18. Andujar, "Interview," 10.

19. Weeks, "Texas: Land of Conservative Expansiveness," *Changing Politics of the South,* 223.

20. See more on the rise of conservatism in David W. Reinhard, *The Republican Right Since 1945* (Lexington, Ky.: University Press of Kentucky, 1983).

21. Ben Johnson, *Arkansas in Modern America, 1930–1999* (Fayetteville, Ark.: University of Arkansas Press, 2000): 165; Bartley, *The New South,* 389.

22. Bartley, *The New South,* 389.

23. Ibid., 393.

24. "Texas Secretary of State," www.sos.state.tx.us.

25. Chandler Davidson, *Race and Class in Texas Politics* (Princeton, N.J.: Princeton University Press, 1990): 80–83.

26. "Texas Secretary of State," www.sos.state.tx.us.

27. Ann Fears Crawford and Jack Keever, *John B. Connally: Portrait in Power* (Austin: Jenkins Publishing Co., 1973): 426.

28. Richard K. Scher, *Politics in the South: Republicanism, Race, and Leadership in the Twentieth Century* (Armonk, N.Y.: M. E. Sharpe, 1997): 149.

29. Malcolm E. Jewell, *Parties and Primaries: Nominating State Governors* (New York: Praeger, 1984): 215.

30. Olien, *From Token to Triumph,* 238.

31. Earl Black and Merle Black, *The Vital South: How Presidents Are Elected* (Cambridge, Mass.: Harvard University Press, 1992): 296.

32. Davidson, *Race and Class in Texas Politics,* 234, 236.

33. Ibid., 202.

34. Martin Schram, *Running for President, 1976: The Carter Campaign* (New York: Stein and Day, 1977): 229.

35. Olien, *From Token to Triumph,* 238.

36. Ibid.

37. Robert P. Steed et al., eds., study the demographics and ideologies of southern party activists in the 1980s and 1990s in *Party Organization in the American South* (Tuscaloosa, Ala.: University of Alabama Press, 1998).

38. Davidson, *Race and Class in Texas Politics,* 201.

39. David R. Goldfield, *Black, White, and Southern: Race Relations and Southern Culture, 1940 to Present* (Baton Rouge, La.: Louisiana State University Press, 1990): 196.

40. *Texas Observer,* October 18, 1977.

41. Louis, Bowles, and Grove to Tower, March 1978, John Tower Papers.

42. Goldfield, *Black, White, and Southern,* 197.

43. Scher, *Politics in the New South,* 151.

44. Ronald Briggs, "Demography of a Sunbelt State," in *Texas at the Crossroads: People,*

Politics, and Policy, ed. Anthony Champagne and Edward J. Harpham (College Station, Tex.: Texas A&M Press, 1987: 15–41), 35.

45. Barry J. Kaplan, "Houston: The Golden Buckle of the Sunbelt," in *Sunbelt Cities: Politics and Growth Since World War II,* ed. Richard M. Bernard and Bradley R. Rice (Austin: University of Texas Press, 1983: 196–212), 196, 201.

46. Heywood T. Sanders, *Urban Texas: Politics and Development,* Char Miller and Heywood Sanders, eds. (College Station, Tex.: Texas A&M University Press, 1990), 30; Martin V. Melosi, "Dallas-Fort Worth: Marketing the Metroplex," in *Sunbelt Cities: Politics and Growth Since World War II,* ed. Richards M. Bernhard and Bradley R. Rice (Austin: University of Texas Press, 1983: 162–95), 169.

47. McCleskey et al., *The Government and Politics of Texas,* 103.

48. *Texas Observer,* October 18, 1977.

49. See Florence Shapiro, "Interview with Florence Shapiro, August 17, 1993," interview by Kristi Strickland (Denton: University of North Texas, 1993).

50. *Dallas Morning News,* November 5, 1977.

51. Ibid.

52. John Morrison, "The Abrasive Candidacy of Bill Clements," *D Magazine* (March 1978): 106.

53. *Texas Observer,* February 3, 1978.

54. Carolyn Barta, *Bill Clements: Texian to His Toenails* (Austin: Eakin Press, 1996): 188.

55. Tarrance, Interview with the author, October 8, 2002.

56. Fred Agnich, "Interview with Rep. Fred Agnich, September 7, 1977," interview by Ron Marcello (Denton: North Texas State University, 1977): 23.

57. Tarrance, Interview with the author, October 8, 2002.

58. Barta, *Clements,* 5.

59. *Dallas Morning News,* November 1, 1977.

60. Martin T. Katzman and Patricia J. Osborn, "Energy Policy," in *Texas at the Crossroads: People, Politics, and Policy,* ed. Anthony Champagne and Edward J. Harpham (College Station, Tex.: Texas A&M University Press, 1987: 129–53), 135.

61. Ibid.

62. Hicks, "Advanced Industrial Development," 50.

63. Barta, *Clements,* 4.

64. George W. Bush, *A Charge to Keep* (New York: William Morrow and Co., 1999): 172.

65. Davidson, *Race and Class in Texas Politics,* 74.

66. Ibid.

67. Barta, *Clements,* 8–9.

68. Ibid., 5–7.

69. Ibid., 7–8.

70. Ibid., 8.

71. *Dallas Morning News,* November 11, 1978.

72. Ibid.

73. Barta, *Clements,* 189; *Dallas Morning News,* November 17, 1977.

74. *Dallas Morning News,* November 17, 1977.

75. Bill Clements, interview with the author, Dallas, Texas, May 10, 2004.

76. Ibid.

77. *Texas Observer,* February 17, 1978.

78. Barta, *Clements,* 190.

79. Robinson, "The Electorate in Texas," 87.

80. Barta, *Clements,* 193.

81. Clements, Interview with the author, May 10, 2004.

82. Barta, *Clements,* 194.

83. Morrison, "The Abrasive Candidacy of Bill Clements," 155.

84. Barta, *Clements,* 194.

85. Morrison, "The Abrasive Candidacy of Bill Clements," 106.

86. Ibid.

87. *Texas Observer,* April 28, 1978.

88. *Dallas Morning News,* March 23, 1978.

89. Ibid.

90. Ibid.

91. Joseph A. Aistrup, *The Southern Strategy Revisited: Republican Top-Down Advancement in the South* (Lexington, Ky.: University Press of Kentucky, 1996), 117.

92. George Norris Green, "Some Aspects of the Far Right Wing in Texas Politics," in *Essays on Recent Southern Politics,* ed. Harold M. Hollingsworth (Austin: University of Texas Press, 1970: 58–94), 58.

93. Ibid., 82.

94. Ibid., 85.

95. Tom Creighton, "Interview with Sen. Tom Creighton, July 15, 1975," interview by Ron Marcello (Denton: North Texas State University, 1976): 2.

96. *Dallas Morning News,* April 6, 1978.

97. Ibid.

98. *Dallas Morning News,* April 27, 1978; *San Antonio Express,* May 1, 1978.

99. *Dallas Morning News,* April 27, 1978.

100. *San Antonio Express,* May 1, 1978.

101. *Houston Post,* May 3, 1978.

102. Ibid., May 5, 1978.

103. *Austin American-Statesman,* April 26, 1978.

104. Ibid.

105. *Houston Post,* May 5, 1978.

106. Ibid., May 2, 1978.

107. Ibid., May 1, 1978.

108. Ibid.

109. *Dallas Morning News,* May 2, 1978.

110. Ibid.

111. Ibid.

112. *Houston Post,* May 1, 1978.

113. Ibid.

114. *Fort Worth Star-Telegram,* March 1, 1978, clipping in Dolph Briscoe Papers, Center for American History, University of Texas, Austin.

115. *Dallas Morning News,* March 16, 1978.

116. Ibid.

117. *Houston Post,* May 1, 1978.

118. Ibid.

119. Ibid.

120. *Dallas Morning News,* April 27, 1978.

121. *Dallas Times Herald,* May 5, 1978.

122. *Houston Post,* May 5, 1978.

123. Ibid., May 6, 1978.

124. Ibid.

125. Ibid., May 5, 1978.

126. *San Antonio Express,* April 30, 1978, Dolph Briscoe Papers; *Austin American-Statesman,* May 6, 1978.

127. *Dallas Times Herald,* May 5, 1978.

128. *Dallas Morning News,* April 23, 1978.

129. *Houston Post,* May 5, 1978.

130. Ibid., May 6, 1978.

131. *Dallas Morning News,* May 5, 1978; *Austin American-Statesman,* May 5, 1978.

132. *Houston Post,* May 3, 1978.

133. Ibid.

134. *Dallas Times Herald,* May 7, 1978.

135. Ibid.

136. *Houston Post,* May 3, 1978.

137. *Dallas Morning News,* May 4, 1978; *Houston Post,* May 3, 1978.

138. Davidson, *Race and Class in Texas Politics,* 238.

139. David Dean, Interview with the author, Dallas, Texas, November 26, 2002.

Chapter 4

1. *Texas Observer,* May 26, 1978.

2. *Dallas Morning News,* June 15, 1978.

3. John Hill, *Oral Interview with the Honorable John L. Hill Jr.,* Sheree Scarborough, ed. (Austin: Texas Bar Foundation, 1999): 44.

4. Hill, Interview with the author, Houston, Texas, September 26, 2002.

5. *Austin American-Statesman,* May 12, 1978; *Dallas Times Herald,* May 11, 1978, clipping in Dolph Briscoe Papers, Center for American History, University of Texas, Austin.

6. Ibid.

7. Ibid.

8. Martin Schram, *Running for President, 1976: The Carter Campaign* (New York: Stein and Day, 1977): 138.

9. Ibid., 304–305.

10. Kandy Stroud, *How Jimmy Won: The Victory Campaign from Plains to the White House* (New York: William Morrow and Co., 1977), 398.

11. John Connally, *In History's Shadow: An American Odyssey* (New York: Hyperion, 1993): 287–291.

12. John G. Tower, *Consequences: A Personal and Political Memoir* (Boston: Little, Brown and Co., 1991), 236.

13. David W. Reinhard, *The Republican Right Since 1945* (Lexington: University Press of Kentucky, 1983), 238.

14. Hill, *Oral Interview,* 30–31.

15. *Dallas Morning News,* November 26, 1978.

16. *Austin American-Statesman,* May 8, 1978.

17. *Dallas Morning News,* May 17, 1978.

18. Ibid.

19. Jimmy Carter, *Public Papers of the Presidents of the United States: Jimmy Carter, 1978: Book I—Jan. 1 to June 30, 1978* (Washington, D.C.: U.S. Government Printing Office, 1 978), 934.

20. *Dallas Morning News,* May 18, 1978.

21. Robert Krueger, Interview with the author, New Braunfels, Texas, March 25, 2004.

22. David Dean, Interview with the author, Dallas, Texas, November 26, 2002.

23. *Dallas Morning News,* July 1, 1978.

24. Ibid., August 5, 1978.

25. Ibid., May 18, 1978.

26. Ibid.

27. Carter, *Public Papers,* 1168.

28. *Dallas Morning News,* August 26, 1978, September 5, 1978.

29. Krueger, Interview with the author, March 25, 2004.

30. Ibid.

31. Dean, Interview with the author, November 26, 2002.

32. *Dallas Morning News,* May 18, 1978.

33. Hill, Interview with the author, September 26, 2002.

34. Hill, *Oral Interview,* 30.

35. *Dallas Morning News,* October 26, 1978.

36. *Austin American-Statesman,* June 18, 1978.

37. *Dallas Morning News,* November 2, 1977.

38. Mike Kingston et al., ed. *The Texas Almanac's Political History of Texas* (Austin: Eakin Press, 1992), 308–11.

39. David Montejano, *Anglos and Mexican in the Making of Texas, 1836–1986* (Austin: University of Texas Press, 1987), 290.

40. Ibid., 296.

41. James Jennings, "Blacks and Latinos in the American City in the 1990s: Toward Political Alliances or Social Conflict?," *Pursuing Power,* F. Chris Garcia, ed. (Notre Dame, Ind.: University of Notre Dame Press, 1997: 472–78): 474.

42. Harold W. Stanley, *Voter Mobilization and the Politics of Race: The South and Universal Suffrage, 1952–1984* (New York: Praeger, 1987): 5–6.

43. Montejano, *Anglos and Mexicans in the Making of Texas,* 289.

44. Stanley, *Voter Mobilization,* 13.

45. Ibid., 82.

46. William F. Flanigan and Nancy H. Zingale, *Political Behavior of the American Electorate,* 6th ed. (Boston: Allyn and Bacon, 1987): 30.

47. Ibid., 43.

48. Hill, Interview with the author, September 26, 2002.

49. Ibid.

50. *Dallas Morning News,* May 18, 1978.

51. Ibid., May 20, 1978.

52. *Dallas Times Herald,* May 9, 1978.

53. *Austin American-Statesman,* June 18, 1978.

54. Oscar Mauzy, "Interview with Sen. Oscar Mauzy, October 23, 1978," interview by Ronald E. Marcello (Denton: North Texas State University, 1979): 44.

55. *Dallas Morning News,* July 5, 1978.

56. Chandler Davidson, *Race and Class in Texas Politics* (Princeton, N.J.: Princeton University Press, 1990): 128.

57. Ibid., 126.

58. Ibid.

59. Ibid., 130–31.

60. Hill, Interview with the author, September 26, 2002.

61. Bill Clements, Interview with the author, Dallas, Texas, May 10, 2004.

62. Sarah M. Morehouse, *The Governor as Party Leader: Campaigning and Governing* (Ann Arbor: University of Michigan Press, 1998): 42.

63. *Austin American-Statesman,* May 10, 1978.

64. Ibid.

65. *Dallas Morning News,* June 6, 1978.

66. Ibid., June 16, 1978.

67. Dean, Interview with the author, November 26, 2002.

68. Ibid.

69. Lance Tarrance, Interview with the author, Denton, Texas, October 8, 2002.

70. Ibid.

71. Ibid.

72. Ibid.

73. O. H. Harris, "Interview with O. H. (Ike) Harris, November 27, 1978," interview by Ron Marcello (Denton: North Texas State University, 1979): 26–27.

74. Tarrance, Interview with the author, October 8, 2002.

75. Dean, Interview with the author, November 26, 2002.

76. John G. Tower, *Consequences: A Personal and Political Memoir* (Boston: Little, Brown and Co., 1991): 208.

77. Untitled internal notes, October 1978, John Tower Papers.

78. Ibid.

79. *Dallas Morning News,* November 26, 1978.

80. Ibid.

81. Ibid.

82. Ken Towery to Nola Heale, July 13, 1978, John Tower Papers.

83. Krueger, Interview with the author, March 25, 2004.

84. *Dallas Morning News,* June 16, 1978.

85. Hill, Interview with the author, September 26, 2002.

86. *Dallas Morning News,* June 19, 1978.

87. Ibid., June 22, 1978.

88. Ibid.

89. Dolph Briscoe, *Report to the 66th Legislature of Texas From Dolph Briscoe, Governor of Texas, 1973–1979* (Austin: State of Texas, 1979) 14–15.

90. *Dallas Morning News,* July 1, 1978.

91. Ibid.

92. Harris, "Interview," 5.

93. *Dallas Morning News,* July 1, 1978.

94. Ibid., July 11, 1978.

95. Ibid.

96. Mauzy, "Interview," 2–3.

97. Harris, "Interview," 4.

98. *Dallas Morning News,* July 12, 1978.

99. Briscoe, *Report,* 14–15; *Dallas Morning News,* August 10, 1978.

100. *Dallas Morning News,* August 10, 1978.

101. Ibid.

102. Mauzy, "Interview," 7.

103. *Austin American-Statesman,* July 9, 1978, clipping in Dolph Briscoe Papers.

104. Bill Clayton, "Interview with Speaker Bill Clayton, November 16, 1978," interview by Ron Marcello (Denton: North Texas State University, 1979): 7.

CHAPTER 5

1. Carolyn Barta, *Bill Clements: Texian to His Toenails* (Austin: Eakin Press, 1996): 202.

2. David Dean, Interview with the author, Dallas, Texas, November 26, 2002.

3. Ibid.

4. Ibid.

5. Ibid.

6. Ibid.

7. Untitled Clements campaign staff list, July 7, 1978, John Tower Papers, Special Collections, Southwestern University, Georgetown, Texas.

8. Dean, Interview with the author, November 26, 2002.

9. *Austin American-Statesman,* May 12, 1978.

10. Dean, Interview with the author, November 26, 2002.

11. Ibid.

12. Mike Kingston et al., *The Texas Almanac's Political History of Texas* (Austin: Eakin Press, 1992).

13. V. O. Key, "Partisanship and County Offices: The Case of Ohio," *American Political Science Review* 47 (June 1953): 525.

14. James W. Lamare, J. L. Polinard, and Robert D. Wrinkle, "Texas: Lone Star (Wars) State," in *The New Politics of the Old South: An Introduction to Southern Politics,* ed. Charles S. Bullock III and Mark J. Rozell, eds. (New York: Rowman & Littlefield Publishers, 1998: 245–60), 248.

15. Ibid., 249.

16. *Dallas Morning News,* July 1, 1978.

17. Charles L. Prysby, and John W. Books, *Political Behavior and the Local Context* (New York: Praegar, 1991): 125.

18. *Dallas Morning News,* June 19, 1978.

19. Roger M. Olien, *From Token to Triumph: The Texas Republicans Since 1920* (Dallas: SMU Press, 1982): 254–255.

20. *Dallas Morning News,* June 19, 1978.

21. Olien, *From Token to Triumph,* 254–255.

22. *Dallas Morning News,* July 1, 1978.

23. Ibid.

24. Barta, *Clements,* 203.

25. Betty Andujar, "Interview with Sen. Betty Andujar, September 6, 1979," interview by Ronald E. Marcello (Denton: North Texas State University, 1979): 35.

26. Prysby, and Books, *Political Behavior and the Local Context,* 111.

27. Ibid., July 1, 1978.

28. Dean, Interview with the author, November 26, 2002.

29. Barta, *Clements,* 206.

30. Bill Clements, Interview with the author, Dallas, Texas, May 10, 2004.

31. Dean, Interview with the author, November 26, 2002.

32. Ibid.

33. Olien, *From Token to Triumph,* 247.

34. Ibid., 249–50.

35. Ibid., 248.

36. Ibid., 251.

37. *Dallas Morning News,* August 4, 1978.

38. Ibid.

39. Ibid., August 5, 1978.

40. Ibid.

41. Clements speech to supporters, September 4, 1978, John Tower Papers.

42. "Bill Clements and Doctors," August 1978, John Tower Papers.

43. *Dallas Morning News,* September 5, 1978.

44. Clements speech to supporters, September 4, 1978, John Tower Papers.

45. Ibid.

46. Ibid.

47. Ibid.

48. Ibid.

49. Clements speech to Texas Republican Convention, September 9, 1978, John Tower Papers.

50. Ibid.

51. Ibid.

52. *Dallas Morning News,* November 26, 1978.

53. Ibid., September 3, 1978.

54. Ibid.

55. Ibid., September 7, 1978.

56. *Houston Post,* September 13, 1978.

57. *Austin American-Statesman,* September 13, 1978; *Houston Post,* September 13, 1978.

58. Ibid.

59. *Dallas Morning News,* September 13, 1978.

60. Ibid., September 16, 1978.

61. Ibid.

62. Ibid., September 19, 1978.

63. Ibid., September 28, 1978.

64. Ibid., September 25, 1978.

65. Ibid., September 19, 1978.

66. *Houston Post,* September 20, 1978, clipping in Dolph Briscoe Papers, Center for American History, University of Texas, Austin.

67. *Dallas Morning News,* September 25, 1978.

68. *Austin American-Statesman,* September 29, 1978; *Dallas Times Herald,* September 29, 1978, clipping in Dolph Briscoe Papers.

69. *Austin American-Statesman,* September 29, 1978.

70. *Dallas Morning News,* September 29, 1978.

71. Ibid.

72. Dean, Interview with the author, November 26, 2002.

73. Ibid.

74. Fred Agnich, "Interview with Rep. Fred Agnich, August 11, 1975," interview by Ron Marcello (Denton: North Texas State University, 1976): 5.

75. Robert Krueger, Interview with the Author, New Braunfels, Texas, March 25, 2004.

76. Bill Clements, Interview with the author, Dallas, Texas, May 10, 2004.

77. Ibid.

78. *Dallas Morning News,* October 10, 1978.

79. Ibid.

80. *Austin American-Statesman,* October 16, 1978.

81. *Dallas Morning News,* October 22, 1978; *Austin American-Statesman,* October 22, 1978.

82. Krueger, Interview with the author, March 25, 2004.

83. Gibson D. Lewis, "Interview with Rep. 'Gib' Lewis, August 29, 1979," interview by Ron Marcello (Denton: North Texas State University, 1980): 51.

84. Oscar Mauzy, "Interview with Sen. Oscar Mauzy, October 23, 1978," interview by Ron Marcello (Denton: North Texas State University, 1979): 6.

85. *Dallas Morning News,* October 1, 1978.

86. Ibid.

87. Ibid.

88. Ibid., October 2, 1978.

89. Ibid., October 3, 1978.

90. Ibid., October 4, 1978.

91. *Austin American-Statesman,* October 5, 1978.

92. Ibid., October 8, 1978.

93. Olien, *From Token to Triumph,* 258.

94. Ibid.

95. *Austin American-Statesman,* October 4, 1978.

96. Barta, *Clements,* 212.

97. *Dallas Morning News,* October 6, 1978.

98. *Austin American-Statesman,* October 18, 1978.

99. Ibid., October 19, 1978.

100. *Dallas Morning News,* October 22, 1978; *Austin American-Statesman,* October 22, 1978.

101. Ibid.

102. Ibid.

103. *Austin American-Statesman,* October 22, 1978.

104. Ibid.

105. *Dallas Morning News,* October 24, 1978.

106. Clements, Interview with the author, May 10, 2004.

107. John Tower, *Consequences: A Personal and Political Memoir* (Boston: Little, Brown, 1991): 211.

108. *Houston Post,* September 28, 1978, Dolph Briscoe Papers.

109. Tarrance to Tower, October 1978, John Tower Papers.

110. Ibid.

111. Ibid.

112. Tarrance to Ken Towery, John Knaggs, and John Davis, October 25, 1978, John Tower Papers.

113. Untitled campaign analysis notes, November 2, 1978, John Tower Papers.

114. *Dallas Morning News,* September 2, 1978.

115. Ibid., October 27, 1978.

116. *Austin American-Statesman,* November 1, 1978.

117. *Dallas Times Herald,* November 2, 1978; *Dallas Morning News,* November 1, 1978.

118. *Dallas Times Herald,* November 2, 1978.

119. *Austin American-Statesman,* November 1, 1978.

120. John Hill, Interview with the author, Houston, Texas, September 26, 2002.

121. Barta, *Clements,* 194.

122. *Dallas Morning News,* October 14, 1978.

123. Ibid.

124. Ibid.

125. For more on the rising costs of political campaigns in Texas and the rest of the United States in the 1970s and 1980s, see Glenn A. Robinson, "The Electorate in Texas," in *Texas at the Crossroads: People, Politics, and Policy,* ed. Anthony Champagne and Edward J. Harpham (College Station, Tex.: Texas A&M Press, 1987: 68–107), 83; and Chandler Davidson, *Race and Class in Texas Politics* (Princeton, N.J.: Princeton University Press, 1990), 133.

126. Ibid., 133.

127. *Houston Post,* November 1, 1978.

128. *Dallas Morning News,* November 5, 1978.

129. *Dallas Morning News,* November 4, 1978; *Austin American-Statesman,* November 4, 1978.

130. *Dallas Times Herald,* November 5, 1978.

131. Barta, *Clements,* 209.

132. Hill, Interview with the author, September 26, 2002.

133. *Dallas Morning News,* November 5, 1978.

134. Barta, *Clements,* 213.

135. Ibid.

136. *Texas Spectator,* 1978, John Tower Papers.

137. *Dallas Morning News,* November 5, 1978.

138. Barta, *Clements,* 212.

139. John Hill, *History Interview with the Honorable John L. Hill Jr.,* Sheree Scarborough, ed. (Austin: Texas Bar Foundation, 1999): 44.

140. Bartley, *The New South,* 16; Doris Kearns Goodwin, *Lyndon John and the American Dream* (New York: St. Martin's Griffin, 1991), 93, 101; Robert A. Calvert, Gregg Cantrell, and Arnoldo De Leon, *The History of Texas,* 3rd ed. (Wheeling, Ill.: Harlan Davidson, 2002), 332, 381–82, 393.

141. Ray Barnhart to Bill Perrin, President of the Texas Republican County Chairs Association, July 13, 1978, John Tower Papers.

142. Untitled campaign notes, October 1978, John Tower Papers.

143. *San Antonio Express,* November 2, 1978.

144. *Dallas Morning News,* November 1, 1978.

145. Ibid.

146. Ibid.

147. Memo, November 1, 1978, John Tower Papers.

148. *Dallas Times Herald,* October 28, 1978.

149. *Houston Post,* November 3, 1978.

150. *Dallas Morning News,* November 3, 1978.

151. *Houston Post,* November 3, 1978.

152. *Dallas Morning News,* October 29, 1978.

153. Ibid.

154. *Houston Post,* November 3, 1978.

155. Ibid., November 1, 1978.

156. Ibid.

157. Ibid.

158. Ibid.

159. *Dallas Times Herald,* November 2, 1978.

160. *Austin American-Statesman,* November 2, 1978.

161. Andujar, "Interview," 33–34.

162. *Austin American-Statesman,* October 15, 1978.

163. *San Antonio Express,* November 1, 1978.

164. *Dallas Morning News,* November 1, 1978.

165. Ibid., November 3, 1978.

166. Ibid.

167. Ibid., November 2, 1978.

168. Ibid.

169. Ibid.

170. *Texas Observer,* October 20, 1978.

171. *Dallas Times Herald,* October 30, 1978.

172. *Fort Worth Star-Telegram,* November 5, 1978.

173. *Austin American-Statesman,* October 21, 1978.

174. Ibid., November 4, 1978.

175. *San Antonio Express,* November 2, 1978.

176. Ibid.

177. Ibid.

178. *Austin American-Statesman,* November 2, 1978.

179. Ibid., November 3, 1978.

180. Ibid., October 16, 1978.

181. Ibid.

182. Ibid., October 22, 1978.

183. *Houston Post,* November 3, 1978.

184. *Austin American-Statesman,* November 4, 1978.

185. *Dallas Times Herald,* November 3, 1978.

186. Ibid.

187. Ibid.

188. *Austin American-Statesman,* November 3, 1978.

189. *Houston Post,* November 4, 1978.

190. *Austin American-Statesman,* November 4, 1978; *Dallas Morning News,* November 4, 1978.

191. *Austin American-Statesman,* November 4, 1978.

192. *Houston Post,* November 4, 1978; *Dallas Morning News,* November 5, 1978.

193. *Houston Post,* November 4, 1978.

194. *Dallas Morning News,* November 4, 1978.

195. *Austin American-Statesman,* November 4, 1978.

196. Tarrance, Interview with the author, Houston, Texas, October 8, 2002.

197. *Dallas Morning News,* November 4, 5, 1978.

198. Ibid., November 5, 1978.

199. Hill, Interview with the author, September 26, 2002.

200. Tarrance, Interview with the author, October 8, 2002.

201. *Dallas Morning News,* November 6, 1978.

202. *Houston Post,* November 3, 1978.

203. Davidson, *Race and Class in Texas Politics,* 113.

204. *Houston Post,* November 3, 1978.

205. Ibid.

206. *Austin American-Statesman,* November 7, 1978; *Houston Post,* November 7, 1978.

207. *Dallas Times Herald,* November 7, 1978.

208. *San Antonio Express,* November 7, 1978.

209. Tarrance, Interview with the author, October 8, 2002.

210. Ibid.

211. Ibid.

212. Ibid.

213. Martin Schram, *Running for President, 1976: The Carter Campaign* (New York: Stein and Day, 1977): 329.

214. Tarrance, Interview with the author, October 8, 2002.

215. *Dallas Morning News,* November 5, 1978.

216. Ibid.

217. Ibid.

218. Barta, *Clements,* 212.

219. Ibid., 213.

220. Hill, Interview with the author, September 26, 2002.

221. *Dallas Morning News,* November 5, 1978.

222. Untitled campaign notes, November 1978, John Tower Papers.

223. *Dallas Morning News,* November 5, 1978.

224. *Fort Worth Star-Telegram,* November 6, 1978.

225. Hill, Interview with the author, September 26, 2002.

226. Ibid.

227. O. H. Harris, "Interview with Sen. O. H. Harris, November 27, 1978," interview by Ron Marcello (Denton: North Texas State University, 1979): 19–20; Richard Morehead, *50 Years in Texas Politics: From Roosevelt to Reagan, from the Fergusons to Clements* (Burnet, Tex.: Eakin Press, 1982), 273.

228. Dean, Interview with the author, November 26, 2002.

229. Ibid.

230. Robert Krueger, Interview with the author, New Braunfels, Texas, March 25, 2004.

231. Olien, *From Token to Triumph,* 256.

232. Tarrance, Interview with the author, October 8, 2002.

Chapter 6

1. *Houston Post,* November 7, 1978.

2. "Texas Secretary of State," http://www.sos.state.tx.us.

3. *Dallas Morning News,* November 8, 1978.

4. Ibid.

5. *Amarillo Daily News,* November 8, 1978.

6. *Dallas Morning News,* November 8, 1978.

7. *Houston Post,* November 9, 11, 1978.

8. David Dean, Interview with the author, Dallas, Texas, November 26, 2002.

9. Ibid.

10. *Dallas Morning News,* November 9, 1978.

11. *Austin American-Statesman,* November 9, 1978.

12. Lance Tarrance, Interview with the author, Houston, Texas, October 8, 2002.

13. *Austin American-Statesman,* November 9, 1978.

14. Ibid.

15. *Houston Post,* November 11, 1978.

16. Ibid.

17. Ibid.

18. Ibid.

19. Robert Krueger, Interview with the author, New Braunfels, Texas, March 25, 2004.

20. Ibid.

21. John Tower to Republicans, November 13, 1978, John Tower Papers, Special Collections, Southwestern University, Georgetown, Texas.

22. Ibid.

23. Tower to Republicans, November 15, 1978, John Tower Papers.

24. Rowland Stiteler, "How to Steal an Election," *D Magazine* (November 1978): 114.

25. Ibid., 116.

26. *Dallas Morning News,* November 17, 1978.

27. Ibid.

28. Ibid., November 18, 1978.

29. Ibid.

30. Neil Coleman to Tower, December 5, 1978, John Tower Papers.

31. John Hill, Interview with the Author, Houston, Texas, September 26, 2002.

32. *Dallas Morning News,* December 8, 1978.

33. Ibid.

34. "Texas Secretary of State," www.state.sos.tx.us; Mike Kingston et al., *The Texas Almanac's Political History of Texas,* (Austin: Eakin Press, 1992), 264–67, 308–11.

35. Alexander Lamis, *The Two-Party South,* (New York: Oxford University Press, 1988), 206.

36. Ibid., 205.

37. Ibid., 206.

38. Ibid.

39. "Texas Secretary of State," www.state.sos.tx.us; Kingston et al., *The Texas Almanac's Political History of Texas,* 264–67, 308–11.

40. Ibid.

41. Hill, Interview with the author, September 26, 2002.

42. Krueger, Interview with the author, March 25, 2004.

43. George Norris Green, *The Establishment in Texas Politics: The Primitive Years, 1938–1957* (Westport, Conn.: Greenwood Press, 1979), 230; *Dallas Morning News,* November 9, 1978; *Fort Worth Star-Telegram,* November 8, 1978.

44. "Texas Secretary of State," www.sos.state.tx.us; Kingston et al., *The Texas Almanac's Political History of Texas,* 308–11.

45. *Dallas Morning News,* November 5, 2002; and *Fort Worth Star-Telegram,* November 5, 2002.

46. "Texas Secretary of State," http://www.sos.state.tx.us.

47. Roger M. Olien, *From Token to Triumph: The Texas Republicans Since 1920* (Dallas: SMU Press, 1982): 259.

48. Ibid., 260.

49. Malcolm E. Jewell, *Parties and Primaries: Nominating State Governors* (New York: Praeger, 1984): 192.

50. Ibid., 176.

51. William F. Flanigan and Nancy H. Zingale, *Political Behavior of the American Electorate,* 6th ed. Boston: Allyn and Bacon, 1987), 15.

52. Ibid., 13.

53. Ibid., 15.

54. Carolyn Barta, *Bill Clements: Texian to His Toenails* (Austin: Eakin Press, 1996): 217.

55. Bill Clements, Interview with the author, Dallas, Texas, May 10, 2004.

56. Tower, *Consequences: A Personal and Political Memoir* (Boston: Little, Brown, 1991), 212.

57. *Houston Post,* November 11, 1978.

58. Ibid.

59. Ibid.

60. Ibid.

61. Ibid.

62. Ibid.

63. Ibid.

64. *Dallas Morning News,* November 18, 1978.

65. Ibid.

66. Hill, Interview with the author, September 26, 2002.

67. V. O. Key, "A Theory of Critical Elections," *Journal of Politics* 17 (February 1955, 3–18): 8.

68. Key, "Secular Realignment and the Party System," *Journal of Politics* (May 1959, 198–210): 204.

CHAPTER 7

1. David Dean, Interview with the author, Dallas, Texas, November 26, 2002.

2. *Houston Chronicle,* November 11, 1978.

3. Ibid.

4. *The Texas Observer,* December 1, 1978.

5. *Dallas Morning News,* November 26, 1978.

6. John Hill, Interview with the author, Houston, Texas, September 26, 2002.

7. Ibid.

8. Ben Johnson, *Arkansas in Modern America, 1930–1999* (Fayetteville: University of Arkansas Press, 2000), 230–33.

9. O. H. Harris, "Interview with Sen. O. H. Harris, November 27, 1978," interview by Ronald E. Marcello (Denton: North Texas State University, 1979): 17–18.

10. Ibid., 18.

11. Lance Tarrance, Interview with the author, Houston, Texas, October 8, 2002.

12. *Dallas Morning News,* January 16, 1979.

13. *Austin American-Statesman,* January 16, 1979.

14. *Dallas Morning News,* January 16, 1979.

15. Dolph Briscoe, *Report to the 66th Legislature of Texas from Dolph Briscoe, Governor of Texas 1973–1979* (Austin: State of Texas, 1979), 63.

16. Ibid., 77.

17. Bill Clayton, "Interview with Speaker Bill Clayton, April 2, 1982," interview by Ron Marcello (Denton: North Texas State University, 1982), 1–2.

18. Clayton, "Interview with Speaker Bill Clayton, November 16, 1978," interview by Ron Marcello (Denton: North Texas State University, 1979), 21.

19. *Austin American-Statesman,* January 16, 1979.

20. Ibid.

21. Ibid.

22. Ibid.

23. Ibid.

24. Marvin DeBoer, ed., *Destiny by Choice: The Inaugural Addresses of the Governors of Texas* (Fayetteville: University of Arkansas Press, 1992), 450.

25. Ibid., 453.

26. Ibid., 454.

27. "Texas Secretary of State," www.sos.state.tx.us; Mike Kingston et al., ed., *The Texas Almanac's Political History of Texas* (Austin: Eakin Press, 1992), 308–15.

28. By the late 1980s, the oil industry had collapsed in the state and by 1990, Republican oilman Clayton Williams had mounted a campaign filled with mistakes and embarrassing misstatements that helped State Treasurer Ann Richards win the governor's race. Whether these incidents gave a false appearance of Democratic strength remains unclear, but the Republicans clearly did not have the strength to overcome these issues.

29. "Texas Secretary of State," www.sos.state.tx.us; *Dallas Morning News,* November 3, 2004; *Fort Worth Star-Telegram,* November 3, 2004.

30. Clements, Letter to the author, May 13, 2004.

31. Johnson, *Arkansas in Modern America,* 240–241.

32. Wayne Parent and Huey Perry, "Louisiana: African-Americans, Republicans, and Party Competition," in *The New Politics of the Old South: An Introduction to Southern Politics,* ed. Charles S. Bullock III and Mark J. Rozell (New York: Rowman & Littlefield Publishers, 1998), 110–11.

33. *Atlanta Journal-Constitution,* November 6, 2002.

34. *Lubbock Avalanche-Journal,* October 19, 2003.

35. Hill, *Oral History Interview with the Honorable John L. Hill Jr.,* Sheree Scarborough, ed. (Austin: Texas Bar Foundation, 1999), 55.

36. Hill, Interview with the author, September 26, 2002.

37. Ibid.

38. Hill, *Oral Interview,* 43–44.

39. Hill, Interview with the author, September 26, 2002.

40. Tarrance, Interview with the author, October 8, 2002.

41. Ibid.

42. Dean, Interview with the author, November 26, 2002.

43. Ibid.

44. Robert Krueger, Interview with the author, New Braunfels, Texas, March 25, 2004.

45. *Fort Worth Star-Telegram,* March 29, 2006, May 10, 2006, June 23, 2006, and September 12, 2006; *Austin American-Statesman,* September 21, 2006.

APPENDIX A

1. "Texas Presidential Elections," Texas Secretary of State, www.sos.state.tx.us.

2. "American Ind." refers to the American Independent Party. "Socialist Wrk." refers to the Socialist Worker's Party, "Socialist Lbr." refers to the Socialist Labor Party, and "Independent" refers to any candidate not officially affiliated with a party. Under state law at the time, these candidates may have qualified as candidates themselves, but their parties may not have qualified for ballot status.

3. The "Change in Votes" column refers to the gains or losses political parties gained from the previous election.

APPENDIX B

1. "Texas Secretary of State," www.sos.state.tx.us; Mike Kingston et al., ed. *The Texas Almanac's Political History of Texas* (Austin: Eakin Press, 1992), 264–67.

2. Note: The "Briscoe +/– 1974" column indicates the change in votes for Dolph Briscoe

in each county in 1978 from the 1974 gubernatorial primary. The "County +/– 1974" and "County +/– 1982" columns indicate the difference in total votes cast in the 1978 Democratic gubernatorial primary in each county with the votes cast in the 1974 and 1982 contests.

Appendix C

1. "Texas Secretary of State," www.sos.state.tx.us; Mike Kingston et al., ed. *The Texas Almanac's Political History of Texas* (Austin: Eakin Press, 1992), 308–11.

2. Mario C. Compean ran as the candidate of the La Raza Unida Party.

3. Sara Jean Johnston ran as the candidate of the Socialist Workers Party.

4. Percentages do not always equal 100 percent because of rounding and the effects of the third-party candidates. For example, in Zavala County, Compean won 51.1 percent of the vote.

Appendix D

1. "Texas Secretary of State," www.sos.state.tx.us; Mike Kingston et al., ed. *The Texas Almanac's Political History of Texas* (Austin: Eakin Press, 1992), 264–67, 308–11.

2. "Primary Difference" refers to the total difference in turnout from the Democratic Primary to the actual Democratic turnout in the general election.

3. "Hill Difference" refers to the difference in votes in each county for John Hill from the Democratic Primary to the general election.

Appendix E

1. "Texas Secretary of State," www.sos.state.tx.us; Mike Kingston et al., ed. *The Texas Almanac's Political History of Texas* (Austin: Eakin Press, 1992), 308–15.

2. Note: The columns "Democrats +/– 1974," "Democrats +/– 1982," "Republicans +/– 1974," and "Republicans +/– 1982" indicate the changes in the number of votes cast for a particular party's gubernatorial nominees by county.

Appendix F

1. "Texas Secretary of State," www.sos.state.tx.us; Mike Kingston et al., ed. *The Texas Almanac's Political History of Texas* (Austin: Eakin Press, 1992), 162–65, 308–11.

2. La Raza Unida candidate Luis A. Diaz de Leon won 17,869 votes in the Senate race, or 0.77 percent of the vote. He won only Zavala County, with 2,088 votes, and scored only a handful of votes in the others.

Appendix G

1. "Texas Secretary of State," www.sos.state.tx.us.

Appendix H

1. "Texas Secretary of State," www.sos.state.tx.us; Mike Kingston et al., ed. *The Texas Almanac's Political History of Texas* (Austin: Eakin Press, 1992).

BIBLIOGRAPHY

PRIMARY SOURCES

Manuscripts and Author Interviews

Briscoe, Dolph. Dolph Briscoe Papers. Austin: Center for American History, University of Texas at Austin.

Clements, William P. Jr. Interview with the author. Dallas, Texas, May 10, 2004.

———. Letter to the Author, May 13, 2004.

Dean, David. Interview with the author. Dallas, Texas, November 26, 2002.

Hill, John. Interview with the author. Houston, Texas, September 26, 2002.

Krueger, Robert. Interview with the author. New Braunfels, Texas, March 25, 2004.

Tarrance, Lance. Interview with the author. Houston, Texas, October 8, 2002.

"Texas Secretary of State." www.sos.state.tx.us/elections/historical/70–92.shtml.

Tower, John G. The John G. Tower Papers. Georgetown, Tex.: Special Collections, Southwestern University.

Published Documents and Memoirs

Briscoe, Dolph. *Report to the 66th Legislature of Texas From Dolph Briscoe, Governor of Texas, 1973–1979.* Austin: State of Texas, 1979.

Bullock, Bob. *The Texas Economy—1970 and 1980.* Austin: Comptroller of Public Accounts, 1981.

Bush, George W. *A Charge to Keep.* New York: William Morrow and Co., 1999.

Carter, Jimmy. *Public Papers of the Presidents of the United States: Jimmy Carter, 1978: Book I, January 1 to June 30, 1978.* Washington D.C.: United States Government Printing Office, 1978.

Connally, John. *In History's Shadow: An American Odyssey.* New York: Hyperion, 1993.

DeBoer, Marvin E., ed. *Destiny By Choice: The Inaugural Addresses of the Governors of Texas.* Fayetteville, Ark.: University of Arkansas Press, 1992.

Hill, John L. Jr. *Oral History Interview with the Honorable John L. Hill Jr.,* Sheree
      Scarborough, ed. Austin: Texas Bar Foundation, 1999.
———. *A Practical Primer for Texas Consumers.* Austin: Attorney General's Office,
      State of Texas, 1975.
Morehead, Richard. *50 Years in Texas Politics: From Roosevelt to Reagan, From
      The Fergusons to Clements.* Burnet, Tex.: Eakin Press, 1982.
Pickle, Jake and Peggy Pickle. *Jake.* Austin: University of Texas Press, 1997.
Smith, Preston. *Programs for People.* Austin: State of Texas, 1973.
Texas State Library, Prints and Photographs Collection, Dolph Briscoe, www.tsl
      .state.tx.us/governors/modern/briscoe-p03.html.
Tower, John G. *Consequences: A Personal and Political Memoir.* Boston: Little,
      Brown and Co., 1991.
United States Department of Commerce, Bureau of the Census. *Statistical
      Abstract of the United States, 1979.* Washington, D.C.: U.S. Government
      Printing Office, 1979.
———. *1980 Census of Population: Gross Migration for Counties: 1975 to 1980.*
      Washington, D.C.: U.S. Government Printing Office, 1984.
United States Department of Labor, Bureau of Labor Statistics. *Employment and
      Earnings, States and Areas, 1939–78.* Washington, D.C.: U.S. Government
      Printing Office, 1979.

Interviews

Agnich, Fred. "Interview with Rep. Fred Agnich, August 11, 1975," interview by
      Ronald E. Marcello. Denton: North Texas State University, 1976.
———. "Interview with Rep. Fred Agnich, September 9, 1977," interview by
      Ronald E. Marcello. Denton: North Texas State University, 1978.
———. "Interview with Rep. Fred Agnich, November 30, 1979," interview by
      Ronald E. Marcello. Denton: North Texas State University, 1980.
Andujar, Betty. "Interview with Sen. Betty Andujar, September 6, 1979," interview
      by Ronald E. Marcello. Denton: North Texas State University, 1980.
———. "Interview with Sen. Betty Andujar, September 12, 1993," interview by
      Kristi Strickland. Denton: University of North Texas, 1993.
Box, Alma. "Interview with Alma Box, August 19, 1993," interview by Kristi
      Strickland. Denton: University of North Texas, 1993.
Cahoon, Frank Kell. "Interview with Frank Kell Cahoon, October 24, 1967,"
      interview by E. Dale Odom. Denton: North Texas State University, 1968.
Campbell, Barbara. "Interview with Barbara Campbell, May 6, 1993," interview by
      Kristi Strickland. Denton: University of North Texas, 1993.
Clayton, Bill. "Interview with Speaker Bill Clayton, June 29, 1977," interview by
      Ronald E. Marcello. Denton: North Texas State University, 1977.
———. "Interview with Speaker Bill Clayton, November 16, 1978," interview by
      Ronald E. Marcello. Denton: North Texas State University, 1979.
———. "Interview with Speaker Bill Clayton, August 27, 1979," interview by
      Ronald E. Marcello, Denton: North Texas State University, 1979.
———. "Interview with Speaker Bill Clayton, April 2, 1982," interview by Ronald
      E. Marcello. Denton: North Texas State University, 1982.

Creighton, Tom. "Interview with Sen. Tom Creighton, July 15, 1975," interview by
    Ronald E. Marcello. Denton: North Texas State University, 1976.
Hall, Tip. "Interview with Tip Hall, August 13, 1979," interview by Ronald E.
    Marcello. Denton: North Texas State University, 1980.
Harris, O. H. "Interview with O. H. (Ike) Harris, September 7, 1977," interview by
    Ronald E. Marcello. Denton: North Texas State University, 1978.
———. "Interview with Sen. O. H. Harris, November 27, 1978," interview by
    Ronald E. Marcello. Denton: North Texas State University, 1979.
Lewis, Gibson D. "Interview with Rep. 'Gib' Lewis, August 29, 1979," interview by
    Ronald E. Marcello. Denton: North Texas State University, 1980.
Mauzy, Oscar. "Interview with Sen. Oscar Mauzy, July 17, 1975," interview by
    Ronald E. Marcello. Denton: North Texas State University, 1975.
———. "Interview with Sen. Oscar Mauzy, October 23, 1978," interview by
    Ronald E. Marcello. Denton: North Texas State University, 1979.
———. "Interview with Sen. Oscar Mauzy, August 2, 1979," interview by Ronald E.
    Marcello. Denton: North Texas State University, 1980.
Parker, Walt. "Interview with Walt Parker, February 4, 1970," interview by
    Ronald E. Marcello. Denton: North Texas State University, 1970.
———. "Interview with Walt Parker, July 17, 1973," Ronald E. Marcello. Denton:
    North Texas State University, 1973.
Shapiro, Florence. "Interview with Florence Shapiro, August 17, 1993," interview
    by Kristi Strickland. Denton: University of North Texas, 1993.

Secondary Sources

Books

Aistrup, Joseph A. *The Southern Strategy Revisited: Republican Top-Down
    Advancement in the South.* Lexington, Ky.: University Press of Kentucky, 1996.
Allsup, Carl. *The American G.I. Forum: Origins and Evolution.* Austin: University
    of Texas Press, 1982.
Baker, Gordon E. *Rural Versus Urban Political Power.* New York: Random House,
    1955.
Barr, Alwyn. *Black Texans: A History of African-Americans in Texas, 1528–1995,*
    2nd ed. Norman, Okla.: University of Oklahoma Press, 1996.
Barta, Carolyn. *Bill Clements: Texian to His Toenails.* Austin: Eakin Press, 1996.
Bartley, Numan V. *The New South, 1945–1980.* Baton Rouge, La.: Louisiana State
    University Press, 1995.
Bartley, Numan V. and Hugh D. Graham. *Southern Politics and the Second
    Reconstruction.* Baltimore: Johns Hopkins Press, 1975.
Black, Earl. *Southern Governors and Civil Rights: Racial Segregation as a
    Campaign Issue in the Second Reconstruction.* Cambridge, Mass.: Harvard
    University Press, 1976.
Black, Earl and Merle Black. *Politics and Society in the South.* Cambridge, Mass.:
    Harvard University Press, 1987.
———. *The Vital South: How Presidents are Elected.* Cambridge, Mass.: Harvard
    University Press, 1992.

Buenger, Walter L. and Robert A. Calvert, eds. *Texas Through Time: Evolving Interpretations.* College Station, Tex.: Texas A&M University Press, 1991.

Bullard, Robert D. *Invisible Houston: The Black Experience in Boom and Bust.* College Station, Tex.: Texas A&M University Press, 1987.

Button, James W. *Blacks and Social Change: Impact of the Civil Rights Movement in Southern Communities.* Princeton, N.J.: Princeton University Press, 1989.

Campbell, Randolph B. *Grass-Roots Reconstruction in Texas, 1865–1880.* Baton Rouge, La.: Louisiana State University Press, 1997.

———. *Gone to Texas: A History of the Lone Star State.* New York: Oxford University Press, 2003.

Calvert, Robert A., Gregg Cantrell, and Arnoldo De Leon. *The History of Texas,* 3rd ed. Wheeling, Ill.: Harlan Davidson, 2002.

Casdorph, Paul. *A History of the Republican Party in Texas, 1865–1965.* Austin: Pemberton Press, 1965.

Chudacoff, Howard P. and Judith E. Smith. *The Evolution of American Urban Society,* 4th ed. Englewood Cliffs, N.J.: Prentice Hall, 1994.

Cobb, James C. *Industrialization and Southern Society, 1877–1984.* Lexington, Ky.: University Press of Kentucky, 1984.

———. *The Selling of the South: The Southern Crusade for Industrial Development, 1936–1980.* Baton Rouge, La.: Louisiana State University Press, 1982.

Conn, Jerry D. *Preston Smith: The Making of a Texas Governor.* Austin: Jenkins Publishing, 1972.

Crawford, Ann Fears and Jack Keever. *John B. Connally: Portrait in Power.* Austin: Jenkins Publishing Co., 1973.

Crawford, Ann Fears and Crystal Sasse Ragsdale. *Women In Texas: Their Lives, Their Experiences, Their Accomplishments.* Burnet, Tex.: Eakin Press, 1982.

Davidson, Chandler. *Biracial Politics: Conflict and Coalition in the Metropolitan South.* Baton Rouge, La.: Louisiana State University Press, 1972.

———. *Race and Class in Texas Politics.* Princeton, N.J.: Princeton University Press, 1990.

DeSipio, Louis. *Counting on the Latino Vote: Latinos As a New Electorate.* Charlottesville, Va.: University of Virginia Press, 1996.

Doyle, Don H. *New Men, New Cities, New South.* Chapel Hill, N.C.: University of North Carolina Press, 1990.

Evans, Wanda. *Preston Smith: The People's Governor.* Lubbock, Tex.: Millenia Books, 1999.

Flanigan, William H. and Nancy H. Zingale. *Political Behavior of the American Electorate,* 6th ed. Boston: Allyn and Bacon, 1987.

Fox, Geoffrey. *Hispanic Nation: Culture, Politics, and the Constructing of Identity.* Secaucus, N.J.: Birch Lane Press, 1996.

Franklin, John Hope and Alfred A. Moss Jr. *From Slavery to Freedom: A History of African-Americans,* 8th ed. Boston: McGraw-Hill, 2000.

Goldfield, David R. *Black, White, and Southern: Race Relations and Southern Culture, 1940 to the Present.* Baton Rouge, La.: Louisiana State University Press, 1990.

——. *Region, Race, and Cities: Interpreting the Urban South.* Baton Rouge, La.: Louisiana State University Press, 1997.

——. *Cotton Fields and Skyscrapers: Southern City and Region, 1607–1980.* Baton Rouge, La.: Louisiana State University Press, 1982.

Goldfield, David R. and Paul D. Escott, eds. *Major Problems in the History of the American South, Volume II: The New South.* Lexington, Mass.: D. C. Heath, 1990.

Goodwin, Doris Kearns. *Lyndon Johnson and the American Dream.* New York: St. Martin's Griffin, 1991.

Green, George Norris. *The Establishment in Texas Politics: The Primitive Years, 1938–1957.* Westport, Conn.: Greenwood Press, 1979.

Greenhaw, Wayne. *Elephants in the Cottonfields: Ronald Reagan and the New Republican South.* New York: Macmillan Publishing, 1982.

Hadley, Charles D. and Lewis Bowman, eds. *Party Activists in Southern Politics: Mirrors and Makers of Change.* Knoxville, Tenn.: University of Tennessee Press, 1998.

"The Handbook of Texas Online." www.tsha.utexas.edu/handbook/online/.

Haynes, Sam W. and Cary D. Wintz, eds. *Major Problems in Texas History.* Boston: Houghton Mifflin, 2002.

Heard, Alexander. *A Two-Party South?* Chapel Hill, N.C.: University of North Carolina Press, 1952.

Hill, Patricia Evridge. *Dallas: The Making of a Modern City.* Austin: University of Texas Press, 1996.

Jackson, Kenneth T. *Crabgrass Frontier: The Suburbanization of the U.S.* New York: Oxford University Press, 1985.

Jewell, Malcolm E. *Parties and Primaries: Nominating State Governors.* New York: Praeger, 1984.

Johnson, Ben. *Arkansas in Modern America, 1930–1999.* Fayetteville, Ark.: University of Arkansas Press, 2000.

Key, V. O. Jr. *Southern Politics in State and Nation.* New York: Alfred A. Knopf, 1949.

Kingston, Mike, et al., ed. *The Texas Almanac's Political History of Texas.* Austin: Eakin Press, 1992.

Kraemer, Richard H., Charldean Newell, and David F. Prindle. *Texas Politics,* 6th ed. St. Paul, Minn.: West Publishing, 1996.

Lamis, Alexander P. *The Two-Party South.* New York: Oxford University Press, 1988.

Lea, James F. *Contemporary Southern Politics.* Baton Rouge: Louisiana State University Press, 1988.

Marten, James. *Texas Divided: Loyalty and Dissent in the Lone Star State, 1856–1874.* Lexington, Ky.: University Press of Kentucky, 1990.

McCleskey, Clifton, et al. *The Government and Politics of Texas.* Boston: Little, Brown, 1978.

Montejano, David. *Anglos and Mexicans in the Making of Texas, 1836–1986.* Austin: University of Texas Press, 1987.

Morehouse, Sarah McCally. *The Governor as Party Leader: Campaigning and Governing*. Ann Arbor, Mich.: University of Michigan Press, 1998.

Moreland, Laurence, et al. *Blacks in Southern Politics*. New York: Praeger, 1987.

Olien, Roger M. *From Token to Triumph: The Texas Republicans Since 1920*. Dallas: SMU Press, 1982.

Prysby, Charles L. and John W. Books. *Political Behavior and the Local Context*. New York: Praeger, 1991.

Rae, Nicol C. *The Decline and Fall of the Liberal Republicans: From 1952 to the Present*. New York: Oxford University Press, 1989.

Reinhard, David W. *The Republican Right Since 1945*. Lexington, Ky.: University Press of Kentucky, 1983.

Richardson, Rupert N., Adrian Anderson, and Ernest Wallace. *Texas: The Lone Star State*, 6th ed. Englewood Cliffs, N.J.: Prentice Hall, 1993.

Roland, Charles P. *The Improbable Era: The South Since World War II*. Lexington, Ky.: University Press of Kentucky, 1975.

Rutland, Robert Allen. *The Democrats: From Jefferson to Clinton*. Columbia, Mo.: University of Missouri Press, 1995.

———. *The Republicans: From Lincoln to Bush*. Columbia, Mo.: University of Missouri Press, 1996.

Scher, Richard K. *Politics in the New South: Republicanism, Race, and Leadership in the Twentieth Century*. Armonk, N.Y.: M. E. Sharpe, 1997.

Schram, Martin. *Running for President, 1976: The Carter Campaign*. New York: Stein and Day, 1977.

Shelton, Beth Anne, et al. *Houston: Growth and Decline in a Sunbelt Boomtown*. Philadelphia: Temple University Press, 1989.

Smallwood, James M. *Time of Hope, Time of Despair: Black Texans During Reconstruction*. Port Washington, N.Y.: Kennikat Press, 1981.

Smallwood, James M., Barry A. Crouch, and Larry Peacock. *Murder and Mayhem: The War of Reconstruction in Texas*. College Station, Tex.: Texas A&M University Press, 2003.

Stanley, Harold W. *Voter Mobilization and the Politics of Race: The South and Universal Suffrage, 1952–1984*. New York: Praeger, 1987.

Steed, Robert P., et al., eds. *Party Organization and Activism in the American South*. Tuscaloosa, Ala.: University of Alabama Press, 1998.

Steed, Robert P., Lawrence W. Moreland, and Tod A. Baker, eds. *Party Politics in the South*. New York: Praeger Publishers, 1980.

———. eds. *Southern Parties and Elections: Studies in Regional Political Change*. Tuscaloosa, Ala.: University of Alabama Press, 1997.

Stephens, A. Ray and William M. Holmes, eds. *Historical Atlas of Texas*. Norman, Okla.: University of Oklahoma Press, 1989.

Stroud, Kandy. *How Jimmy Won: The Victory Campaign From Plains to the White House*. New York: William Morrow and Co., 1977.

Strong, Donald S. *Issue Voting and Party Realignment*. Birmingham, Ala.: University of Alabama Press, 1977.

Tindall, George Brown. *The Persistent Tradition in New South Politics*. Baton Rouge, La.: Louisiana State University Press, 1975.

———. *The Emergence of the New South, 1913–1945.* Baton Rouge, La.: Louisiana State University Press, 1967.

Tindall, George Brown and David E. Shi. *America: A Narrative History,* 6th ed. New York: W. W. Norton and Co., 2004.

Weinstein, Bernard L. and Robert E. Firestine. *Regional Growth and Decline in the United States: The Rise of the Sunbelt and the Decline of the Northeast.* New York: Praeger Publishers, 1978.

Articles

Angel, William D. Jr. "To Make a City: Entrepreneurship on the Sunbelt Frontier," *The Rise of the Sunbelt Cities,* David C. Perry and Alfred J. Watkins, eds. (Beverly Hills, Cal.: Sage Publications, 1978): 109–128.

Briggs, Ronald. "The Demography of a Sunbelt State," *Texas at the Crossroads: People, Politics, and Policy,* Anthony Champagne and Edward J. Harpham, eds. (College Station, Tex.: Texas A&M Press, 1987): 15–41.

Campbell, Bruce A. "Change in the Southern Electorate," *American Journal of Political Science* 21 (February 1977): 37–64.

Cassel, Carol A. "Change in Electoral Participation in the South," *Journal of Politics* 41 (August 1979): 907–917.

Dobbs, Ricky Floyd. "Towards A Two-Party South: Allan Shivers and Texas Politics, 1934–1957," Ph. D. diss., Texas A&M University, 1996.

Fleischmann, Arnold. "Sunbelt Boosterism: The Politics of Postwar Growth and Annexation in San Antonio," *The Rise of the Sunbelt Cities,* David C. Perry and Alfred J. Watkins, eds. (Beverly Hills, Cal.: Sage Publications, 1978): 151–168.

Gaddie, R. K., and Scott E. Buchanan, "Oklahoma: GOP Realignment in the Buckle of the Bible Belt," *The New Politics of the Old South: An Introduction to Southern Politics,* Charles S. Bullock III and Mark J. Rozell, eds. (New York: Rowman & Littlefield Publishers, 1998): 205–226.

Green, George Norris. "Some Aspects of the Far Right Wing in Texas Politics," *Essays on Recent Southern Politics,* Harold M. Hollingsworth, ed. (Austin: University of Texas Press, 1970): 58–94.

Hicks, Donald A. "Advanced Industrial Development," *Texas at the Crossroads: People, Politics, and Policy,* Anthony Champagne and Edward J. Harpham, eds. (College Station, Tex.: Texas A&M Press, 1987): 42–67.

Howard, Russell. "Energy for the Growing South," *The Economics of Southern Growth,* E. Blaine Liner and Lawrence K. Lynch, eds. (Durham, N.C.: The Southern Growth Policies Board, 1977): 89–105.

Jennings, James. "Blacks and Latinos in the American City in the 1990s: Toward Political Alliances or Social Conflict?," *Pursuing Power,* F. Chris Garcia, ed. (Notre Dame, Ind.: University of Notre Dame Press, 1997): 472–478.

Johnson, David R. "San Antonio: The Vicissitudes of Boosterism," *Sunbelt Cities: Politics and Growth Since World War II,* Richard M. Bernard and Bradley R. Rice, eds. (Austin, Tex.: University of Texas Press, 1983): 232–254.

Kaplan, Barry J. "Houston: The Golden Buckle of the Sunbelt," *Sunbelt Cities: Politics and Growth Since World War II,* Richard M. Bernard and Bradley R. Rice, eds. (Austin, Tex.: University of Texas Press, 1983): 196–212.

Katzman, Martin T. and Patricia J. Osborn. "Energy Policy," *Texas at the Crossroads: People, Politics, and Policy,* Anthony Champagne and Edward J. Harpham, eds. (College Station, Tex.: Texas A&M Press, 1987): 129–153.

Key, V. O. Jr. "Partisanship and County Offices: The Case of Ohio," *American Political Science Review* 47 (June 1953): 525–532.

———. "Secular Realignment and the Party System," *Journal of Politics* 21 (May 1959): 198–210.

———. "A Theory of Critical Elections," *Journal of Politics* 17 (February 1955): 3–18.

Lamare, James W., J. L. Polinard, and Robert D. Wrinkle. "Texas: Lone Star (Wars) State," *The New Politics of the Old South: An Introduction to Southern Politics,* Charles S. Bullock III and Mark J. Rozell, eds. (New York: Rowman & Littlefield Publishers, 1998): 245–260.

Melosi, Martin V. "Dallas-Fort Worth: Marketing the Metroplex," *Sunbelt Cities: Politics and Growth Since World War II,* Richard M. Bernard and Bradley R. Rice, eds. (Austin, Tex.: University of Texas Press, 1983): 162–195.

Miernyk, William H. "The Changing Structure of the Southern Economy," *The Economics of Southern Growth,* E. Blaine Liner and Lawrence K. Lynch, eds. (Durham, N.C.: The Southern Growth Policies Board, 1977): 35–63.

Parent, Wayne, and Peter A. Petrakis. "Populism Left and Right: Politics of the Rural South," *The Rural South Since World War II,* R. Douglas Hurt, ed. (Baton Rouge, La.: Louisiana State University Press, 1998):149–167.

Parent, Wayne, and Huey Perry. "Louisiana: African-Americans, Republicans, and Party Competition," *The New Politics of the Old South: An Introduction to Southern Politics,* Charles S. Bullock III and Mark J. Rozell, eds. (New York: Rowman & Littlefield Publishers, 1998): 105–120.

Perry, David C. and Alfred J. Watkins. "People, Profit, and the Rise of the Sunbelt Cities," *The Rise of the Sunbelt Cities,* David C. Perry and Alfred J. Watkins, eds. (Beverly Hills, Cal.: Sage Publications, 1978): 277–305.

Robinson, Glenn A. "The Electorate in Texas," *Texas at the Crossroads: People, Politics, and Policy,* Anthony Champagne and Edward J. Harpham, eds. (College Station, Tex.: Texas A&M Press, 1987): 68–107.

Sanders, Heywood T. "Building a New Urban Infrastructure: The Creation of Postwar San Antonio," *Urban Texas: Politics and Development,* Char Miller and Heywood T. Sanders, eds. (College Station, Tex.: Texas A&M University Press, 1990): 154–173.

Weeks, O. Douglas. "Texas: Land of Conservative Expansiveness," *The Changing Politics of the South,* William C. Havard, ed. Baton Rouge, La.: Louisiana State University Press, 1972.

Winters, Donald L. "Agriculture in the Post-World War II South," *The Rural South Since World War II,* R. Douglas Hurt, ed. (Baton Rouge, La.: Louisiana State University Press, 1998): 8–27.

INDEX

ISBN-13: 978-1-60344-009-7
ISBN-10: 1-60344-009-7